Slow Culture and the
American Dream

Slow Culture and the American Dream

A Slow and Curvy Philosophy for the Twenty-First Century

Mary Caputi

LEXINGTON BOOKS
Lanham • Boulder • New York • London

Published by Lexington Books
An imprint of The Rowman & Littlefield Publishing Group, Inc.
4501 Forbes Boulevard, Suite 200, Lanham, Maryland 20706
www.rowman.com

86-90 Paul Street, London EC2A 4NE

British Library Cataloguing in Publication Information Available

Library of Congress Cataloging-in-Publication Data

Names: Caputi, Mary, 1957- author.
  Title: Slow culture and the American dream : a slow and curvy philosophy
    for the twenty-first century / Mary Caputi.
  Description: Lanham : Lexington Books, [2022] | Includes bibliographical
    references and index.
  Identifiers: LCCN 2022005141 (print) | LCCN 2022005142 (ebook) | ISBN
    9781793642400 (cloth) | ISBN 9781793642424 (paperback) ISBN
9781793642417 (ebook)
  Subjects: LCSH: Slow life movement--United States.
  Classification: LCC HN20 .C37 2022 (print) | LCC HN20 (ebook) | DDC
    306.973--dc23/eng/20220324
  LC record available at https://lccn.loc.gov/2022005141
  LC ebook record available at https://lccn.loc.gov/2022005142

To my Sunday Zoom Group that sustained me throughout the lockdown: Richard and Rahael, Pauline and Tony, Carol and Randy, Nancy and Christine, Chris and Maria, Chiara, Adam, and Elena, Lucas and Courtney, Anthony and Mayra

Contents

Acknowledgments

There are a great many people that I need to thank in connection with this project. First and foremost, I would like to thank Jane Close Conoley, president of California State University, Long Beach, for her generous award that allowed me to travel and conduct interviews about the slow movement. President Conoley's award supported me for a year, and with the help of Amelia Marquez I was able to use it for numerous aspects of my research that are invaluable to this book. I am also very indebted to the people from Slow Food International, Slow Food USA, and *Cittaslow* who made time for me; their input and insights taught me a great deal about both movements, and about the slow philosophy in general. They include Carlo Petrini, Cinzia Scaffidi, the late Paolo Saturnini, Pier Giorgio Oliveti, Aldo Graziani, Alice Waters, Anna Mulè, Richard McCarthy, and Andrew Nowak. All of them set aside time to talk with me and I am very grateful for their attention to my work. Pier Giorgio Oliveti was especially generous not only with his time and knowledge, but also in sharing the names of *Cittaslow* mayors, some of whom I eventually interviewed. Thus, I would like to thank the mayors of Positano and San Miniato, Italy; Saint Antonin Noble Val and Mirande, France; Alphen-Chaam, the Netherlands, and Andrea Mearns of Mold, Wales for their invaluable input and dedication to the movement. Many thanks to Rhonda Del Bene for her friendly companionship and help in my travels to France. Colles Stowell and Kevin Scribner spoke with me at length about Slow Fish USA and deepened my understanding of the importance of the oceans to the ecosystem. I am grateful for their time and impressive knowledge of the oceans. Five people were instrumental in teaching me about efforts to introduce the *Cittaslow* philosophy in the United States: Pamela Campbell, Elmire Budak, David Weinsoff, Virginia Hubbell, and Tasha Beauchamp. I am very grateful for their input and interest in my project, and for their stories about how *Cittaslow* fared on American soil.

Julia Wheen kindly met with me twice and gave me much background and insider knowledge regarding the University of Gastronomic Sciences

(UNISG) in Pollenzo, Piedmont, including a tour of the buildings and grounds. She explained how the University has grown and changed over the years, including the ways in which it reaches out to the business community in an effort to go green. A professor at UNISG, Simone Cinotto, allowed me to interview him and he explained a great deal about the academic arm of the University. I am also grateful for the anecdotes of two graduates of the University, Tien Bui and Victoria Ambruso, whose fond memories of their time in Pollenzo speak favorably of the program.

I would also like to thank Geir Berthelsen, founder of The World Institute of Slowness in Kristiansand, Norway, for his explanation of how his Institute seeks to bring the philosophy of slow into everyday life, including into the business community. I am impressed and inspired by his work and the work of his wife, Anna, whose art embellishes the community in Kristiansand. Joanne Byrd and Jeremy Samson taught me a great deal about school gardening programs in Southern California, and Joanne gave me a tour of a gardening site. Many thanks to Kim and Neha for their explanation of how the school garden program is administered in various school systems. Two student assistants, Lucas Madrigal and Lynda Aguayo, researched various aspects of the movement for me when I first began this project, and their findings were invaluable to my writing. I am also indebted to my students Julieta Martinez, Diana Do, and Lindsey Rippert who taught me a great deal about slow fashion; their enthusiasm for the slow movement is inspiring. I would also like to thank friends and colleagues who read portions of the manuscript and recommended texts to me, some of which have proven indispensable to my argument: Ron Schmidt, Judith Grant, Paul Apostolidis, Charlie Mahoney, and Sun Young Kwak gave me excellent advice in this regard. My anonymous reviewers also deserve thanks for their careful reading of my manuscript and many useful suggestions.

I owe a large debt of gratitude to the numerous Slow Food USA and Slow Food International volunteers who allowed me to interview them. Their stories shaped my understanding of the slow movement in various parts of the world and helped me understand how a philosophy comes to be implemented and administered where the rubber hits the road. I thank them for the time they gave me as well as for all they do for the movement. Jim Embry is an inspiration to us all in his commitment to slow principles as well as to bringing social justice center stage in the movement. Fabio Picchi is to be thanked for his commitment to slow principles, especially organic food. Sincere thanks also go to Joseph Parry, Alison Keefner, Sara Noakes, Carter Moran, and Crystal Branson at Lexington Books for their sustained enthusiasm and support. Without their help and guidance, the project would never have seen the light of day. Finally, I would like to thank the team at California State University, Florence, with whom I worked for a year and who took me to Expo 2015 where I first discovered the Slow Food movement. Connie, Paola, Jane, Refugio, Valentina, Marsha, Giulia, other CSU Florence professors, Uta and Giovanni Bernardi: thank you for a wonderful year and for introducing me to the slow movement. I remain deeply indebted to you.

Introduction

Slow Food: Gastronomic Politics for the Twenty-First Century

In 2015, the city of Milan hosted the World Expo, and the focus that year was food. I had the good fortune of being in Italy at the time and so went to the event, not knowing what to expect. What I found was a clamor of wall-to-wall people arriving by busloads from all over the world, sardined in amidst an array of cuisine-themed pavilions that featured exhibits, displays, and demonstrations about food. The crowds were overwhelming and the lines so long at eateries that ironically one could hardly buy anything to eat. Some pavilions were prohibitively packed, and others a bit disappointing in their exhibition: too obvious, too predictable, too unexceptional in their presentation. Others were fun and educational. Many highlighted the culinary tradition of a country or region of the world; others examined the changing politics of food in the globalized economy.

As I wandered hungry through the fairgrounds surrounded by conversations about food, I stumbled upon one pavilion that showcased alternative food movements and their attentiveness to agriculture and climate change. It was there that the Slow Food movement was first made known to me, and I bought a book chronicling its history. I had heard the term "Slow Food" before and had a vague idea that it took aim against fast food. Yet I had no idea how large the movement had become and how serious it was in its mission. Nor had I ever heard of its formidable outgrowth, *Cittaslow,* "slow city," or of the other offshoots that now make up the "slow movement" such as slow fashion, slow parenting, slow travel, and other commitments to deceleration. I wasn't entirely wrong in thinking that the term "slow food" was meant in jest, for as I soon learned the founder of the movement, Carlo Petrini, infuses optimism and humor into much of his work, insisting that in order to change the world one shouldn't don't do it with sadness, but with joy. Nevertheless, while the movement highlights fun, conviviality, and creativity as part of its message, it is serious in its efforts to bring about change, even radical change, in the way we live. It seeks to execute a realignment in our relationship to speed which will in turn realign a host of other relationships: e.g., with the ecosystem and our agricultural practices, with food and its deep cultural and emotional resonances, with our communities and families, even with ourselves and our bodies. And in seeking radical change through our daily practices and everyday choices, Slow Food typifies the slow movement writ large.

With a venerable red snail as its mascot, Slow Food has grown into a well-articulated international movement which, at this writing, is present in roughly 160 countries. Its aim is nothing short of changing the world, not through revolution in the streets or a coup d'état, but in the fields, in the kitchen, and at the dinner table. Revolutionary in aim, its tactics are unconventional and have nothing to do with weaponry or materiel. Food, not fighting, is its focus, for a central premise of the movement stipulates that our relationship to food contains far-reaching social and political implications that our fast-paced, fast-food, McDonaldized world has either forgotten, kept hidden from view, or never understood in the first place. Food and its relationship to agriculture thus define its agenda, its ammunition, and its remedy, since it views how we feed ourselves as a main political linchpin in the era of neoliberal globalization. "I am sure that, through gastronomy, food will make us free . . . ," Petrini writes, "[b]ecause food is freedom."[1] Food determines so many things and is truly global in reach; it operates as a linchpin in world politics and in the future of the planet. As chef Dan Barber explains, everything—but *everything*—comes together in a plate of food: politics, agriculture, technology, culture, philosophy, health, the future of the planet, and of course the delights of gastronomy.[2]

While we may not find *everything* on our dinner plate, I am convinced that a sufficient number of things coalesce there that warrant serious attention. What is on our plate is a revelatory constellation that recounts stories regarding our social and political landscape, our natural environment, our cultural heritage, and even our personalities. As Barber explains, the new gastronomy "helps us recognize that what we eat is part of an integrated whole, a web of relationships . "[3] In these pages, I'm willing to defend the claim that a plate of food tells all, and that it is as much a meal as it is a collection of clues, an expository ensemble that recounts how our society feeds itself—that is to say, how we live. I'm willing to support Petrini's affirmation that we can change the world joyfully and meaningfully through attention to food. After all, as others have noted, haven't many revolutions begun around a table? Moreover, the manner in which the focus on food has expanded outward to inspire a larger movement—the slow movement writ large—convinces me that the snail could conceivably incite a potential sea change in the narratives that Americans live by; it could reorient and reprioritize the American Dream.

In fact, my argument is that Slow Food's gastronomic revolution not only indicts the more pernicious attributes of the modern world, but that it has

Figure 0.1 The red snail serves as the Slow Food mascot. Source: Photograph courtesy of Slow Food Italy, © Paolo Properzi.

bearing on the Western humanist tradition. In ways not always made explicit in the Slow Food literature, nor indeed in the other iterations of slow, this movement goes to the heart of the humanist tradition and exposes the problems created by a human-centric, human-dominated worldview. That worldview places *people*—with all our ambitious initiatives and ancillary sense of entitlement—at its center at the expense of the natural world, and understands human domination over nature to be an accepted given. While philosophers have debated exactly what is meant by Protagoras' assertion that "man is the measure of all things," there can be little doubt that the statement empowers humanity and confers dominion on our earthly existence. Moreover, the precise configuration of that dominion favors certain people to the detriment of others: for instance, the industrialized North over the Global South, economically advanced countries over developing nations, Whites over Indigenous people, Black Americans, and people of color.

Slow Food (and the slow movement in general) claims that we can understand humanity only in terms of our relationship to the earth, for gastronomy links directly to agriculture. "It is impossible to discuss food without discussing agriculture," Petrini insists.[4] In an email exchange with him in September 2021, it became clear to me that he places agricultural practices, and especially the practice of biodiversity, at the top of his agenda. He describes biodiversity as the "fertile terrain of our movement . . . of interest to every living being on this planet " [translation mine]. And this interconnection to "every living being on this planet" links Slow Food to other expressions of slow also seeking to combat our harmful anthropocentric imprimatur and to undo the pernicious blowback of our humanist tradition.

My analysis thus draws on the philosophy of slow in order to demonstrate how much the United States can learn from it. I query the difficult fit between the movement's underlying philosophy with its latent, understated critique of humanism, and the American Dream of upward mobility, unchecked growth, and exceptionalism. Without question, the fit between the philosophy of slow and the predominant American Dream is uncomfortable, since the latter nearly always suggests a synergistic dynamism that expands outward rather than decelerating and turning inward. It always syncopates with an economy of growth, speed, and competition rather than calling growth itself into question. Yet a number of contemporary crises—from climate change to food insecurity to epidemics of obesity and diabetes—clearly indicate that America must change course since the one we are now on is unsustainable, unhealthy, even unlivable.

I use the term "predominant American Dream" because "the American Dream" is such a rich and diverse idea that has no singular interpretation or set lexicon of meanings. As Jim Cullen and others have pointed out, there are several "American Dreams" at play in our nation's history.[5] These include the dream of freedom, of equality and tolerance, of racial blindness and gender non-discrimination; dreams of financial stability and upward mobility, and of America as the unrivaled military leader of the Free World. It brings to mind a stable dwelling place and at least one car in the driveway, television sets, computers, and social media, the ability to enjoy popular culture and rampant consumerism thanks to sufficient earning power. Indeed, it almost always suggests the economic largesse of rags to riches. Moreover, the Dream's epic narrative often makes reference to America the melting pot, the land of opportunity and industrial growth, the country of Martin Luther King, Jr., Barack Obama, and Kamala Harris, and the place where an immigrant can go from being fresh off the boat to being a millionaire.

While these various components help make up the many-faceted American Dream, it is fair to say that all allude to an optimistic, forward-looking ideology that confirms Laurence Shames' "the more factor," the belief that America can always find more, produce more, want more, and obtain more. The grandeur of our collective narrative resides in the fact that, historically, "[t]here was always a second chance, or always seemed to be, in this land where growth was destiny and where expansion and purpose were the same."[6] The United States is fueled by a vitality unparalleled in other parts of the world, or so we tell ourselves, because the land of plenty always has more to give, to provide, to discover.

To be sure, each iteration of our collective definition at least hints at the possibility of making money and improving one's social class. John Archer supports this claim by insisting that an integral component of the American Dream has long been that of home ownership, which of course presupposes steady income and good credit history.[7] Archer demonstrates that while this Dream in many ways assumes a mythical status, and has even been dismissed as chimera, it persists as a staple of the collective American imagination. Although owning one's home has become decidedly out of reach for many Americans, especially since the collapse of the housing bubble in 2008, "the recent history of the American dream demonstrates . . . the degree to which myths are resilient."[8] Hard times represent an aberration on the dominant narrative; even amidst pronounced austerity, the "more factor" displays its resilience as the American Dream continues to include some allusion to prosperity and good times ahead.

More recent expressions of the Dream insist that other elements factor into its expression, components that highlight our current state of political polarization. For some, these include dreams of environmental health and ecological sustainability, of electric cars, solar panels, and windmills dotting the landscape. They desire economic health for the nation but often embrace a model eager to restore the impoverished middle class that has dwindled since the 1970s. They seek to reinvigorate a more robust middle class while aiding the poor and diminishing the power of the one percent, that tiny fraction of the population that owns roughly forty percent of the wealth. Concurrent with this is another American Dream that wants to revive our nation's "greatness" by stringently embracing neoliberal values and a traditional American lifestyle, with "traditional" carrying echoes of the 1940s and 1950s postwar years. It longs to erase the legal precedents and public policies that by now, in its estimation, carry the country too far to the left and stymie our muscle power. This American Dream hopes for the restitution of an earlier time when the mainstream was not beset by identity politics, immigration issues, and the problems of extreme cultural fractiousness.

While all of these versions of the Dream hold interest, I focus especially on the classic dream of upward mobility and economic expansion, of a secure and vibrant society that promises wealth to anyone driven by a Horatio Alger-style commitment to hard work and perseverance. To my mind, this constitutes the "predominant" American Dream because, as a nation of immigrants so attuned to the challenges of demographic shifts, the United States often operates as a metaphor for amplitude and growth, improvement and optimism, a place where fortunes can be made by anyone with the necessary mettle. Moreover, in many ways this version of the American Dream constitutes the common denominator of all other iterations, for the premium on growth and social mobility exists in all its incarnations.

Of course, we are painfully aware of the fact that this version of the American Dream stands imperiled today, and for many represents sheer myth. By any standards, the land of opportunity today offers many fewer opportunities, and the possibilities of a Horatio Alger-style success story stand diminished. The loss of our manufacturing base in the age of globalization, the impoverishment of cities due to a loss of jobs, the shrinking middle class and skyrocketing cost of higher education; these and other factors contribute to the sad reality that today, America as the land of opportunity pales alongside its postwar version when opportunity shone brightly. Robert Putnam writes convincingly of the disappearance of expansionist America, arguing that, in the twenty-first century, it is imperative that our society come to the aid of the needy, especially children whose prospects for the future look dim.[9] Taking into consideration the social cost of young people who have no future—the cost of welfare, health care, imprisonment, drug rehabilitation, and criminal reform—the need to invest now rather than pay later appears urgent. "Even acknowledging the back-of-the-envelope nature of these calculations, one can't help concluding that ignoring the plight of poor kids imposes a substantial economic burden on us all," Putnam writes.[10]

Yet despite this crisis, even *because* of it, the dream of a prosperous America characterized by outward growth and upward climbing remains alive, such that we can still discern its alluring influence in American politics today. Surely advocates of conservative ideology eager to "make America great again" understand this greatness to denote opulent wealth and an economy whose swelling grandeur could, if handled properly, stand unparalleled in recent history. Moreover, reviving hope for the poor or the beleaguered middle class does not belong solely to the political right: the Biden agenda currently seeks to diminish the gaping chasm between rich and poor and reestablish the quality-of-life issues that prevailed in earlier decades.

Alongside this interpretation of the American Dream so enthralled by growth, strength, and expansionism, the slow movement exerts a countercultural pull that swims against the mainstream and slackens the commitment to growth. In many ways the slow philosophy resonates meaningfully with ideas that countervail the prevalent understanding of progress; in this, it shares a degree of overlap with the de-growth literature in political economy that insists that constant economic growth proves counterproductive.[11] The staples of slow to be discussed presently appeal mostly to cultural critics unaligned with the ambitious desires for ever-increasing wealth, size, and influence and the conviction that bigger, faster, and more technologically sophisticated always spells "better." Along with advocates of de-growth, such cultural critics promote the environmentalist movement, the many efforts to revive and respect Indigenous People's culture, and of course the various iterations of slow: Slow Food, *Cittaslow*, slow fashion, slow tourism, slow parenting, slow shopping. I add my voice to this list and hope to demonstrate the urgency in the quest to change course and slow down, to rethink a staple of Western humanism that puts human sovereignty at its center to be replaced by the exhortation to "go slow and curvy."[12]

The Canadian journalist Carl Honoré deserves much credit for having already brought the virtues of slow into the mainstream of American consciousness. Honoré has written extensively and given many public speaking engagements, including TED Talks on the topic of slow, always seeking to convince his audience that our culture's signature frenzy proves detrimental and indeed counterproductive. His book, *In Praise of Slowness: How a Worldwide Movement Is Challenging the Cult of Speed,* perhaps counts among his most famous publications, and can be credited for having made the American public aware of slowness as a way of life, a philosophical commitment to deceleration and a more deliberate approach to family, parenting, work, social commitments, and all that demands our time.[13] Other books by Honoré, such as *The Slow Fix: Solve Problems, Work Smarter, and Live Better in a World Addicted to Speed* and *Under Pressure: Rescuing Our Children from the Culture of Hyper-Parenting,* offer practical insights and advice on how to counter the ubiquitous message that we need to double down and do everything faster and more efficiently.[14]

In making my case for a revised and revisited American Dream that embraces the philosophy of slow, I focus primarily on the Slow Food movement and its urban outgrowth, *Cittaslow,* to be discussed in chapter One. I do this because I have had the opportunity to interview and meet with persons involved in various aspects of slow, but especially in Slow Food and *Cittaslow.* Having participated in fifty-two interviews regarding slow—some in person, some over Zoom or by telephone, and some via email—and having learned from ten students about slow fashion, I draw out the dangers that inhere in a human-centered worldview that privileges people above other forms of life. And interestingly, this indictment of a human-centered worldview does not negate the claim that adherence to the slow philosophy in fact encourages "a rebirth of humanism," a seeming paradox that I discuss throughout these pages.[15] Principal among the scholars and texts that I cite are the works of Frankfurt School authors, Annemarie Mol's insightful *Eating in Theory,* and Dehyun Sohn, Hee-Jung Jang, and Timothy Jung's *Go Slow and Curvy: Understanding the Philosophy of the Cittaslow^{slowcity} Phenomenon.*[16]

It must be stated, of course, that the slow philosophy is neither the first nor the only movement to pioneer in this direction, to "go curvy" rather than straight. Sohn, Jang, and Jung cite the Korean scholar, Dasan Yak-Yong Jeong (1762–1836), as well as the ancient Chinese philosopher, Laozi, who founded Taoism, both of whom maintained that only if something is bent, curvy, and meandering is it complete. For these thinkers, curvaceous lines far exceed those that are straight, for "the secret of life is hidden in 'slow' and in a curve that only God knows."[17] They therefore draw on the belief of Indigenous People that when one travels, it is important to pause so that the soul can catch up to the body.

Of course, the United States has its own deep thinkers who have recognized the value of going slow and curvy. The cultural impact of environmentalists such as Rachel Carson, John Muir, Wendell Berry, and Ansel Adams cannot be denied, as will be discussed in chapter Three. Their voices and images, along with contemporary ecopoets, ecocritics, and green political theorists, surely factor in the overall American experience, offering an alternative to modernity's status quo; collectively, their legacy exemplifies the kind of modern re-enchantment and re-engagement with the world that Jane Bennett so thoughtfully links to ethics.[18] Organizations such as the Sierra Club, Greenpeace, and the Nature Conservancy all owe a debt of gratitude to the groundbreaking work of Carson and others who worked to change our sensibility and raise awareness about the need for conservation. Moreover, Native American and other Indigenous People embrace a variety of rich and long-standing cultures all of which uphold an ethos that differs dramatically from that of capitalists, industrialists, and developers. Today an alternative sensibility critical of America's land grabs, abuse of the earth, and genocide against the first inhabitants has gained ground, and many call for reparations for the harm done to Native Americans. It is a new sensibility more aligned with going slow and curvy, embracing a philosophy that "involves the patience of 'sitting with' the world . . . to dwell, to stop, to reflect. "[19]

The time may be propitious for reconsidering our self-understanding and redefining the American Dream that we live by—painfully aware of life's vulnerability and finitude, we may be ready to take the teachings of slow seriously. Given the malaise that we now face thanks to climate change and covid-19, it may well be an opportune moment to write about the possibility of social change. Before delving into the philosophy of slow, Slow Food, and *Cittaslow*, then, let us first consider the current context. Is it conceivable to envisage "a new beginning that grows out of the past," something different that emerges from a worldview honoring slowness, smallness, and an Old World sensibility now revalued as something *new*?[20]

SPEED AND CLIMATE CHANGE, "THE ROAD TO EXTINCTION"

All iterations of the slow movement identify speed as a pernicious virus that infects contemporary society. True, they cannot take full credit for bringing the problem of speed into the public consciousness, for other scholars have already examined the topic with great expertise. Paul Virilio, Hartmut Rosa, and Honoré are all to be credited with treating the topic with the seriousness it deserves.[21] Yet since its inception in the late 1980s, the slow movement has sought to address social ills through its attention to a slower, more mindful pace of life that combats what it deems the "virus of speed." As stated in the international Slow Food Manifesto, the movement diagnoses the current historical era as one riddled with problems, suffering from an array of troubles that emanate from modernity's dysfunctional understanding of progress. For indeed, today it is often difficult to disentangle the concept of "progress" from the attribute of speed, to imagine that something has progressed beyond an earlier stage without accelerating its pace and quickening its tempo. Stated differently, it appears inconceivable that something has progressed when it now adopts a slower pace and returns to an older, less tech-savvy lifestyle that approaches life more slowly and on a smaller scale. Yet this is precisely what the slow movement advocates, presenting something old as something new.

While one cannot deny that faster is often better, the Slow Food Manifesto affirms in no uncertain terms that the benefits of an industrialized, mechanized culture have by now "enslaved" humanity and held us captives to the "shackles" of speed that pauperize our lives. "Speed became our shackles," the Manifesto affirms, causing us to "fall prey" to an insidious enemy that "fractures our customs and assails us even in our own homes." More than this, the Manifesto affirms that the prevailing ideology so "assails" modern life that we now succumb to a "universal madness" whose pernicious harm we often fail to recognize. The Manifesto states:

Born and nurtured under the sign of Industrialization, this century first invented the machine and then modelled its lifestyle after it. Speed became our shackles. We fell prey to the same virus: 'the fast life' that fractures our customs and assails us even in our own homes, forcing us to ingest "fast-food."

Homo sapiens must regain wisdom and liberate itself from the "velocity" that is propelling it on the road to extinction. Let us defend ourselves against the universal madness of 'the fast life' with tranquil material pleasure.

Against those—or, rather, the vast majority—who confuse efficiency with frenzy, we propose the vaccine of an adequate portion of sensual gourmandise pleasures, to be taken with slow and prolonged enjoyment.

Appropriately, we will start in the kitchen, with Slow Food. To escape the tediousness of "fast-food," let us rediscover the rich varieties and aromas of local cuisines.

In the name of productivity, the "fast life" has changed our lifestyle and now threatens our environment and our land (and city) scapes. Slow Food is the alternative, the avant-garde's riposte.

Real culture is here to be found. First of all, we can begin by cultivating taste, rather than impoverishing it, by stimulating progress, by encouraging international exchange programs, by endorsing worthwhile projects, by advocating historical food culture and by defending old-fashioned food traditions.

Slow Food assures us of a better quality lifestyle. With a snail purposely chosen as its patron and symbol, it is an idea and a way of life that needs much sure but steady support.[22]

This allusion to "tranquil material pleasure" that guards against our current malaise thus promises more than mere gastronomical delight. It presents itself as the antidote to the current harms that lead down "the road to extinction," an antidote that can reverse the perilous direction in which we are headed. What is meant by "the road to extinction"? Having written the Manifesto in 1989, Petrini and co-author Folco Portinari may well have been aware of the connection between how we grow, transport, and sell food and the then-incipient global problems that accompany climate change. But they could not possibly have imagined to what extent the "road to extinction" brought on by global warming would loom large in the twenty-first century, and to what degree the life-threatening problems existing in 1989 would be exacerbated on a grand scale in the form of severe weather patterns, rising sea levels, the extinction of plant, animal, and bird species, and the massive displacement of communities. If the global crisis at the time constituted a "universal madness," how much more insane is the state of affairs in the twenty-first century.

As will be demonstrated, the movement approaches these troublesome speed-related issues—especially that of climate change—that threaten the globe from a number of angles; it has exhibited a good deal of creativity and imagination, as well as sheer administrative know-how, in its praxis. Slow Food and *Cittaslow*, for instance, actively embrace and address such topics as agriculture and agribusiness; seed-saving; farming techniques from around the world; the promotion of small-scale farmers and protection of migrant workers; the importance of safeguarding plants, animals, and insects faced with extinction; the value in preserving the cuisines of Indigenous Peoples; and the urgent need to eradicate food deserts. Other iterations of slow, such as slow fashion and slow tourism, strive to reduce our carbon footprint by fighting various industries that contribute to greenhouse gases. They promote low-tech or even no-tech practices that go against the grain of neoliberal habits of consumption. Yet even as justice infuses the slow philosophy, the focus on "tranquil material pleasure" is never lost, and the "right to pleasure" remains a focal point.

This search for pleasure inflected with a focus on social justice thus deliberately proceeds at a snail's pace and on a small scale, aiming to fight the globalized food industry at the grassroots level of everyday life. Famed restauranteur and Slow Food advocate Alice Waters insists that "less is more" as she exhorts others to "trust the power of the small scale."[23] The message is to keep it simple, small, and slow, to oppose the ideology and practices of fast in ways that will in turn have widespread ramifications (for instance, in how we farm, in where our clothing comes from and how often we replenish our wardrobe, and the carbon footprint left by travel). "Appropriately, we will start in the kitchen," the Manifesto avers, just as other iterations of slow start in our closets, our automobiles, or on our airplanes, for slow "is the alternative, the avant garde's riposte. Real culture is to be found here."[24]

"Real culture if to be found here." This starkly articulated phrase gives pause and invites reflection, for it reveals a large claim. In the twenty-first century so attuned to multiculturalism and postmodern displacements, who dares make pronouncements about "real" culture? The phrase expresses an idea heavy with value judgments and aesthetic preferences, positing assertions that for many operate against the grain in an irritating fashion. At the extreme, it sounds out of step with intellectual trends. Yet the slow movement indeed makes such claims, and without apology. Moreover, it does so while identifying itself as "the avant garde's riposte," the pushback of a *progressive* movement rather than the jeremiad of an old-fashioned position out of synch with the times. It insists that reconnecting to former rhythms, former lifestyles, and former ways of cultivating the earth delivers a superior and politically progressive culture that rescues us from our current misalignment. Going slow and curvy might thus be described as a forward-looking movement inflected with an Old World sensibility, a visionary politics that draws deeply on time-honored traditions and old-school, artisanal practices.

In its focus on urban life, *Cittaslow* similarly combats the virus of speed seeking to redefine "progress" along lines that are less harried and less tech-savvy. Deliberately taking its cues from the Slow Food mission, it concurs in the claim that speed represents a scourge on humanity such that achieving a more desirable lifestyle resides not in ramping up our mechanized, electronic, technology-dependent lifestyle, but in reducing it. Modern rhythms have become so accelerated, and modern lifestyles so cut off from nature, that a "progressive" solution actually resides in going back to a simpler time that allowed for a less hurried way of life. The *Cittaslow* Manifesto unequivocally indicts the modern world with imposing an inhumane pace on everyday life.

In the beginning man fed himself. He then sought shelter and protection: homes, villages, towns were founded. Finally, the time of the machines came with their increasingly hectic, frenetic rhythms of life. Today, man dreams of liberation from the many anxieties that his own progress has created. He is looking for a more serene, calm, reflective way of life. A wise man at the end of the contradictory and restless twentieth century would propose salvation through the model of the

Towns Where Living is Good

The new *Cittaslow* international movement wants to bring together, with a programme of the exchange of our towns' civilisations, industrious yet peaceful as they are, based on the serenity of daily life [sic]. The towns, be they large, medium-sized or small, share common features and aim towards the same end.

Towns animated by people "curious about time reclaimed," rich in squares, theatres, workshops, cafes, restaurants, spiritual places, unspoilt landscapes and fascinating craftsmen, where we still appreciate the slow, benevolent succession of the seasons, with their rhythm of authentic products, respecting fine flavours and health, the spontaneity of their rituals, the fascination of living traditions. This is the joy of a slow, quiet, reflective way of life.

The national and international association wanted by the participating towns and the Slow Food movement will be a continuous laboratory for a rebirth of humanism at the beginning of the third millennium.[25]

The *Cittaslow* movement thus seeks to enlarge the slow philosophy by extending that movement's commitment to a slower city pace, respect for the environment, respect for community and traditions, and an eagerness to hold on to local ties. According to Executive Director Pier Giorgio Oliveti, with whom I met in Orvieto, Italy, in the fall of 2019, it is only when the soul of the city, its *anima*, comes to life that the locale resists the "banal" commercialization of neoliberal globalization; it then becomes a place "where the living is good." For *Cittaslow,* the red snail of Slow Food morphs into one that is orange and that appropriately carries a city on its shell. At this writing, 278 cities around the globe have earned the title "*Cittaslow.*"[26]

Hence the task of Slow Food and *Cittaslow,* as with the entire slow movement, is to unmask the cunningly disguised, toxic harm so entangled in modern "progress" and propose something else in its place, disentangling our lives from the time-space compression that prevails in much of the industrialized world. True, the American Dream may still have a pre-industrial, agrarian element in its repertoire striving to keep alive a romantic closeness to the earth. Yet the virus of speed so crucial to the McDonaldization of society has

rete internazionale delle città del buon vivere

Figure 0.2 The *Cittaslow* mascot is an orange snail that carries a town on its shell. Source: Photograph courtesy of *Cittaslow* International.

largely eclipsed such notions of a return to the earth and instead glamorized the ability to become automated, mechanized, and increasingly accelerated. This triumph of industrialization has enlarged and deepened our carbon footprint exponentially, even as processed food has taken a toll on our health. Many have commented on the industry's efforts to shield the consumer from knowing where our food comes from and how it got here, and from learning that much of what we eat is not food at all.

Food critics Michael Pollan and Eric Schlosser deserve fulsome credit for having educated the American public along these lines and for working tirelessly to introduce a different sensibility where food is concerned.[27] "What is most troubling, and sad, about industrial eating is how thoroughly it obscures all these relationships and connection," Pollan writes. "To go from the chicken (*Gallus gallus*) to the Chicken McNugget is to leave this world in a journey of forgetting that could hardly be more costly. "[28] Schlosser reveals that a fast-food strawberry milkshake contains little food, but does contain amyl acetate, benzyl isobutyrate, cinnamyl isobutyrate, cognac essential oil, diacetyl, ethyl lactate, 4-methylacetophenone, methyl heptane carbonate, orris butter, rum ether, and y-undecalactone, among other things. Before the industrialized food system became so large, what people ate traveled a short distance from where it was raised to the dinner table. Today, Waters points out, "[i]t's fifteen thousand miles on average from where food is grown to where it's consumed. "[29] For the slow movement, this disconnect between our consumption and our realization of how consumption operates, the carbon footprint it leaves, encapsulates why a slow and curvy philosophy is so needed today.

But has the experience of lockdown and the grim reality of covid-19 changed our infatuation with the machine and its signature speed?

Covid-19 and Its Variants

The coronavirus pandemic that has ravaged our society since 2019 has forced Americans to adjust to an ethos that in many ways goes against the principles of the hard-working, profit-oriented American Dream. Covid-19 and its variants have wreaked havoc on Americans' ability to live out the traditional dream, and have forced us to countenance loss, economic hardship, and a sense of despair that hardly resonates with our time-honored optimism. The pandemic brought our society to a sudden and unexpected standstill that for considerable swathes of time seemed to indicate our going backward rather than forward, confirming a collective helplessness in the face of adversity. At this writing, the virus is again surging in ways that deeply disappoint former hopes of recovery. As is well known, the pandemic has exposed the injustices commonly experienced by many Americans, and especially by Black Americans, Indigenous people, people of color, the poor, and the undocumented.[30] Worldwide, the virus has caused a tremendous spike in the number of people suffering starvation.[31] All in all it has been a dismal time of unprecedented setbacks, with low-wage earners being hit eight times harder than high-wage earners.[32]

A decidedly slower pace of life has thus been thrust on American culture due to the pandemic, and sheltering in place has replaced the usual rhythms. Forced to adapt to a slower tempo, and for many a diminished if not disappearing income, it could be a moment when the slow philosophy more broadly construed exerts an influence on how Americans interpret the democratic experience, capturing the American imagination in a renewed, slow, and curvy fashion. Covid-19's scourge has forced us to consider doing things differently, to get creative in coming up with solutions and figuring out how we can surmount obstacles. It has mandated under pressure that we be resourceful in thinking outside the box and being inventive in our approach to work, family, friends, and community. "This virus is making us reevaluate our lives, our values, our ways of being," writes Yohana Agra Junker, "the ways in which we have (not) been present to one another, and how we must take a deep look at all our relationships with each other, with societal institutions, and with the Earth."[33]

One unexpected benefit of the pandemic's tragedy, then, resides in our recognizing that the American way of life is malleable. Our lifestyle and the Dream that accompanies it can undergo renegotiation. Working from home in sweatpants, having get-togethers on Zoom, attending drive-in religious services, remotely-held graduation ceremonies, and drive-by birthday parties: if we can reimagine these activities, what else can we do differently? How else can we get creative? We have the resources; what is needed are ingenuity and political will.

Slow Culture and the American Dream is divided into six chapters. Chapter 1, "What Is 'Slow Food'? What Are 'Slow Cities'?" presents the Slow Food and *Cittaslow* movements to the reader, explaining what they stand for, how they got started, and why they believe that "there is no smart without slow." The chapter chronicles the origins of Slow Food, which began in Rome's Piazza di Spagna where crowds protested the arrival of fast food. It also recounts the beginnings of *Cittaslow*, conceived in a mayor's office amidst the vineyards of Tuscany in an effort to bring the principles of Slow Food more fully into urban life. As it lays out the guiding ideas of slow, the chapter zeroes in on how we define modernity and how Americans in particular bind the topic of "the modern" to issues of speed. In order to provide more context on the slow movement, the chapter discusses other iterations of slow, specifically slow fashion and slow parenting.

Chapter 2, "What's So Great about Slow?" takes up this discussion by examining several political theorists' inquiries into the relationship between speed and democracy. It counters the claim that speed always encourages what William Connolly deems a tolerant pluralism and an inclusive lifestyles given that speed exposes people to alternative worldviews. It does this by citing examples of an openness to foreign cultures and unfamiliar mindsets that existed long before the age of industrialization, automation, and information technology. Without dismissing the many and irrefutable benefits of speed, the chapter demotes the virtues of fast by suggesting that perhaps fast is not what opens the mind; other things do that. An accelerated pace need not go hand in hand with a desirable cosmopolitanism. Hence the chapter insists that a commitment to slow proves imperative if we are serious about addressing climate change, for changing our relationship to the earth and to food in ways that will restore the ecosystem can only be done with a great deal of patience. To illustrate this point, the chapter discusses John Chester's film, *The Biggest Little Farm,* which chronicles a seven-year adventure in transforming an abandoned, moribund farm from a devitalized wasteland into a thriving, prosperous estate respectful of biodiversity.

Chapter 3, "Prometheus versus Noah: A New Humanism In the Twenty-First Century," delves into the many-layered meanings of two iconic figures in the Western tradition. In his writing, Petrini juxtaposes the modern Prometheus with the ancient patriarch, Noah. This juxtaposition illustrates that our time-honored understanding of modernity—epitomized in the forward-looking, risk-taking Prometheus—proves outdated, for in the twenty-first century we should emulate the venerable, obedient Noah who saves humanity through his humble caretaking and closeness to the natural world. This contrast between Prometheus and Noah shapes the chapter's argument and grounds the discussion regarding the uneasy fit between American industriousness and the slow philosophy.

Prometheus, the daring Titan trickster, defied the Olympian gods and stole fire in order to give it to humanity. Prometheus committed this theft out of love for humanity, since the gift of fire would of course prove immeasurably useful in terms of humanity's ability to advance. The chapter focuses on the significance of Prometheus' willingness to challenge the Olympian gods and take matters in his own hands, a gesture diametrically opposed to Noah's obedience to God's orders to build an ark, fill it with animals, and endure a deluge. Taking matters into one's own hands in the name of a humanity-centered progress as opposed to working with nature so as to save humanity constitutes the focal point of the Prometheus/Noah contrast. And while no one flatly dismisses the value of progress—Prometheus loved humanity and stole for our sake—we live in a time in which we should urgently reassess our relationship to nature. But can the Old Testament patriarch really become an American hero? Does Noah's caretaking deference to God's order jibe with the ever renewed, ever energized American Dream? The chapter asks whether a Noah-like sensibility could ever become mainstream.

Chapter 4, "Imagined Communities, USA: Crosses, Flags, Arches," examines the relationship between food and the cultural imaginary. It argues that food plays a pivotal role in the collective narrative of any nation such that taste and its surrounding associations prove integral to creating the stories that allow a country to cohere even if its stories, images, and underlying emotions do not always correspond to empirical reality. Food not only partakes of the imagined communities that we live by, it is one of its defining pillars. As Kennan Ferguson argues in his engaging *Cookbook Politics*, food creates communities and defines the parameters of who belongs.[34] It is central to how we define ourselves because it represents far more than calories and nutrients that sustain the body; it appeases hunger but also inspires the imagination, connecting us to a history, a family, a tradition, and even an entire country. And because the United States defines itself as the paradigmatic modern nation, fast food's association with speed, technology, automation, and standardization explains at least in part why it, and not Slow Food, has made such inroads into the collective American imagination. For while ethnic cuisines surely play an important part in constructing the American culinary landscape, the appeal of fast food seems unparalleled to our palate overall: it appears so universally accepted that for many the Golden Arches represent quintessential Americana, the epitome of the United States' cultural imaginary, the DNA that we all share. Yet the alternative food movement indicates that a cultural shift may be underway.

If so much of this book examines the relationship between food and the larger cultural imaginary, chapter 5 insists on our private, idiosyncratic relationship with food that defies standardization, or even explanation. Titled "The Rescuing Ark: The Art, the Music, the Place," this chapter argues that the aesthetics of food as witnessed in an expanding foodie culture may reveal a desire to resist the incursions of the ever-growing, ever-invasive neoliberal ethos epitomized in "workism." Following the argument of Dwight Furrow's lively and engaging *American Foodie*, the chapter explores the possibility that the explosion in foodie culture in the United States perhaps explains itself as a reaction against the incursions of a workaholic society so bent on sustaining its "progress" in the administered, standardized, technologically saturated world. America's pronounced interest in gastronomy may well reveal the desire to replace the formal logic of instrumental rationality with beauty and pleasure, allowing an aesthetic sensibility to flourish in place of an overvalued techno-savvy productivity.

Chapter 6, "Conversations with Snailblazers and the Charge of Elitism," tells of my conversations with employees, volunteers, mayors, and advocates of the slow movement, as well as an employee and students at the University of Gastronomic Sciences (UNISG) in Pollenzo, Italy. It documents a variety of different interpretations about where the slow movement is today and what it stands for. Conversations with mayors and an employee at UNISG were conducted in Europe where I had the opportunity to visit a number of *Cittaslow* cities as well as the university. I interviewed mayors recommended to me by the Executive Director of *Cittaslow*, Pier Giorgio Oliveti. Other interviews totaling roughly forty-five hours took place in the United States with Slow Food and *Cittaslow* volunteers and employees either in person, by Zoom, telephone, or email. The chapter considers the future of Slow Food, the difficulty of establishing *Cittaslow* cities in the United States, and the many strides that UNISG has made in terms of training students in the philosophy and practices of the slow movement. The chapter offers a realistic report from within the trenches about the impact that the movement has had thus far, and how it contributes to our ability to redefine our relationship to modernity. There is room for optimism: in the words of Richard McCarthy, a former Slow Food USA employee, "we are winning."

Slow Culture and the America Dream seeks to convince its readers that there is much to learn from the red and orange snails whose practical, every-day recommendations are within reach. As we seek to redefine ourselves amidst this pandemic and concurrent efforts to confront the urgency of climate change, the political praxis of slow as expressed in its various iterations has much to offer. If our redefinition of the American Dream incorporates at least some of the slow movement's teachings, my purpose in writing this book will be accomplished.

NOTES

1. Carlo Petrini, *Food & Freedom: How the Slow Food Movement Is Changing the World Through Gastronomy*, trans. John Irving (New York: Rizzoli Ex Libris, 2015), 239.

2. *Chef's Table,* Season One, Episode Two, "Dan Barber." David Gelb. Netflix, April 26, 2015.

3. Dan Barber, *The Third Plate: Field Notes on the Future of Food* (New York: The Penguin Press, 2014), 21.

4. Petrini, *Slow Food Nation: Why Our Food Should Be Good, Clean, and Fair*, trans. Clara Furlan and Jonathan Hunt (New York: Rizzoli Ex Libris, 2005), 23.

5. See Jim Cullen, *The American Dream: A Short History of an Idea That Shaped a Nation* (Oxford: Oxford University Press, 2004). See also Lawrence R. Samuel, *The American Dream: A Cultural History* (Syracuse: Syracuse University Press, 2012), and *The American Dream in the 21st Century*, edited by Sandra L. Hanson and John Kenneth White (Philadelphia: Temple University Press, 2011).

6. Laurence Shames, "The More Factor," in *Signs of Life in the USA*, ed.Sonia Maasik and Jack Solomon(Boston: Bedford/St. Martin's, 2003), 57.

7. John Archer, "The Resilience of Myth: The Politics of the American Dream," *Traditional Dwelling and Settlements Review,* vol. 25, no. 2 (Spring 2014): 7–21.

8. Archer, "The Resilience of Myth," 20.

9. Robert D. Putnam, *Our Kids: The American Dream in Crisis* (New York: Simon & Schuster, 2015).

10. Putnam, *Our Kids*, 233.

11. See especially Serge Latouche, *Farewell to Growth*, trans. David Macey (Cambridge, UK: Polity Press, 2009), and Ekaterina Chertkovskaya, Alexander Paulsson, and Stefania Barca, eds., *Towards a Political Economy of Degrowth (Transforming Capitalism)*, (Lanham, MD: Rowman & Littlefield Publishers, 2019).

12. The term "slow and curvy" is taken from Dehyun Sohn, Hee-Jung Jang, and Timothy Jung's *Go Slow and Curvy: Understanding the Philosophy of the Cittaslow slowcity Phenomenon* (Cham, Switzerland: Springer, 2015).

13. Carl Honoré, *In Praise of Slowness: How a Worldwide Movement Is Challenging the Cult of Speed* (New York: HarperCollins Publishers, 2004).

14. Honoré, *The Slow Fix: Solve Problems, Work Smarter and Live Better in a Fast World* (London, UK: William Collins, 2014), and *Under Pressure: Rescuing Our Childhood from the Culture of Hyper-Parenting* (New York: HarperCollins Publishers, 2008).

15. "The *Cittaslow* Manifesto," *Cittaslow*: International Network of Cities Where the Living Is Good, https://www.cittaslow.org/content/cittaslow-manifesto, accessed December 16, 2021.

16. Annemarie Mol, *Eating in Theory*, (Durham, NC: Duke University Press, 2021); for Sohn, Jang, and Jung, see note no. 12.

17. Sohn, Jang, and Jung, *Go Slow and Curvy*, 5.

18. See Jane Bennett, *The Enchantment of Modern Life: Attachments, Crossings, and Ethics,* (Princeton: Princeton University Press, 2001).

19. Michelle Boulous Walker, *Slow Philosophy: Reading Against the Institution*, (London, UK: Bloomsbury, 2018), xv.

20. Petrini, *Slow Food Nation*, 27.

21. See Paul Virilio, *Speed and Politics*, trans. Mark Polizzotti, (Los Angeles, CA: Semiotex(e), 2006); Hartmut Rosa, *Social Acceleration: A New Theory of Modernity,* trans. Jonathan Trejo-Mathys (New York: Columbia University Press, 2015). For Carl Honoré, see notes 13 and 14.

22. "The Slow Food Manifesto," http://slowfood.com/filemanager/Convivium%20 Leader%20Area/Manifesto_ENG.pdf, accessed August 18, 2018.

23. Alice Waters, *We Are What We Eat: A Slow Food Manifesto* (New York: Penguin, 2021), 163.

24. "The Slow Food Manifesto."

25. "The *Cittaslow* Manifesto."

26. https://www.cittaslow.org/, accessed November 18, 2021.

27. See Eric Schlosser's *Fast Food Nation: The Dark Side of the All-American Meal,* (New York: Harper Perennial, 2004); Michael Pollan, *In Defense of Food: An Eater's Manifesto* (New York: Penguin, 2009); Pollan, *Omnivore's Dilemma: A Natural History of Four Meals*, (New York: Penguin, 2007); see also Alice Waters *We Are What We Eat: A Slow Food Manifesto*, (New York: Penguin Press, 2021).

28. Michael Pollan, *The Omnivore's Dilemma,* 10.

29. Waters, *We Are What We Eat*, 36.

30. See, for example, Harmeet Kaur, "The Coronavirus Pandemic Is Hitting Black and Brown Americans Especially Hard on All Fronts," CNN, May 8, 2020.

31. The United Nation's World Food Program subsequently received the Noble Peace Prize in 2020, and its executive director, David Beasley, affirms that due to the virus those afflicted by starvation now number 270 million, up from the pre-covid 135 million. See "Leader of Nobel Peace Prize-Winning World Food Programme on Global Starvation Crisis," *The PBS Newshour*, Amna Nawaz, October 9, 2020.

32. See "The Deeply Unequal Consequences of the Pandemic," *The PBS Newshour*, Amna Navaz, October 2, 2020.

33. Yohana Agra Junker, "On Covid-19, U.S. Uprisings, and Black Lives: A Mandate to Regenerate All Our Relations," *Journal of Feminist Studies in Religion*, vol. 36, no. 2 (Fall 2020): 117.

34. Kennan Ferguson, *Cookbook Politics* (Philadelphia: University of Pennsylvania Press, 2020).

Chapter 1

What Is "Slow Food"? What Are "Slow Cities"?

In twenty-first century America, the culture of food is alive and well. A variety of new and different gastronomical ventures strive to improve the quality of our lives and to reeducate our palates, each promising a long list of benefits once our culinary habits change. Conceivably, we might separate these new eating philosophies into two separate camps. One is health-oriented and focused on the well-being of our bodies and the planet. Plant-based vegans, gluten resisters, Paleolithic cavemen, and fat-consuming Ketos all exemplify a healthful food culture that targets the well-being of our bodies as well as our planet. In good faith, they pursue a clean-eating culinary philosophy that seeks to counter America's love of fast food, our overconsumption of processed ingredients, and the agribusiness that controls farming while ignoring the importance of biodiversity. Collectively, they do an enormous business as they seek to correct a misalignment in our relationship to our bodies and to Mother Nature.

Side by side with this health-oriented approach there flourishes another camp. It consists of a well-articulated gourmet culture initiated in the mid-twentieth century and now eminently visible on television and throughout the media. This thriving American epicureanism produces a host of talented foodies who educate us about the pleasures of a refined and ethnically diverse gastronomy long absent from mainstream American cuisine. These gifted chefs and purveyors of haute cuisine, indigenous foods, and exotic ingredients introduce us to new culinary experiences that render our palate more cosmopolitan and make us more daring as cooks. Typically, this camp is less concerned with health and more committed to flavor, culinary experimentation, and widening the repertoire of what Americans eat. *Chopped*'s "Impossible Mystery Basket Ingredients," for instance, has been known to include Buddha's hand, squid ink, black garlic, and reindeer pâté, while *Guy's Grocery Games* has asked celebrity chefs to cook only with ingredients

beginning with the letter F. These energized, worldly epicureans focus especially on the *aesthetics* of food: the flavors, the texture, the presentation. We
can even describe certain foodie cookbooks as "gastroporn."

Whether health-oriented, gastronomically inspired, or both, all elements of
America's now booming foodie culture today proceed full throttle, insisting
that Americans need to become more health- and food-savvy by adopting a
new culture of food. Although these camps part company over certain issues,
they agree that a retooled diet is vital to our health, our politics, and our relationship to nature. Food for them represents a topic that expands outward from
our dinner plate to embrace the entire planet; so much is at stake when we
shop, cook, and eat. Thus, a robust, sophisticated, politically aware culinary
culture now stands in competition with our most deeply embedded habits,
rivaling America's signature love of fast food and simpler, downhome fare.

Indeed, even as foodie sensibilities take root and expand in everyday
American life, it remains the case that fast food has already burrowed deep,
very deep, and constitutes the manner in which many Americans feed themselves regularly. As George Ritzer convincingly argues, McDonalidization is
now our way of life. The alternative food cultures—one health-oriented, one
committed to fine cuisine—offer pushback against the embedded Goliath of
fast and processed food, but Goliath's embeddedness is formidable.[1]

Slow Food joins ranks with the expanding foodie enterprise eager to change
our habits and combat the culture of fast food. Most Americans have never
heard of Slow Food, in part thanks to its commitment to remaining grassroots
and keeping things local (despite some measure of organization and bureaucracy). It is by now an international movement which began in Italy in the late
1980s and has grown exponentially. Although some critics debate its status as
a bone fide social movement, this gastronomically grounded form of politics
entertains revolutionary ambitions and advertises its ability to meaningfully
impact the world.[2] The Slow Food movement interprets food as a nexus of
contemporary political issues with great transformative potential, for it views
our relationship to what we eat as linked to such pressing topics as climate
change, food insecurity and food deserts, the well-being and survival of
Indigenous Peoples, diabetes, and obesity. The movement actively safeguards
the ecosystem in its promotion of agroecology and biodiversity, thereby challenging the sinister side of large-scale industrialized farming, globalization,
and neoliberal policies.

Yet through all this, it never sacrifices a commitment to pleasure, for its
defining devotion to gastronomic mindfulness promotes the importance of
taste, the taste that carries emotional and cultural weight, linking us to our
childhoods, our family histories, and to our real or imagined memories. In the
words of Slow Food USA's executive director, Anna Mulè, taste occupies a
central position in the movement's philosophy; hence, we never want to "take

out the delicious." Life is too short to eat bad food, the movement maintains, demanding that we not only ingest, but enjoy in epicurean fashion.

Unlike other players who dot the alternative food landscape, the gastronomical philosophy of Slow Food thus underscores the vital importance of food's emotional weight that our frenetic, prepackaged lifestyle threatens to erase. Perhaps more than any other food-reforming advocate, it argues that when you say "food," you mean not simply something that you swallow for energy. Food means love (and hate?), childhood, a familiar kitchen or dining room, holidays, recipes, the means by which we connect. It means noisy get-togethers with copious spreads, but also the silent, single-minded coffee of Edward Hopper's *Nighthawks,* or the iconic bar scene in *Lost in Translation.* Food means our ability to recollect if not reexperience the past; it means the centrality of taste and smell in our highly idiosyncratic narratives, the structure of a feeling and the power of reminiscence. "One of the most important ingredients in his food is memory," says food critic Faith Willinger of chef and Slow Food advocate Massimo Bottura. "His memory of tasting things and the way things were made."[3] Ferguson similarly argues that recipes "participate in a kind of eternal return, each time the reading process is begun anew, yet also ghosted by past preparations . . . overlapping echoes of taste and temporality while also existing in the here and now."[4] In sum, food is part of our embeddedness inside a many-layered experience that envelops us, including the atomized individualism of lone eaters who appreciate the privacy of their car.

Because it reaffirms pleasure as a crucial emotional need as well as a right—the "right to taste"—the slow philosophy that emanates from the Slow Food movement recognizes the extensive reach of food. Petrini has tirelessly stressed the importance of bringing a slower pace to bear on the topic of food, thereby reeducating not only our palates but our relationships, including our relationship to the earth. Food and a slower pace are inextricably linked. Because he believes that the rhythms and practices of modern life have ravaged our gastronomic habits in ways that are detrimental to our everyday eating as well as to the earth, he places food at the center of this movement that is simultaneously backward leaning and forward moving, an effort to revive an Old World sensibility in the name of progressive politics. "Food is thus becoming an instrument of liberation," he writes, acknowledging that what we consume wields great political power.[5] Not just calories and nutrients, food is a means of freeing the world from the harms of modernization, a liberator from the problems wrought by the industrialized, globalized food system.[6] "Liberation, at last," Petrini writes, "from the most scandalous of yokes and cages: inequality, oppression, the damage it wreaks on the environment and people, the scandal of hunger and malnutrition."[7]

By joining the topic of *food* to the philosophy of *slow*, then, the movement imbues what we eat with renewed and broadened political force. For while food has always been political, "slow" indicates a commitment that takes aim at the pervasive malaise of the contemporary world. It doesn't simply describe a de-accelerated tempo but reveals an entire politics of resistance against the perils of a frenzied world whose frenzy has endangered the very planet we live on. "Slow" takes aim at globalization and the neoliberal ethos of conspicuous consumption, for in slowing down we reevaluate our priorities and rethink our choices. Hence the various guises of the slow movement—Slow Food, *Cittaslow*, slow fashion, slow travel, to mention a few—offer a unique combination of old-fashioned practices and forward-looking politics, a desire to revive artisanal methods devoted to quality while also seeking to address contemporary global problems. This duality of purpose thus unites a conservative impulse to resuscitate and retain something forgotten with a clarion call regarding the perils of modernization. Phrased differently, it believes that safeguarding older practices against the incursions of modernity in fact represents the wave of the future.

SLOW FOOD: GASTRONOMIC POLITICS
IN THE TWENTY-FIRST CENTURY

The Slow Food movement initially emerged due to pivotal events that reveal the sinister underside of modernity's focus on growth and speed. Petrini's inspired activism, always informed by a sense of humor that injects lightness into politics, came into focus in 1986 with two things that caught national attention. One was the death of twenty-three people and the hospitalization of many others due to the presence of methanol in Piedmontese wine. In an effort to cut costs, a wine distributor had tampered with his wares by mixing his vintage with methanol. The subsequent deaths and hospitalizations greatly damaged the reputation of Italian wine and caused exports to seriously nosedive. This adulteration of a hallowed staple of the Italian diet—"in the beginning was wine"[8]—brought many things into focus for Petrini and a cohort of similar-minded gastronomes worried not only about Italy's reputation on the world market, but about the livelihood of those whose income depended on the sale of wine. What about those who grew grapes, worked the soil, tended the vineyards, oversaw the harvest, and produced Barolo, Chianti, Valpolicella, Soave, Pinot Grigio, and a host of others; what would happen to their income? The sanctity of wine had been desecrated, and what was "closely intertwined with the lives of people [had been] ruined by the speculation of a bunch of crooks."[9] Thus the guiding principles and emergent mantra of the nascent Slow Food movement—"Good, Clean, Fair"—were keenly felt. Even today, Slow Foodies insist that food should not only be gastronomically delectable ("good"), but also carefully and ethically produced ("clean") in ways that consider the larger ecological and socio-economic context of all involved ("fair"). Each Slow Food principle matters as much as the others: never forgetting the delicious, we also never contaminate the product, never promote ecocide, and never exploit those who help deliver the food.

Changing the world with gastronomical joy thus first denotes the "good," the centrality of "tranquil material pleasure" to our lives that we should be able to savor with "slow and prolonged enjoyment." This "good" highlights our need to reclaim the "right to taste" by savoring "the rich varieties and aromas" of the kitchen and a heightened interest in *local* cuisines. The movement is careful to acknowledge that the gastronomical "good" will vary from culture to culture and from place to place, always avoiding standardization. Slow Food's presence in so many countries mandates this cultural sensitivity, as the movement values local traditions and cuisines including those of Indigenous Peoples. Indeed, the "Good, Clean and Fair: A Manifesto for Quality" pays tribute to a discerning palate: "A food's flavor and aroma, recognizable to educated, well-trained senses, is the fruit of the competence of the producer and of choice of raw materials and production methods, which should in no way alter its naturalness."[10]

Moreover, the "good" differs depending on the season of the year, offering variety according to time as well as place. The seasons introduce another form of diversification that both Slow Food and *Cittaslow* capitalize on, one that detracts from the homogenized uniformity of fast and pre-packaged food. For at the extreme, these foods' corporatized cultures alienate us from the seasonal aspect of food's availability and the fact that food exists as a direct outgrowth of the earth's temporality. True, fast-food eateries feature holiday items reflecting the seasons: Christmastime milkshakes and summertime spare ribs are clearly popular items that allow these corporate chains to honor the seasons. Yet the perennial availability of menu staples—hamburgers, French fries, breakfast sandwiches, apple pie—is what brings people back, and this reality alienates consumers from what is locally grown and temporarily available. "It's possible to get peaches in Alaska in December," writes Waters, an advocate of the Slow Food philosophy. "Evian is sold in Nairobi. You can buy sushi in Dubai."[11] Yet the "good" that the slow movement promotes strives to increase our respect for the seasonality of food, even if year-round availability has its appeal.

The second component of the mantra, "clean," reveals Slow Food's (and *Cittaslow*'s) opposition to the practices of large-scale monofarming agribusiness, practices that have substantially impacted how food is grown in recent decades. Large-scale agribusiness pursues an approach whose profit-driven motive encourages the cultivation of fewer crops in greater volume; much of it adheres to principles of the Green Revolution that a larger yield of fewer crops is what is needed to feed the world. This ethos is driven by the principle that bigger is better and that more is always desirable, something that Paolo Saturnini, the founder of *Cittaslow,* emphatically disliked and thus sought to oppose in outlining *Cittaslow* principles. The corporate takeover of traditional farming methods has thus given rise to the increased use of pesticides and chemical compositions derived from the herbicide Agent Orange, to GMOs (genetically modified organisms) and the ability to patent seeds, all of which greatly diminishes the latitude that farmers traditionally enjoyed. "[T]he problem with more-is-better," writes Waters, "is that we're not seeing the consequences to our environment and to our health."[12]

Cultivation of one or of few crops defies the principles of biodiversity so necessary to maintaining the balance of the ecosystem. "Clean" denotes food whose growth supports biodiversity without depleting the soil of carbon, food that does not upset the earth's delicate balance and thus eschews harmful chemicals, GMOs, and patented seeds. "Every stage in the agro-industrial production chain, consumption included, should protect ecosystems and biodiversity, safeguarding the health of the consumer and the producer," explains the Slow Food document "Good, Clean, and Fair: the Slow Food Manifesto for Quality."[13] And in an email exchange with me from March 2021, Petrini insisted that biodiversity has always constituted a central concern of the movement since it "is of interest to every living thing that inhabits the planet, from micro-organisms that enrich the soil . . . to the most developed forms of life" (translation mine).

Importantly, "clean" also designates an aversion to waste, a desire to make use of nature's generosity in a spirit of gratitude rather than of squandering. The ideas in play thus disagree with certain premises of the Green Revolution, such as the argument that technology and pesticides are key to producing higher yields of food, and that a more bounteous crop is inherently desirable regardless of its costs to the environment or to people's health. Rather than producing food in copious amounts, Slow Food and *Cittaslow* maintain that the manner in which it is produced supercedes its volume. Both maintain that "[t]here is food for everyone on this planet, but not everyone eats."[14]And if food works to promote rather than destroy health, it is crucial that it remain "clean," comprising "the sustainability and durability of all food-related processes . . . from distribution to end consumption, without waste, and based on conscious choices."[15]

The mention of "conscious choices" previews that final term in the mantra: "fair." Now we are explicitly in the realm of ethics, the realm of deliberate choices and policies that concern the innumerable persons who grow, harvest, distribute, and sell our food, as well as the many animals involved. An important premise of both Slow Food and *Cittaslow* is that the ethical treatment of persons and animals cannot be separated from the quality of the food; we cannot enjoy culinary delights and deem them "good" if there has been mistreatment in whatever form along the way. Slow Food and *Cittaslow* thus remain highly attentive to the ethical weight that surrounds all aspects of gastronomy, and explicitly link their recommended "sensual gourmandise pleasures" to a moral treatment of the world. They mandate that food be produced "without exploitation, direct or indirect, of those who work in the countryside . . . valorizing equity, solidarity, donation, and sharing."[16] The fact that their presence has expanded beyond Europe into so many regions of the world gives this premise ample articulation, for both movements have initiated projects and joined local forces fighting to eradicate harmful practices. For instance, in winter 2021, Slow Food USA donated money to two local projects in Puerto Rico, *Centro de Apoyo Mutuo La Olla Común* and *Comedores Sociales de Puerto Rico*, both of which work to combat hunger which has only grown worse with the pandemic.[17]

Another illustrative example is the adaptation of "narrative labels" used by Slow Food's "Presidia," which are collectives that work to protect plants and animals in danger of extinction, and that subsequently collaborate with local, traditional farming methods in an effort to safeguard what is threatened. These Presidia frequently operate against the interests of large-scale agribusiness since they work to protect endangered items—often catalogued in Slow Food's Ark of Taste—that do not promote the interests of monofarming. Thus, it is not enough to simply proclaim a product "organic" or ethically grown. More than that, the "narrative labels" tell the story of the food in an effort to impart knowledge about its history, its composition, how it is grown or raised, and so forth. This allows consumers to understand their food in ways that differ markedly from the advertising which often obscures so much. Narrative labels exemplify on a small scale the changed culture of food that the movement seeks to encourage, "through the pursuit of balanced global economies; through the practice of sympathy and solidarity; through respect for cultural diversities and traditions."[18]

The second event that marks Slow Food's inception had nothing to do with savoring wine, but involved French fries, hamburgers, and a high-profile fracas in Rome's Piazza di Spagna. This public square in downtown Rome constitutes an iconic locale where tourists flock to the famous Spanish Steps and one of the city's many fountains. Here, a McDonald's restaurant first sought to alter the Eternal City's historic center by offering an element of quintessential Americana. This meddling with Romans' beloved cityscape produced an outcry and the "Save Rome" committee, which mobilized urban natives to rally against a fast-food establishment's efforts to insinuate itself in the historic center. The culture of the Golden Arches, they argued, does not belong amidst ancient ruins, Baroque churches, and the leisurely lunch.

The mere thought of McDonald's happy meals assuming residency alongside marble statues of ancient deities and stern-faced emperors seemed intolerably dissonant.

Romans thus worried that the smell of French fries and presence of discarded hamburger wrappers would sully the piazza's aesthetic appeal and countervail the meaning of "when in Rome." Would food on the run now replace the unhurried repast and siesta so integral to the Roman way of life? Would Italians now consume meals on Vespas, in Fiats or Maseratis, with the fast-food chain's rounded capital M becoming as familiar as SPQR, the insignia of the ancient Roman Republic? Fashion designer Valentino, aghast at the thought of hamburgers and Coke permeating Italian culinary culture, did his best in a Roman court to stop this from happening. Valentino spoke for many when he argued that the "Americanization" of Italian culture brought "noise and disgusting odors" to the Eternal City. Meanwhile, throngs of supporters fearing "the degradation of Rome" shared plates of penne *al fresco* in the piazza as they listened to impassioned protest speeches from a makeshift podium. Political activism thus took the form of eating together, and pasta prepared "in vast iron skillets" assumed its role as a politically charged trope.[19]

Petrini's belief in gastronomy as serious cultural capital had in fact been in play long before either the wine scandal or McDonald's efforts to set up shop. He had been actively involved in organizations that sought to bring attention to food, such as the "Free and Praiseworthy Association of the Friends of Barolo" as well as "*Arcigola*." The latter represents an outgrowth of the national organization, ARCI (*Associazione Ricreativa Culturale Italiana*), a recreational association of the Italian left founded in the late 1950s. As Petrini explains, the name "*Arcigola*" represents a play on words, with "Arci" referring not only to the national organization but also to the prefix "arch." When attached to "*gola*"—meaning throat, but also implying appetite, gourmandizing, gluttony—*Arcigola* thus suggests "archgluttony," or the many pleasures of food and drink.[20] It has always demonstrated a lighthearted side that takes pleasure seriously, referring to itself as a group of "new big forks" (*neo-forchettoni*), "democratic and anti-fascist gluttons" (*golosi democratici e antifascisti*), and a collection of "new hedonists" (*nuovi edonisti*).[21]

Since the Italian left had long been associated with "the spirit of Franciscan poverty"[22] that frowns on material indulgence, *Arcigola* sought from its beginning to disabuse people of this association and to underscore the importance of gastronomy to all points on the political spectrum, including the left. It wanted to change the association between good food and bourgeois materialism, to revive culinary practices and remind all Italians, regardless of political stripe, of the importance of food to their collective identity. *Arcigola* sought to safeguard the centrality of pleasure to the Italian way of life broadly speaking and not allow the hurried demands of neoliberal McDonaldization to overshadow the nonchalant elegance of *sprezzatura,* the time-honored Italian commitment to an unhurried, unruffled demeanor dating back to the Renaissance.[23] *Sprezzatura* denotes one who knows how to enjoy life, to savor the moment and not spoil things through hurry. It implies the seemingly effortless grace of one who refuses to be harried, who never appears ruffled, and who knows the importance of pleasure. In an effort to combat the homogenizing influence of the post-war world dominated by American popular culture, *Arcigola*'s focus was on a more leisurely, deliberate, enjoyable way of life that emphasizes beauty, reflection, and the cultivation of human relationships. For instance, members of *Arcigola* would practice the Piedmontese ritual called *canté i'euv,* or "singing for eggs," during the Easter season. Congregated below farmers' bedroom windows at inconvenient hours, they would serenade them in the night and be repaid with food.

Yet alongside this playfulness stands the conviction that the virus of speed truly infects daily life. Worry that the globalizing economy was causing Italians to lose their focus when it comes to the pleasures of the table had already been on the mind of many Italians. If food is home, family, and identity, the burgeoning Slow Food movement was concerned that an important part of Italians' sense of self was being lost. It was no accident, for instance,

Figure 1.1 Carlo Petrini (center), founder of Slow Food, has been a leading inspiration since the movement's inception. Source: Photograph courtesy of Slow Food Italy and Carlo Petrini, © Tullio Puglia

that gastronomic politics arose in that country after Silvio Berlusconi popularized consumerist sensibilities and American-style soap operas, encouraging Italians to be avid shoppers and devotees of popular culture.[24] Although the industrialization of food had been part of Italy's post-war "economic miracle," Berlusconi's radical altering of Italian television and efforts to mainstream neoliberal sensibilities brought the country's signature celebration of *la dolce vita* more in line with *Dallas* and *Dynasty*.[25] "I'm in favor of everything American before even knowing what it is!" Berlusconi told *The New York Times* in 2001.[26] And the Italian public, "sick of terrorism and ideological paroxysms,"[27] was ready to enjoy the prosperity and Americanized culture that these goods represented. To many Italians, leaving behind old-fashioned traditions and the trappings of an earlier era signaled "progress" at that historical juncture. Hence, they embraced with enthusiasm mini-marts, 99-cent stores, Halloween costumes, and American television dubbed into Italian.

The Americanizing shift in cultural sensibility brought about by Berlusconi's 1980s commercialized television empire lent the movement a polarizing weight and helped clarify what it sought to oppose. Not everyone appreciated the loud game shows, the sometimes pornographic late-night viewing, the repeating infomercials, and the opportunities to win consumer goods that accompanied this shift. In an effort to oppose this commercializing trend, the emergent Slow Food movement placed emphasis on food and agriculture, not unnecessary spending and technological know-how. Seeking to preserve traditional culinary practices and the regionally distinct, slower-paced culture so focused on gastronomy, the movement viewed food as central not only to one's health, but also to one's identity and cultural embeddedness. It thus sought to preserve the regional identity of Italy's distinct areas and to safeguard these against a homogenizing McDonaldization. For as is well known, Italian cuisine is marked by distinct regional differences throughout the peninsula; this is the central theme of Stanley Tucci's *Searching for Italy* wherein Tucci takes us on a gastronomical tour of various Italian regions as he explores the country's differing cuisines.[28] For this reason, the term "Italian food" is a bit of a misnomer.

Ultimately, McDonald's succeeded in occupying a space at some remove from Piazza di Spagna, albeit in a modest, unimposing manner: the small Golden Arches are visible only on the awnings. Yet this incident, so rich with geo-political, cultural, and temporal significance, can be credited with spawning the Slow Food movement, which officially began with the signing of its Manifesto in 1989. And because an anti-commercial, anti-corporate sentiment provided a keynote to the movement's inception, it is little wonder that Slow Food remains a less well-known exponent of the multi-dimensional alternative food movement in the United States. With European fashion heavyweights like Valentino taking aim at our culinary habits, many Americans subsequently dismiss Slow Food as a coterie of elitist snobs educated in olive oil and wine but out of touch with American reality. My aim is to prove them wrong, to argue that the movement, like the slow movement in general, has much to teach us and shares a good deal with our fundamental beliefs.

Even at the movement's inception, Italians themselves seemed determined that Slow Food's corrective to our harried pace of life is for everyone, not just Europeans. Those protesting with penne from a large iron skillet also sported tee-shirts and held up posters featuring the face of Clint Eastwood with a scruffy beard and cowboy hat. Eastwood had recently been elected mayor of Carmel, California, and an initial gesture once in office involved discourag ing fast-food establishments in his city. Thanks to this anti-fast food stance, Romans hailed Eastwood as a cultural hero aligned with their sensibilities, indeed with *anyone's* sensibilities, provided a commitment to a slower pace, the preservation of local culture, and love of fine cuisine are present. They commended his standing up to the fast-food industry in order to protect the unique ambience of Carmel. The posters read: "Clint Eastwood, you should be our mayor."[29]

Points of overlap between European and American cultures thus emerge, as Eastwood's mayoral pronouncements dovetail with Romans' efforts to defensively block the infiltration of burgers and fries. An actor in a cowboy hat turned politician surely embodies a number of traditional *American* values: self-reinvention, rugged individualism, going it alone. If these qualities were appealing to Romans eager to preserve their cultural heritage, there must be similarities between Slow Food's mission and Americans' respect for those who take matters into their own hands. The bold individual daring to confront a larger, more established organization is the stuff of many an American cultural icon: Rosa Parks refusing to give up her seat, Daniel Ellsberg leaking the Pentagon Papers, Bernstein and Woodward breaking Watergate. In many ways, this is how the Slow Food movement sees itself: as a grassroots David taking aim at the entrenched Goliath.

Yet if as Americans we are *both* the David and the Goliath, it represents a tall order to favor one identity over the other. For on the one hand, the movement's goals resonate with the American cultural narrative: brave individuals rooting out a behemoth. But on the other, American fast food and its accompanying ideology *are* the behemoth in question. Indeed, the pejorative attributes of "Americanization" are not without validity, and my main concern lies in examining the difficulty of squaring a "slow and curvy" philosophy with America as *the* modern nations *par excellence*. For too many, "Americanization" operates as code signifying other cultures' willingness to jettison traditions and simply push forward in the name of progress: shops open on Sundays, ubiquitous laptops that transform any place into a workstation, family members all staring at screens, texting, messaging, tweeting, FaceTiming morning, noon, and night, each person eating separately.

The polarized nature of contemporary American culture may be partly responsible for our resistance to the movement. Given its European origins, and with Slow Food growing out of such cultural staples as the long lunch, afternoon siesta, aperitif, and commitment to *sprezzatura*, the reasons for an American resistance hardly need explaining. Added to this is the American politicization of food itself, given that it now carries heavy left/right, blue/red, green politics/development overtones. Without question, at this historical moment there is as much polarization in food as there is in party politics. To a good degree, food in America is locked in an ideological debate that pits one side against the other, such that the food itself becomes ideologically red or blue. Hence the alternative food movement is saturated with value-laden resonances and positioning; Slow Food is not exempt from the fray. Aaron Bobrow-Strain thus correctly points out that nearly every shade of the alternative food movement—organic, vegan, Keto—is now codified as "hipster." When we shop at farmers' markets, grow our own vegetables, and avoid the store-bought loaf by baking our own, we are in a political conversation whether we know it or not. Even a commonplace comestible such as bread operates as a trope freighted with political meaning, for "[t]he story of bread is the story of how social structures shape what we eat, and how what we eat shapes social structures."[30] In America as elsewhere, food functions as both bodily sustenance and ideological marker as witnessed in various food-grounded expressions: "crunchy granolas," "white-breaded wonder," "eat more kale."[31]

Yet I have to be careful in characterizing the slow movement as being uniquely leftist and progressive in orientation, for many of its arguments resonate on the American right. Rod Dreher assures us that "counter-cultural conservatives" share many points of overlap with progressives on the left as witnessed in their Birkenstocks, ecology-mindedness, and love of organic food.[32] He insists that elements of the right also endorse a back-to-the-land, agro-ecological worldview consistent with Slow Food's focus on "good, clean, and fair," community involvement, and the need to stave off an invasive bureaucratic, technocratic, expert-heavy ideology. Coming from the contemporary right, Dreher insists that many conservative Americans willingly offer pushback to the culture of fast and processed food. "[W]e're 'crunchy,' as in the slang for 'earthy,'" he writes, "because we stand alongside a number of lefties who don't buy in to the consumerist and individualist mainstream of American society."[33] Thus, eating low on the food chain as protest against ecocide, diabetes, and obesity does not automatically indicate a leftie: some strains of American conservatism are just as devoted to back-to-the-land basics as are progressives.

But surely former President Trump's love of fast food encapsulates the spirit of America's populist base; when asked by a journalist to identify what part of Trump is not elitist, his Communications Director Anthony Scaramucci pointed to the president's love of fast food. "How about the cheeseburgers, how about the pizzas that we eat?"[34] During his presidency, Trump's love of cheeseburgers and fast food affirmed this distinction between a refined palate and the nearby drive-through while imbuing it with a wide array of cultural, political, and emotional meanings. Trump's promotion of fast-food culture thus accompanies the sartorial semiotics of his long red tie, solidifying the association between an indignant populism and the fast-food industry. Contrasting sharply with Michelle Obama's vegetable garden outside the White House, Trump encourages "the bland nourishment of Americana . . . burgers and meatloaf, Caesar salads and spaghetti, See's Candies and Diet Coke."[35] And when the White House endorses Americana, the latter's aesthetic bores ever more deeply into the collective imagination and receives a special benediction. In 2016, Ashley Parker of *The New York Times* wrote that Trump "is hoping to become the nation's first fast food president," since in the former president's own words, "The Big Macs are great. The Quarter Pounder. It's great stuff." Summing it all up, "He'll have fries with that."[36]

For Slow Food and other foodie alternatives, part of the difficulty therefore arises from the fact that establishing a viable counternarrative takes place in a highly politicized context. In these anxious, polarized times it is hard to offer criticism of the American mainstream without entering a contentious fray. Left and right claim deeply entrenched territory; hence topics of discussion that might be kept free of political overtones are in fact saturated and even operate as code: kale probably signals left, while homeschooling may well signal right.

Slow Food USA, thus, insinuates itself into a culture that is increasingly aware of food, and increasingly political about its meanings.[37] Of course, those who pioneered new approaches to gastronomy and now serve as the avant garde of foodie culture did not think in political terms, at least not overtly. Julia Child, James Beard, Craig Claiborne, and Alice Waters have exerted great influence on the American gastronomical sensibility, operating out of the simple love of fine cooking. Together these influential chefs opened new vistas for the American palate in the mid-to-late twentieth century, and helped it move from eating to dining, from frying and baking to sautéing, braising, fricasseeing, and fondueing. "I was learning to take *time*—hours, even—and *care* to present a delicious meal . . . (since) [m]y teachers were fanatics about detail and would never compromise,"[38] Child writes of her time at the Cordon Bleu in Paris. There can be little doubt that the influence of these progenitors has deeply impacted the contemporary American palate, since in David Kamp's words, it is now "a great time to be an eater . . . [since] food is one area of American life where things just continue to improve."[39]

Still, for many, downhome Americana means fast food, packaged food, and simple methods of cooking. Without question, today fast food and other forms of industrialized eating are thriving in America, and a McDonaldized model that promotes efficiency, calculability, predictability, and control has been adopted by many businesses. Fast food's appeal remains grounded in familiar tastes, low cost, the time-space compression of eating in one's car, and the commitment to speed so integral to the American Dream. Since the 1950s, this approach to eating has become "traditionally" American and associates simpler, ready-to-eat food with our shared values. One need hardly do extensive research to perceive the extent to which the fast-food industry and its related culture of ready-to-go dominates American life: a visit to any medium-sized American urban center illustrates this point resoundingly, for there are fast food eateries galore, even within grocery stores and gas stations. True, McCafé now serves cappuccinos, macchiatos, and lattes, but these hardly obscure the main attraction, i.e., burgers and fries.

To recognize a politics of food clearly confers ideological meaning onto the latter, imbuing what we ingest with distinctly social attributes. Yet several authors have probed even further, insisting that not only food, but eating itself is an act fraught with philosophical implications. *Philosophers At Table: On Food and Being Human* and *Philosophy Comes to Dinner: Arguments of the Ethics of Eating* offer important arguments surrounding the philosophical meaning and morality of food.[40] For instance, they consider how the act of eating burrows deeply into the Western tradition's mind/body split, the privileging of sight over taste, and the ethics of how we obtain what we eat.

Yet to my knowledge it is Annemarie Mol who goes furthest in her analysis of eating, for her *Eating in Theory* reveals the deepest implications about our connection to the earth and to others as embodied in the everyday act of ingesting food. Mol convincingly illustrates how the act of eating undermines the sovereign subject and offers a radically different vision of human beings as bodies enmeshed in the social and natural worlds. By its very nature, eating makes trouble for a human-centered, humanly sovereign, human-dominated world with the individual at its center, for the very act of ingesting food countervails our supposed control. We are in fact deeply interconnected with the outside world, both natural and social:

> My eating body . . . far from remaining distinct, incorporates bits and pieces of the outside world. And while externally entangled, internally I am differentiated. A gastrointenstinal tract here, lungs there, welcoming different kinds of matter . . . But if there is traffic across bodily boundaries, there is also transformation as I eat, my food stops being food and becomes a part of me. . . . while,

as walker, I move through the world, when I eat, it is the world that moves through me.[41]

Our reliance upon food thus gives the lie to our reputed insular self-control and self-directed agency, drawing upon a host of dependencies, interconnections, and permeable boundaries: seeds that morph and grow, geographic boundaries that are crossed, food that digests and is either absorbed or expelled. These actions go dramatically against the grain of the individual's primacy; they unravel our supposed dominance over nature and instead underscore our status as *part of* nature. The food we ingest changes shape and substance as it literally becomes part of the eater, the eater who depends on food's nutrients in order to stay alive. "In eating, then, I *am* a semipermeable, internally differentiated being, getting enmeshed in intricate ways with pieces of my surroundings," Mol writes.[42]

Thus, the eater is not an individual entirely in charge of the process; although choices can be made about what, when, and where to eat, or with whom, so much of the ensuing physical experience operates against the grain of a sovereign subject who dictates what happens. Because the body incorporates, assimilates, and digests food in ways that constantly permeate boundaries and put into question the subject's authority, we can posit eating as an anti-humanist trope, a metaphor that undermines our sovereign status. Eating magnifies human interdependency, just as the need for food underscores the individual's dependency on the surrounding physical environment and economic setting needed to provide sustenance. Even before arriving at our plates, a vast array of things have happened involving a great number of people; moreover, the process of digestion has already begun in the cooking process which breaks food down in ways palatable to our systems.

Eating clarifies how much of our well-being and indeed survival has nothing to do with thinking, since our use of food takes place in regions other than the brain. Human agency is not even in play, for we stand on a continuum with nature, not above it. "Eating suggests a model of *being* in which the body that *is* overflows into her surroundings," Mol explains just as the surroundings—the food that she ingests—overflow into her.[43] "Overflowing" suggests water, something meandering and malleable, something that bends and curves like a river. If the human subject overflows into her surroundings as the latter overflow into her, then a slow and curvy ethos is in place whether the eater recognizes it or not.

By countervailing the intellectual hubris of the sovereign subject, the act of eating undercuts the claims of instrumental rationality, that form of rationality that sustains the myth of human sovereignty so integral to the Western tradition. "What human beings seek to learn from nature is how to use it to dominate wholly both it and human beings," Max Horkheimer and Theodor

Adorno write of the Enlightenment's legacy. "Nothing else counts."[44] Yet in the twenty-first century things other than *dominating* nature count very much, such as reversing climate change and confronting the humanitarian crises that it unfortunately fosters. If the legacy of the Enlightenment has been nature-dominating in principle, it is clearly time to undo that legacy; it is time to take seriously the anti-humanist argument that human mastery needs dethroning.

Importantly, then, what I am calling the implicit "anti-humanism" of the Slow Food movement (and, to a good degree, of the entire slow movement) appears to others as a repurposed and rehabilitated form of humanism, a refreshed version of an old doctrine that demands reconsideration in the contemporary context. In a 2009 interview with *The Guardian*, for instance, Petrini explained that the time is ripe for this repurposing, such that the "false global economy" will give rise to "a new humanism . . . a change in values and a change in . . . what richness is . . . Rather than constant consumption it might be better to recycle and to give."[45] In short, a version of anti-humanism can function as the new humanism.

A new humanism based not on sovereign individualism but on interconnection and permeable boundaries proves to be one of the greatest contributions of the slow movement, and of Slow Food. It represents a shift in paradigm that radically reorients the expansionist American Dream away from the playlist of impressive achievements and exceptional individuals toward something rooted in permeable boundaries and interdependence. In the case of Slow Food this underscores the urgent need to rethink the meaning and role of processed and fast food in American life, a way of feeding ourselves that dismantles agribusiness and the drive-through, single-serving lifestyle that now contributes to our unsustainable relationship to the earth. Authors such as Jonathan Kauffman, whose work is discussed later, come to my aid in this rethinking, for Kauffman convincingly demonstrates how something as originally countercultural as yogurt and granola—"hippie food"—can eventually become mainstream, everyday fare.[46] Paradigm shifts can and do occur provided they have enough enthusiastic backers behind them.

Yet the new humanism—the anti-humanist humanism—promulgated by Slow Food does not confine itself to the topic of food. One of the movement's most influential outgrowths, *Cittaslow*, elaborates its philosophy in an extension to civic life, bringing the slow and curvy worldview to bear on the organization and administration of cities, towns, and villages. We now turn to the topic of "slow cities" and their vision for an improved, humane urban lifestyle that values quality of life above all else.

"Slow Cities," The Mission of *Cittaslow*

A major outgrowth of Slow Food is to be found in *Cittaslow,* or "slow cities." *Cittaslow* embodies these principles in an effort to redefine civic life, pulling it away from modernity's time-space compression and rethinking the trend toward constant urban growth and acceleration.

While it must be admitted that certain slow cities promote their "*Cittaslow*" status as a means of attracting "slow tourism" and thus raising revenue, they nevertheless do so out of a commitment to certain tenets of slow tourism: preserving architecture and infrastructure, featuring heritage foods and artisanal products, encouraging communal space free of traffic.[47]

This movement originated thanks to the vision of the late Paolo Saturnini whom I had the pleasure of meeting in November of 2019. Saturnini thrice held the office of mayor in Greve, a small town in Tuscany famous for its wine. A friend of Petrini's and advocate of the slow philosophy, he explained to me how, as mayor, the principles of Slow Food seemed to him eminently applicable to the government of urban life, and that what Petrini envisioned in the realm of gastronomy he in turn envisioned for urban living. He supported Slow Food, and saw its wider application to cities and towns, enhancing the quality of life such that the *Cittaslow* label would designate "an international network of cities where the living is good."[48]

Saturnini thus trailblazed the effort to apply Slow Food principles at the municipal level, exhorting mayors to promulgate the philosophy of slow in keeping with each city's particular history, culture, and demographics. Saturnini can thus be credited with having conceived of a movement that today has an international reach extending at this writing to 278 cities in 31 countries. While the movement is especially strong in Italy, Turkey, Poland, Germany, the Netherlands, and France, a good number of designees also exist in China and South Korea, with several in Japan. Dehyun Sohn, mentioned above, has been a strong advocate of the movement in the Korean context. Still other *Cittaslow* cities dot the landscape in Africa, Australia, New Zealand, and Latin America. The movement thus balances both expansionist and anti-expansionist tendencies, for while it welcomes its own growth in numbers, it promotes a small-is-beautiful, slower-is-better, artisanal and locavore lifestyle. Although currently not present in the United States, it represents an influential and successful outgrowth of the Slow Food movement.

A humble and amiable man, Saturnini met with me in his former office to discuss how the idea of *Cittaslow* came to him and how he carried it out. He was eager to share his ideas and in no way exuded a proprietary attitude toward the movement. Of primary concern to him was the manner in which the globalizing economy was bringing an unwelcome uniformity to modern life, altering the landscapes and changing the rhythm and values of our lives

Figure 1.2 Paolo Saturnini (left) is the founder of *Cittaslow*, an outgrowth of Slow Food. Source: Photo taken by author.

in ways that lose touch with rich traditions. Under a globalized regime, various species of plants were facing extinction and he wished to see them preserved for both ecological and culinary reasons (precisely the mission of Slow Food's Ark of Taste and Presidia). Industrial farming was playing havoc with the earth's delicate balance, producing something unnatural—"*snaturato*"—and potentially sinister. Because Saturnini's native region in Tuscany produces a good deal of wine, Chianti being among them, and also attracts a fair number of visitors, it is easy to understand why he might be motivated to implement the basic principles of *Cittaslow*, striving to safe-guard "identity, memory, environmental protection, justice and social inclu-sion, community as well as an active citizenship."[49]

Seeking to bring the slow philosophy to life through the city, *Cittaslow* therefore emphasizes the beauty of (mostly small) cities and farms which "have a soul" worth preserving. History, architecture, food, music, and art arc things that the movement identifies as crucial to its efforts to go slow and curvy; they are the things that create memory rather than the "standardized and meaningless spaces" of so many modern cities.[50] *Cittaslow* maintains that large-scale industrial farming exerts a depraved influence on small-scale farms, delivering an unnatural output that goes against the rhythms and needs of Mother Nature. In many ways, then, the movement is aligned with the concept of "degrowth" in political economy, which argues against the prem-ise that sustained, unchecked economic growth always represents a desirable goal.[51] Yet in an effort to remain flexible, this principle of degrowth is not uniformly enforced.

Still, the movement's philosophy embodies principles that are astutely forward-looking and worth fighting for. It was in his mayoral office, located in a beautifully preserved medieval palazzo, that Saturnini thus met with Petrini in 1999 to found the *Cittaslow* movement. Together with the mayors of three other Italian cities—Bra, Orvieto, and Positano—they worked to produce the original charter outlining the movement's central tenets and pro-moting an "international network of cities where living is good." While legal channels represent one way in which communities can fight the influence of globalization, Saturnini explained, *Cittaslow* represents a different and more philosophically comprehensive approach to fighting the industrialized, globalized world's pauperizing influence. For him, twenty-first-century neo-liberal values deliver a homogenized, standardized culture highly inflected with commercialism and a consumerist lifestyle and come at too high a price. Similarly, at the 2011 *Cittaslow* International Assembly in Lidzbark Warmiski, Poland, Sohn commented on how quickly South Korea had devel-oped since the 1950s, energetically rebounding from a state of dire poverty to one of advanced industrialization and a modernized lifestyle. Yet amidst this remarkable achievement, Sohn maintains, "we lost a lot of things: cultures and environment . . . so we love the *Cittaslow* philosophy."[52]

If a city or town wishes to become *Cittaslow* certified, it must apply for this title and undergo an examination process, the "Cittaslow Certification Scheme." The *Cittaslow* Charter stipulates 72 principles that cities carrying the *Cittaslow* label must strive to uphold, one of them being that, unless the Coordinating Committee rules otherwise, they cannot have a population exceeding 50,000 residents. These 72 principles are in turn grouped into seven subdivisions that articulate the movement's philosophy, including 1) energy and green environmental policies; 2) infrastructure policies that encourage walking, biking, and the availability of benches; 3) the quality of urban life, focusing attention on the repurposing and reuse of marginalized areas; 4) agricultural, touristic, and artistic policies undertaken with a view toward rekindling traditional crafts and small-scale farming; 5) best practices that encourage hospitality and social integration; 6) social cohesion, including concern for disabled persons, minorities, and those who experience discrimination; and 7) partnerships with other communities in an effort to promote organic farming and artisanal foods. Above all, the focus is on retaining a city's uniqueness and local identity rather than resembling any other locale. "By now everyone knows there is no 'good life' without slowness," affirms "Innovation by Tradition," an in-house *Cittaslow* document, "even if we need to change lifestyles and rethink our behaviour in production and consumption."[53]

Headquartered in Orvieto, Italy, this movement represents "an international network of cities where living is good." While participating cities must honor the charter in order to be counted, Executive Director Oliveti insists that a certain degree of flexibility is in order. Petrini concurs that rules and regulations are necessary, but that one needn't become "ridiculous" in their execution: "there are still a great many people wandering around in gastronomic straightjackets."[54] Every city, every culture, every history is different, and it is more important to spread the philosophy of slow than it is to be meticulous about protocol.

I met with Director Oliveti in September of 2019, and we discussed the movement for several hours. I was impressed with his enthusiasm and confidence in the movement, as well as his generous flexibility in terms of cities' differing needs. Going slow and curvy plays out differently in different settings, he insists; if the aim is to restore the uniqueness of a given culture, then homogeneity is to be avoided. For at the extreme, becoming dogmatic regarding *Cittaslow*'s charter could go against its very principles and ironically spoil its mission. Already globalization has cast its "standardized, banalized" pall over things; the point for *Cittaslow* is to go in the opposite direction.

This explains why mayors' offices participating in the movement have a special charge in carrying forward the slow philosophy. While growth is not wholly frowned upon, it is the general consensus of *Cittaslow* advocates— mayors as well as "Supporters" and "Friends" of the movement—that urban growth be undertaken only with the principles articulated above. Examples

Figure 1.3 Pier Giorgio Oliveti (right) is now the executive director of *Cittaslow*. Source: Photo courtesy of Pier Giorgio Oliveti.

from *Cittaslow* South Korea and China dramatically illustrate efforts to countervail the influence of rapid modernization and economic growth. The region of Yaxi, China features the annual Golden Rape Flower Festival and Land Art Festival in an effort to reestablish a harmonic relationship between inhabitants and their landscape, showcasing the beauty of bamboo, lavender, pear trees, and sunflowers. In Wando, South Korea, the annual Slow Walking Festival encourages leisurely strolls, and its beautiful walkways are known as "a nature gallery without a roof." Hadong is the site of the country's first wild green tea plantations, grown naturally without the use of agricultural chemicals. Jeonju Hanok Village features 735 traditional "hanok" houses, whose graceful sloping roofs and well-manicured walkways surely correspond to the aspirations of a "slow and curvy" philosophy.[55]

From my visits, phone calls, and emails with cities that carry the *Cittaslow* label, I discern an obvious effort to preserve what is unique to that locale and to cultivate what cannot be reproduced elsewhere. Not only the food, wine, and teas, but the city layout, the architecture, the singularity of the urban *Gestalt* constitute defining features that participating mayors seek to safeguard against big box influence conveying "anywhere." This was brought home to me when I visited Positano in late September 2019. In many ways,

this Southern Italian city has changed little over the years, such that my suit-
case was lifted up to my hotel located high on a hill by placing it in a rusty
metal box suspended by a steel chord. The hotel functions nicely without
going high tech. In Olivetti's analogy, *Cittaslow* is the yeast while the existing
cities are the flour. "And the yeast works!" ("*Il lievito sta lievitando!*") he told
me with great enthusiasm.

As will be discussed in chapter 6, there are currently no American cities
that carry the label *Cittaslow*, although Sonoma, Sebastopol, and Fairfax all
gave it an honest try for several years in Northern California. Thus, while
Slow Food has made inroads on American soil, *Cittaslow* has fared less well.
"*Aspetto gli Stati Uniti!*" "I am waiting for the United States!" exclaimed
Director Oliveti, throwing open his arms when I noted that the movement is
virtually unknown in my homeland.

"Festina Lente": Other Expressions of Slow

Let us now consider other expressions of slow in order to gain a fuller picture
of the philosophy under discussion, and to appreciate how the slow movement's curvy appeal has articulated itself in things other than food and city
life. For as Gabriel Rockhill correctly argues, this new aesthetic must be
based not only on ambitious ideas and good wishes, but on concrete institu-
tional change and planning that is often hard and emotionally trying. It asks
not only that we envisage doing things differently, but "requires a patient and
resolute construction of alternative practices, communities and institutions."[56]
Here, I consider The World Institute of Slowness, slow fashion, and slow
parenting.

As mentioned, many Americans have never heard of Slow Food, and there
are currently no *Cittaslow* urban spaces in the United States. Nevertheless,
the slow movement writ large has made an impact on our country as it has
on other advanced industrialized nations. The ideas that sustain the slow
movement have burrowed deeply into societies around the world, producing
literature, promoting practices, and giving rise to organizations that uphold
the slow philosophy. Indeed, by now there are numerous expressions of
slow: not only the lesser-known Slow Food and *Cittaslow*, but also slow
fashion, slow parenting, slow money, slow tourism, slow art, and slow shopping. Honoré deserves much credit for bringing the philosophy mainstream
through his books, Ted Talks, and website that features a list of "slow links."
There also exists a think tank, The World Institute of Slowness, founded by
Geir Berthelsen in Kristiansand, Norway, whose aim is to explore the many
ways that slowness can penetrate modern life, seep into our consciousness,
and reshape our metric of progress. The key component of the Institute's philosophy centers around altering how we think about time and honoring not a

sequential, chronological approach to our lives but one more aligned with the ancient Roman motto, "*Festina Lente*," meaning "make haste slowly."

Trained in physics and industrial psychology, Berthelsen has counseled the private sector in an effort to introduce a new work ethic into the workplace, one that reduces stress and makes the environment more collaborative and even fun. Indeed, the ultimate goal strives to make work feel more like play inasmuch it is driven not by an output-oriented sense of urgency, but by a team effort and sense of synergistic collaboration. Berthelsen believes strongly that stress exerts a negative effect on our performance; when we feel hurried, anxious, and race with the clock, we actually perform more poorly than when we are relaxed and having fun, because fun makes us feel engaged. "The more stress we feel, the dumber we are," he asserted when I interviewed him via Zoom in September 2021.

In a video explaining The World Institute of Slowness, Berthelsen correctly points out that the Greeks had two fundamentally different understandings of time: kronos, or chronological time that operates sequentially, and cairos, whose meaning invokes not linear direction but the fulfilled present, the ability to step out of a serial progression and instead experience an amplitude in the here and now. "Fulfilled" time might of course mean a number of things: in religious parlance, it invokes eternity and the ability to step out of the terminus of chronology; in psychological and aesthetic terms, it refers to moments of great insight and inspiration in which a newfound clarity enlightens an array of other things, moments when many things come together and seemingly surpass temporal limits. In his analysis of modernity's futile efforts to reestablish meaning, Walter Benjamin refers to this possibility as *Jetztzeit*, that moment when a truly definitive break might be made and history could experience a redemptive new beginning, something other than the repetitive emptiness of capitalism's time. "History is the subject of a structure whose site is not homogeneous, empty time," he writes, "but time filled by the presence of the now [*Jetztzeit*]."[57] Another Frankfurt School scholar, Herbert Marcuse, also develops the notion of an alternative "aesthetic dimension" which stands in opposition to the prevalent instrumental rationality that typifies a task-oriented world. "The memory of gratification is at the origin of all thinking," Marcuse affirms, "and the impulse to recapture past gratification is the hidden driving power behind the process of thought."[58]

This occluded aesthetic dimension that is so unlike the work-centered ethos of our world necessarily engenders an alternative understanding of time more aligned with cairology's non-linear, non-sequential reading of experience. Of course, the slow movement cannot claim to straightforwardly realize cariological time and reorient our hardwired attitudes. Yet it does claim to promote a different angle on time that hopes for a change, a rupture in our thinking and doing that will adhere less to the dictates of efficiency-oriented instrumental

rationality. A "curvy" approach to life reassesses the modern world's emphasis on speed and output, diminishing a sequential reading of things in favor of
one that revalues and rehabilitates the importance of the present.

Berthelsen's wife, Anna Berthelsen, is an artist whose creative rehabilitation of public space might be deemed an example of the aesthetic dimension.
Through her artwork, she transformed an unpleasant, unwelcoming public
space underneath a bridge in Kristiansand into an area where children's artwork is now on display. The dark, foreboding quality of that space was radically altered when Anna painted the walls underneath the bridge a welcoming
shade of sky blue and commissioned no fewer than 5,300 school children up
to the age of sixteen to paint their dream on a small piece of glass. These
pieces of glass exhibiting the children's dreams reflect sunlight and thus con-
fer a glimmering, almost radiant feel to the space, now called "Slow Bridge."
Transformed from something foreboding into something soothing and imagi-
native, the area invites pedestrians to pause and consider the many drawings.
As Sohn, Jang, and Jung write, slow does not resonate with the linear tendencies of an accelerated pace. Rather, the slow philosophy always tends toward
what is "curvy," meandering, pensive, and aware of beauty. While man-made
items adhere to a "straight" mentality of sharp right angles and a mission-
oriented need to save time, the authors argue, nature always prefers to go
"curvy," to take its time at the appropriate pace. "Fast is straight," the authors
write, "but slow is curvy and patient . . . It is time to learn the slowness,
mildness, and composure in a life and how to love from the curvy."[59] As the
mascot of both Slow Food and *Cittaslow,* the snail's deliberate and dawdling
pace proceeds under a shell characterized by voluptuous curves.[60]

Slow fashion represents another expression of slow that especially takes
seriously its commitment to green politics. It represents a movement eager
to raise awareness about the significant changes that have taken place in the
realm of the clothing industry and clothes-buying over roughly the past forty
years. It opposes "fast fashion," which emerged in the 1980s, an industry
devoted to "the production of trendy, inexpensive garments in vast amounts at
lightning speed in subcontracted factories, to be hawked in thousands of chain
stores."[61] Slow fashion seeks to meaningfully counter these business practices
of the fast fashion industry and raise awareness about the economic, social,
and ecological harm that it does.

Today, our consumption of clothing differs drastically than that of our
parents and grandparents, for by any standards we go through wardrobes
more quickly and in greater volume than in the past. Shopping represents
a national pastime in the United States, and we have come to expect many
more garments to fill our closets only to remain there for shorter and shorter
time spans. But where do these clothes come from at such record speed? Slow

Figure 1.4 Slow Bridge represents the artwork of Anna Berthelsen, whose husband Geir Berthelsen founded The World Institute of Slowness. Source: Photo courtesy of Anna and Geir Berthelsen.

fashion seeks to instruct consumers who may be unaware of the voraciousness of their habits and the heavy cost of their frenzied buying.

Slow Fashion reveals that, tied to aesthetic allure and commercial trendiness of clothing, there are implications for the future of our planet, social inequities and labor exploitation, and the American loss of its manufacturing base. As is well known, the fashion industry represents a billion-dollar enterprise, yet the act of shopping hardly seems a political act. The vertical business model of the fast fashion industry promotes an economic model allowing those at the top to reap enormous benefits thanks to the sweatshops and slave labor conducted abroad. Having successfully encouraged the buying public to shop for new garments at least every season, a practice that was less common in former generations, fast fashion thrives on the overproduction and overconsumption of cheaply made clothing sold at low prices and manufactured in sweatshops abroad or on American soil, especially in Los Angeles.[62]

The benefit of operating such objectionable entities of course resides in the companies' ability to pay low wages and to hire child labor, to avoid the demands of labor unions and other pro-worker agents, and to do business in countries with little to no environmental protection. Companies operating abroad in such countries as the Philippines, India, Pakistan, and Bangladesh, or that maintain obscured sweatshops on American soil, therefore greatly reduce costs when compared to the price of doing business above board in the United States, as they avoid the vigilant gaze of the Environmental Protection Agency or National Labor Relations Board. Subsequently, thanks to reduced costs and the abundance of cheap labor, the clothing produced can be sold at relatively low prices.

Moreover, with its shortened production cycle consistently glutting department store racks and filling the storefront display windows, fast fashion habitually results in overproduction. One need only visit popular retail stores to appreciate the supernumerary overflow of hastily made garments cramming the racks. Not all of these garments sell. In response to their overproduction of low-cost items, the companies responsible for this excess simply burn immense piles of unbought, unused, unnecessary attire that their sweatshops delivered. As with the industrialized food system, there is an enormous waste of resources and human labor along with waste that harms the environment. Yet demand remains high, for according to Tabitha Whiting consumers now keep their clothing for half as long as they used to prior to 1992. "The fashion industry churns out over 1 billion items of clothing every year, producing 1.2 billion tons of CO2 equivalent at the same time, accounting for 5% of global greenhouse gases."[63] Insatiable demand feeds overproduction and vice versa. Low-cost items keep customers returning to shop at ever shorter intervals: according to Liliana Castelhanos, the time needed to complete a cycle of production and place garments in retail stores is now only five weeks.[64]

Despite these objectionable practices, however, many of the companies market themselves as eco-friendly, environmentally conscious, attuned to a hipster sensibility that seeks to go green in every area of life. Through their use of advertising language and nature-based images—leaves, trees, and grass, drawn or photographed in earth tones—they present a politicallyaware image which is in fact chimera, the illusion of social and ecological rectitude whose sinister underside belies its appearance. Words such as "environmentally conscious," "eco-friendly," "go green," and "organic" hide the fact that fast fashion lacks social responsibility and instead benefits from the suffering of low-paid workers and the degraded environment. The companies involved thus engage in "greenwashing," that is, in convincing the public that they are ecofriendly and committed to social justice even as they sponsor unsafe and unsanitary working conditions, pay an unlivable low wage, employ the und-eraged, refuse benefits, and disregard their establishments' harm to animals and the environment. They cleverly market themselves as environmentally proactive, yet the 2013 collapse of a garment factory in Dhaka, Bangladesh, which killed 1,134 people and injured approximately 2,500 others, remains a sorry testimony to the harm done by the world of fast fashion.

In response to this pervasive reality abetted by the seductive appeal of advertising, Slow Fashion strives to propose alternatives. In ways that parallel Slow Food's mission, this undertaking first seeks to educate the general public about the reality of fast fashion whose dealings remain so hidden from view. A number of scholarly publications such as Dana Thomas' *Fashionopolis: The Price of Fast Fashion—and the Future of Clothes*, Safia Minney's *Slow: Aesthetic Meets Ethics* (2016), and Tansy E. Hoskins' *Stitched Up: The Anti-Capitalist Book of Fashion* (2014), to name but a few, carefully unmask the often horrifying realities that lurk behind popular clothing labels.[65] In addition to this education, practices that support the Slow Fashion ethos include recycling clothing, learning to sew, repair, or repurpose existing gar-ments, checking labels in order to avoid synthetic, non-biodegradable fabrics, and simply buying fewer items. Regardless of one's style, the emphasis is on shopping less and owning fewer articles of clothing. By decreasing the demand for fast fashion's offending overkill, it is hoped that an array of benefits will ensue i.e., less use of water, less abuse of animals, less use of synthetics that harm the environment, and the eradication of sweatshops.

While these mindful, politically conscious aspects of going slow and curvy impact our shopping habits, other forms are simply concerned with decelerat-ing our pace. Here, slow parenting offers an excellent example of what the slow philosophy stands for, for it represents a version of things that especially highlights the need to slow down and reevaluate. Slow parenting seeks to counter the current trend that exerts social, academic, and artistic pressure on children as it takes stock of how this pressure can be damaging. Hoping to decrease parents' desire to manage their children in the pursuit of excellence, the aim is to distance oneself from the output-oriented ethos of instrumental rationality that forever expects a return on an investment and discernable, quantifiable output relative to the effort expended. Because neither children nor families operate in terms of corporate culture, slow parenting urges a slackened and more thoughtful pace when it comes to organizing children's lives, for less is often more and unstructured downtime delivers the most bountiful yield. As against the claim that only proactive, deeply involved parenting will help children attain their full potential, the philosophy of slow promotes deceleration as the path to enrichment, a slow and curvy attitude toward family life.

The current trend in the United States errs in the direction of keeping children busy with little room for leisure, fun, and games. Parents oversee an often crowded schedule that they hope will allow their children to excel, for in today's culture being an average child almost appears tantamount to having failed. With the best of intentions, parents therefore prod, promote, advocate, and lobby for their children in hopes that their efforts will produce a winning result. Their children are their projects, in other words, projects that often dictate parents' schedules and command considerable amounts of their income. None of this is inherently objectionable. Yet with slow parenting, the focus is on keeping things simple when it comes to children's schedules and taking a slow approach to the rate at which children are introduced to the ways of the world.

Honoring the irreplaceable domain of childhood means deemphasizing the need to excel and instead indulging the imagination in unscripted play without strictures or expectations. This school of thought opposes the overscheduling and interference that typifies helicopter parents whose good motives and admirable forethought nevertheless crowd their children's lives to an often intolerable degree. In an effort to help prepare their offspring for the realities that lie ahead, they normalize an excessively busy schedule and perceive overstimulation as equal to being informed about the world and wise to its practices.

Parents who overdo social planning, extracurricular activities, and the rage for excellence often fall prey to what Honoré terms "hyper-parenting."[66] While such focus on children's success undoubtedly has its rewards and is at times necessary, according to the slow philosophy it errs in the direction of normalizing harried, task-oriented time as though it were the only time available. The speed and efficiency that accompany instrumental rationality take pride of place while the merits of the aesthetic dimension stand diminished. Yet as is well known, a purely sequential understanding of things breeds depression and anxiety, since there is always more to do, and one can never really rest. We seek to dominate time and nature rather than be part of the natural order, while Indigenous Persons know that the earth has all the time in the world. Honoré thus examines the emotional and interpersonal damage done to parents and children alike when life devolves into a race for high-achieving results that augment social standing. "The yearning for an über-child has always been there, buried deep within the DNA of every parent," he avers, while insisting that it often breeds unsettling results. Children "grow up terrified of failure and expecting everything on a silver platter."[67]

No one, of course, should be without sympathy for parents who overdo it since there are excellent reasons why they push their children so hard. Objectively, it *is* a more competitive world that children are facing, and the expectations placed upon young people are higher than a generation ago.

Hence it is now a commonplace for parents to make "a new race of alpha children" their project.[68] For if the gifted child now counts as the norm rather than the exception, it is not fair to blame parents who simply want what is best for their offspring.

Nevertheless, other concerns surround ambitious, at times aggressive childrearing. Because so much of contemporary hyper-parenting involves technology in the form of computers, iPads, iPhones, and online learning, the mandate to go slow and curvy has other, far-reaching implications for the brain. Children spend a great deal of time looking at screens and engaging in web-surfing in the pursuit of readily available information; subsequently, the effect is not only interpersonal but physiological, for our brains respond palpably to over-engagement with the screen. Here the work of Nicholas Carr proves useful, for his book, *The Shallows: What the Internet is Doing to Our Brains,* carefully analyzes the two-way street that characterizes our engagement with technology. Carr convincingly explains how the very manner in which our brains' neurons transmit information changes depending on the medium with which it interacts. The patterns by which the brain communicates internally is not solidified, but due to its plasticity and malleable quality actually morphs in accordance with what it is encountering. When it habitually engages with an agent such as a search engine that features short bursts of information in the form of sound bites, headlines, extracted quotes, and a cacophony of links, the brain itself alters accordingly. It is led toward scanning and skimming, and actually begins to imitate that shallowness in its own activity. Its malleable neural circuitry—which transmits information to other nerve cells, muscles, or gland cells—not only becomes accustomed to shorter intervals and fleeting thoughts, but eventually reproduces that.

Subsequently, we ourselves come to desire faster, shorter, quicker thoughts; we want knowledge in a hurry and confuse information for thinking itself. We forget that reflection takes time and that knowledge of a person, a field of study, a musical instrument, or social problem can take years to acquire. Thus, it seems reasonable to ask, as Carr does, whether such inventions as the world wide web reveal themselves as truly pharmacotic at their core: i.e., as something that aids humanity's progress while also sending us back, offering a venue for intellectual advancement while simultaneously destroying our ability to think at all. "The intellectual ethic is the message that a medium or other tool transmits into the minds and culture of its users," Carr argues.[69]

Because thinking is itself a slow process, slow parenting must surely discourage excessive interaction with technology and cultivate a more balanced, slow-and-curvy approach to helping children learn. If we consider slow fashion and slow parenting together, it becomes clear that both promote a mindfulness that stresses interconnection with the world: an interconnection among those living locally, among cultures and economies around the globe, and importantly, interconnection with Mother Nature. "The secret of life is hidden in the 'slow' and 'curvy' that only God knows," writes Sohn et al.; "only if something is bent, it is complete."[70] A straight, streamlined approach thus misses something, for it fails to understand interconnection, nuance, and context. Slow and curvy deconstructs the sovereign subject and puts us all on a continuum, in a context, in relationship to things outside ourselves.

Honoré's antidote to micromanaging children in inadvertently harmful ways centers around listening to one's parental instincts while backing off from an ambitious to-do list. Insisting that there is no single formula for how parents might ease up on pressure, he writes in assuring tones that simply listening to children's particular needs and responding to them as individuals proves sufficient. Child-rearing resists a formulaic model by its very nature; thus, focus should be on giving attention and guidance without promoting an overbearing set of expectations. Because it savors imagination, playtime, time spent outdoors, and the pleasure of the everyday, slow parenting resonates strongly with the central tenets of both Slow Food and *Cittaslow* for which relishing the here and now stands paramount.

Despite its European origins, then, surely certain aspects of the slow movement resonate with Americans. The effort to inspire something new while preserving something old, to go back to the land and cherish our roots while opposing those in power: isn't that quintessential Americana? Surely the notion of individuals taking aim at entrenched giants resonates with the American cultural imaginary: the stories, the traditions, and even the myths that sustain our shared narrative about who we are. Still, some wonder "what's so great about going slow?" This is the topic of the next chapter.

NOTES

1. George Ritzer, *The McDonaldization of Society,* (Thousand Oaks: Sage Publications, 2013).

2. For a discussion of the slow movement's emergence, see Michael Clancy, "Practicing Slow: Political and Ethical Implications," in *Slow Tourism, Food, and Cities: Pace and the Search for 'the Good Life,'* Michael Clancy, ed., (New York: Routledge, 2018), 63–73.

3. *Chef's Table*, Season One, Episode One, "Massimo Bottura." David Gelb, Netflix, April 26, 2015.

4. Kennan Ferguson, *Cookbook Politics*, 34.

5. Petrini, *Food & Freedom,* 8.

6. For an analysis of the emotional and cultural weight of food, see also the work of Massimo Montanari, author of *Italian Identity in the Kitchen, or Food and the Nation*, trans. Beth Archer Brombert (New York: Columbia University Press, 2013).

7. Petrini, *Food & Freedom*, 9.

8. Ibid., 10.

9. Ibid., 11.

10. "Good, Clean, and Fair: The Slow Food Manifesto for Quality," https://www.slowfood.com/wp-content/uploads/2015/07/Manifesto_Quality_ENG.pdf, accessed August 2, 2021.

11. Waters, *We Are What We Eat,* 33.

12. Waters, *We Are What We Eat,* 69.

13. "Good, Clean, and Fair," accessed August 2, 2021.

14. Petrini, *Food & Freedom*, 35.

15. Petrini, *Food & Freedom*, 35.

16. Petrini, *Food & Freedom*, 35.

17. "Fueling Food Sovereignty in Puerto Rico," https://slowfoodusa.org/fueling-food-sovereignty-in-puerto-rico/, December 16, 2021. Accessed December 18, 2021.

18. https://www.slowfood.com/wp-content/uploads/2015/07/Manifesto_Quality_ENG.pdf, accessed August 2, 2021.

19. Mary Davis Suro, "Romans Protest McDonald's," *New York Times*, May 5, 1986, accessed July 28, 2017, http://www.nytimes.com/1986/05/05/style/romans-protest-mcdonald-s.html.

20. Petrini, *Slow Food, The Case for Taste*, trans. William McCuaig (New York: Columbia University Press, 2001), 6.

21. Petrini, *Slow Food, The Case for Taste,* 11.

22. Petrini, *Slow Food, The Case for Taste,* 10.

23. See Baldassare Castiglione, *The Book of the Courtier,* trans. George Bull, (New York: Penguin Books, 1976).

24. See Geoff Andrews, *The Slow Food Story: Politics and Pleasure* (Montreal: Montreal-Queens University Press, 2008).

25. See Andrews, *The Slow Food Story, chap. 1.*

26. Quoted in Alexander Stille, *The Sack of Rome*: *How a Beautiful European Country with a Fabled History and a Storied Culture Was Taken Over by a Man Named Silvio Berlusconi,* (New York: Penguin, 2006): 11.

27. Stille, *The Sack of Rome*, 8.

28. *Searching for Italy*, Episodes 1–6. Stanley Tucci, Raw Television, February 14–March 21, 2021.

29. See note 17.

30. Aaron Bobrow-Strain, *White Bread: A Social History of the Store-Bought Loaf* (Boston: Beacon Press, 2012), 6.

31. While kale generally indicates left, then, Dreher does have a point: the intense polarization that characterizes contemporary American politics is not as starkly drawn as one might think, and it is my aim in these pages to draw out the ideological points of overlap that allow Slow Food to resonate with the American Dream. In Bobrow-Strain's words, "conservatives who look carefully find that the alternative food movement expresses many of their values" (Bobrow-Strain, 106).

32. Rod Dreher, *Crunchy Cons: How Birkenstocked Burkeans, Gun-Loving Organic Gardeners, Evangelical Free-Range Farmers, Hip Homeschooling Mamas,*

Right-Wing Lovers, and Their Diverse Tribe of Counter-cultural Conservatives Plan to Save America (or at Least the Republican Party)(New York: Crown Forum, 2006).

33. Dreher, *Crunchy Cons*, 12.

34. See www.aol.com/article/news/2017/07/27/scaramucci-says-trump-s-love-for-burgers-and-pizza-proves-hes-n/23052702/, accessed July 30, 2017.

35. Ashley Parker, "Donald Trump's Diet: He'll Have Fries With That," www.nytimes.com/2016/08/09/us/politics/donald-trump-diet.html, accessed June 3, 2018.

36. Parker, accessed June 3, 2018.

37. See Darryl Furrow, *American Foodie: Taste, Art, and the Cultural Revolution,* (Lanham, MD: Rowman & Littlefield, 2016). Furrow's excellent book analyzes the explosion of interest in gastronomy in ways that dovetail with the Slow Food philosophy, for he interprets the current desire to grow, shop, cook, and eat differently in terms of a need for pleasure, uniqueness, and something other than the standardized, processed fast food that characterizes the iron cage.

38. Julia Child, *My Life in France*, with Alex Prud'homme (New York: Alfred A. Knopf, 2006), 82.

39. David Kamp, *The United States of Arugula: How We Became a Gourmet Nation* (New York: Broadway Books, 2006), xi.

40. Raymond D. Boisvert and Lisa Heldke, *Philosophers at Table: On Food and Being Human,* (London: Reaktion Books, 2016); Andrew Chignell, Terence Cuneo, and Matthew C. Halteman, *Philosophy Comes to Dinner: Arguments About the Ethics of Eating,* (New York: Routledge, 2016).

41. Mol, *Eating,* 49.

42. Ibid., 36.

43. Ibid., 43.

44. Max Horkheimer and Theodor Adorno, *Dialectic of Enlightenment*, trans. Edmund Jephcott, (Stanford University Press, 2002), 2.

45. Leo Hickman, "Slow Food: Have We Lost Our Appetite?" *The Guardian*, February 4, 2009, https://www.theguardian.com/environment/2009/feb/04/slow-food-carlo-petrini, accessed September 20, 2021.

46. Jonathan Kauffman, *Hippie Food: How Back-To-The-Landers, Longhairs and Revolutionaries Changed the Way We Eat* (New York: William Morrow, 2018).

47. See especially Gabriele Manella, "*Cittaslow*, the Emilia-Romagna Case," in *Slow Tourism, Food and Cities: Pace and the Search for the Good Life,* edited by Michael Clancy (London: Routledge, 2018), 145–165.

48. https://www.cittaslow.org/, accessed March 27, 2020.

49. "Cittaslow International Charter," accessed March 27, 2020, https://www.cittaslow.org/sites/default/files/content/page/files/257/charter_cittaslow_en_05_18.pdf.

50. Giovanni Tocci, "Slow and Intelligent Cities: When Slow Is Also Smart," in *Slow Tourism, Food and Cities*, ed. Michael Clancy (New York: Routledge, 2019), 118.

51. See, for instance, Serge Latouche, *Farewell to Growth*, trans. David Macey (Cambridge, UK: Polity Press, 2009); and *Towards a Political Economy of Degrowth,*

ed. Ekaterina Chertkovskaya, Alexander Paulsson, and Stefania Barca (Lanham, MD: Rowman & Littlefield, 2019).

52.   https://www.youtube.com/watch?v=kyNdzzHUqC4,   accessed September 6, 2021.

53. *Cittaslow*, "Innovation by Tradition," in-house publication, 7.

54. Petrini, *Food and Freedom*, 14.

55. Another hanok village in South Korea, Jeonju Hanok Maeul, also promotes Slow Food culture such as the traditional Korean bowl, Bibim-Bab, along with traditional music in the village. Shinan County further demonstrates the value of traditionally produced, high-quality sun-dried salt or tideland salt, slowly produced in tideland salt fields, and was recognized as UNESCO's World Network of Biosphere Reserves (WNBR) in May 2009. Meanwhile, Yeongyang strives to conserve the lifestyle and culture of Yangban, or "traditional nobility"; for example, it has restored and follows the recipes of a 400-year-old cookbook written in Korean. The book is highly valued historically and academically, and also contains the recipes of traditional Korean liquor, proving that the county has the oldest brewery in Korea. I am grateful to Sun Young Kwak for her research regarding *Cittaslow*, South Korea.

56. Gabriel Rockhill, *Interventions in Contemporary Thought: History, Politics, Aesthetics* (Edinburgh: Edinburgh University Press, 2016), 3.

57. Walter Benjamin, "Theses on the Philosophy of History," in *Illuminations*, trans. Harry Zohn (New York: Harcourt Brace Jovanovich, 1968), 261.

58. Herbert Marcuse, *Eros and Civilization: A Philosophical Inquiry into Freud*, (Boston: Beacon Press, 1966): 31.

59. Sohn, Jang, and Jung, *Go Slow and Curvy,* 4.

60. The snail is a creature imbued with an array of attributes depending on its cultural setting and time period. The Sumerians and Babylonians believed that snails were immortal, while in Mesoamerican religious art, it symbolized the life god, Quetzalcoatl. In the Aztec culture, snails were also imbued with sacred meaning. The Greek poet Hesiod wrote that when snails climbed to the top of plants it was time to harvest. Similarly in medieval painting, the snail would on occasion indicate the Virgin Mary, whose announcement of a new understanding of time marked a definitive break in history.

61. Dana Thomas, *Fashionopolis: The Price of Fast Fashion–and the Future of Clothes* (New York: Penguin Press, 2019), 4.

62. For a description of Los Angeles sweatshops, see Thomas, *Fashionopolis,* chapter 2.

63. Tabitha Whiting, "'Sustainable Style': The Truth Behind the Marketing of H&M's Conscious Collection," accessed September 2, 2021, https://tabitha-whiting.medium.com/sustainable-style-the-truth-behind-the-marketing-of-h-ms-conscious-collection-805eb7432002. I am grateful to Julieta Martinez, Diana Do, and Lindsey Rippert for explaining this to me.

64. Liliana Castelhanos, "Fast Fashion vs. Slow Fashion," https://www.youtube.com/watch?v=nkjsdNlVnAI&t=2s, accessed September 4, 2021.

65. In addition to Thomas, see Tyler Little, *The Future of Fashion: Understanding Sustainability in the Fashion Industry* (Potomac, MD: New Degree Press, 2018); Safia

Minney, *Slow: Aesthetic Meets Ethics* (Oxford, UK: New Internationalist Publications Ltd, 2016); Minney, *Slave to Fashion* (Oxford, UK: New Internationalist Publications Ltd, 2017); Clare Press, *Wardrobe Crisis: How We Went from Sunday Best to Fast Fashion* (New York: Skyhorse Publishing, 2018). See also Robert Ross, *Slaves to Fashion: Poverty and Abuse in the New Sweatshops* (Ann Arbor, MI: University of Michigan Press, 2004), and Tansy E. Hoskins, *Stitched Up: The Anti-Capitalist Book of Fashion* (London, UK: Pluto Press, 2014). Additionally, Minney can be credited with having founded the pioneering enterprise People Tree, a Fair Trade and sustainable fashion brand that pursues "an enlightened capitalism" through its commitment to transparency, rigorously ethical business standards, and ecofriendly practices.

66. Carl Honoré, *Under Pressure: How the Epidemic of Hyper-Parenting Is Endangering Childhood,* Alfred A. Knopf, 2008.

67. Honoré, *Under Pressure*, 258.

68. Honoré, *Under Pressure,* 11.

69. Nicholas Carr, *The Shallows: What the Internet is Doing to Our Brains,"* (New York: W.W. Norton & Co., 2020).

70. Sohn, Jang, and Jung, *Go Slow and Curvy*, 4.

Chapter 2

What's So Great about Slow?

The virtues of a slow, curvy lifestyle are not obvious to everyone. There are skeptics who take issue with the movement's fundamental principles and doubt its longevity. Some see it as a fad comparable to the end-of-millennium infatuation with angels and Gregorian chant; others view it as a romantic effort to recover a preindustrial lifestyle that simply is not tenable in today's world, for once the wheels of progress spin at such high speed there is no stopping them. In October of 2019, I spent a few days in Paris and in my hotel's dining room struck up a conversation with an American traveler. When I told him that I was researching the slow movement as it expresses itself through Slow Food, *Cittaslow*, and other exponents, he laughed and said that these movements would never catch on in the United States. Americans frequently go in for food fads, he argued regarding Slow Food, while secretly consuming the ready-made fare that we all love. Slow Food is a passing fancy that will never infiltrate America's social fabric, for we are too addicted to speed to ever decelerate and embrace a locavore lifestyle. Take a look in a so-called gastronome's freezer, he said, and you will find a cache of pre-packaged, brand-name foods ready to be microwaved.

As with the skeptical American who summarily dismissed the movement over his *café au lait*, not everyone is convinced that "the living is good" in a slow and curvy world. For some, slow simply means slow with all its unflattering implications, while the movement's claims to "real culture" represent high-minded utterances of those nostalgic for times gone by. Such critics of the snail genuinely enjoy the stimulation of a busy schedule, the adrenalin rush that keynotes an urban existence, and the creative invigoration that drives our version of progress. Why slow down if speed is not only thrilling, but gets the job done faster? It's a fair question, especially in light of the criticism that will be addressed in chapter six: namely, that the slow movement embodies an often-hidden elitism that militates against the principles of a democratic society. Those who oppose its philosophy are known to say that with slow, the living *is* good for the economically advantaged, but not for many Americans who long to pursue the classic American Dream yet struggle to pay their bills.

SPEED'S RHIZOMATIC AMBIGUITIES

It is my argument that the United States represents an especially difficult context in which to promote the principles of slow, since we so define ourselves as a nation wherein progress and modernity are understood in terms of technological advancement. While in older cultures, the term "modern" invokes early shifts in philosophical and religious paradigms perhaps beginning in the sixteenth century, in the United States "modern" has more recent, industrial connotations and invokes iron, steel, the Gold Rush, and the economic impetus behind the Gilded Age. Thus, in the West historians might think of "modern" as Copernicus at work on a heliocentric cosmology sometime in the early 1500's, or of Galileo with his telescopes running afoul of the Church around 1615. They might think of Sir Isaac Newton experimenting with the laws of physics somewhere in the late seventeenth century. More recently, previously colonized countries might associate "modernity" with the arrival of unwelcome foreign powers or the incursions of global capital that permanently altered a former way of life.

Yet in our own country, Americans more readily associate "the modern" with industrial and technological giants connected to oil, steel, the stock market, real estate, and information technology. Separating the industrial from the preindustrial, agrarian era, we typically cast technology as a key axis around which "modernity" defines itself. We think of titans of industry such as Andrew Carnegie (1835–1919), a self-made man who worked his way up and ultimately exerted influence over technological advancements such as the railroads, the automobile industry, factory life, and what was later termed the military-industrial complex. We think of John D. Rockefeller and J. P. Morgan, Bill Gates, Steve Jobs, and Mark Zuckerberg, all of whom revolutionized industries while creating massive amounts of wealth. For many Americans, "modernity" means rapid exponential growth, going big in chrome or steel, surpassing the speed of sound.

Indeed, the emergence of modernity with its signature acceleration differs considerably from one country to another. Moreover, for those unconvinced that speed is an altogether reprehensible thing, a persuasive argument as to why we might want to decelerate and go curvy has yet to present itself, especially as relates to the workplace. After all, there are many benefits to speed: email, text messaging, Instagram, snap deposits, online banking. And we have all become accustomed to the microwave, 24-hour news feeds, consult-a-nurse, and the conveniences of online shopping. Thus, if we instinctively associate "modernity" with contemporary democratic principles, practices, and institutions, it would seem that we also associate it with a fast-paced lifestyle; at the extreme, perhaps democracy itself is now defined in terms of speed. As William E. Scheuerman correctly states, for better or worse, the fast-paced world, or at least certain aspects of it, is here to stay. Since "[e]xtreme busyness is endemic to modern society," those of us advocating the slow philosophy need to accept this premise and work from there.[1] Creating a paradigm shift in favor of slow must articulate a more robust defense; lamenting busyness itself is not enough.

Scheuerman concerns himself especially with the impact that speed has on modern citizenship and the democratic process. He worries that the frenetic pace of modern life exerts a largely detrimental effect on our involvement in civic life and commitment to democratic principles; after all, deliberative democracy necessitates listening, patience, a willingness to compromise, and the ability to engage in agonistic politics without always needing to win. It means tolerating opinions we do not share and allowing our own agendas to be revisited; much of the time, it affirms Sartre's astute pronouncement that "hell is other people." Democratic practices thus run counter to quick solutions and instead demand our time as well as our forbearance. So much of technology claims to free up our time; why then are we so pressed for it, unable to engage in the demands of citizenship and participate in the democratic process?

Since we simply don't have time to devote to the activities that characterize traditional civic involvement, we hand over the decision-making process to those in business and industry, financial institutions, corporate titans, and as Bernie Sanders reminds us, to millionaires and billionaires who increasingly run our country. At the extreme, the time-space compression squeezes out the activities that we formerly made time for in the name of civic participation. Subsequently, it delivers a nation not operating according to democratic principles, but to the logic of a technocratic/oligarchic/plutocratic elite that runs things from the top. Hence much of the democratic process now operates through technological networks that keep us informed and up to date, yet ironically contribute to our being frantically over-committed.

Today, "civic engagement" rarely means town hall meetings, volunteering for a political campaign, knocking on doors in the precinct, or giving our energies to a worthy cause. Rather, it finds expression in condensed, easy-breezy acts that more closely resemble the *suggestion* of civic engagement rather than bone fide engagement itself: click here, donate there, fill out this questionnaire. Advancements in technology have made it easy for us to perform simple, shall we say ersatz forms of civic involvement that prove far less time-consuming than the old-fashioned iterations. Drawn-out, contentious meetings, canvassing, helping others register to vote; while recent,

sustained protests against police brutality and efforts to alter the voting process certainly qualify as a form of civic engagement, they stand alongside
a political *disengagement* that technological advancement has conferred on
twenty-first-century life. With one click of the computer, we can now make
a donation to a political cause, sign a petition online, or endorse a candidate,
thereby freeing up time for other things. Thus, it is easy for us to tell ourselves
that we are politically "engaged" and have done our bit. Without discounting the meaningful political activism that recently expressed opposition to
police brutality and voting restrictions, nor the earlier Occupy Movement that
also took to the streets, this more passive form of politics has by now taken
root and is unlikely to be displaced anytime soon. While "it remains unclear
whether even such high-speed forms of citizen involvement are normatively
satisfactory," we must come to terms with their entrenchment in modern life.[2]
Moreover, we must be selective about what forms of democratic engagement
we want to rehabilitate and be realistic in terms of their impact.[3]

Speed's relationship to democratic politics has its defenders, especially
in this age of a globalized economy with its massive shifts in demographics
and subsequent problematics surrounding citizenship. For some, the "virus
of speed" is simply the more sinister underside of speed's commendable
efficacy, the fact that we can now computerize problems and solve electronically what formerly would have taken a painfully long time. The damaging
virus represents the shadow of the positive advancement, the malevolent flip
side of progress. Both positive and negative elements characterize modern
advancements, and both have serious political consequences.

Wondering why slow is better, William E. Connolly has convincingly
argued in favor of the progressive elements embedded in a world marked by
ever-increasing acceleration.[4] For those truly disadvantaged and in need of
assistance, speed can often be a boon. Connolly admits that there are harmful
aspects of the modern world's frenetic pace; in many ways, Virilio's sinister
interpretation of speed's centrality to modern warfare culture rings true, for
speed is often aggressive and dangerous ("What makes war convenient is
transportation . . . the armored car . . . offers a whole new geometry to speed,
to violence," Virilio writes).[5] Yet Connolly more willingly concedes the *benefits* of speed in helping promote an open-minded, cosmopolitan sensibility
more compatible with peaceful ambitions and democratic aims. He believes
that the deeply interpenetrated, "rhizomatic" nature of the globalized world
features an interlacing that necessarily promotes a more democratic culture;
heightened interpenetration contributes to a refined democratic sensibility in
a world of comingled, variegated elements. Despite the dangers and brutality
of acceleration, Connolly insists that a fast-paced world of increased travel
and finely networked cultural exchange necessarily promotes a cosmopolitan
sensibility whose tolerance and open-mindedness help dispel the dogmatic

dark ages. Speed thus accommodates tolerance as much as it does warfare; it harmonizes as much as it introduces dissonance. Because it enlarges our judgment and quells a narrow-minded provincialism based on self-referencing, speed's effects "also improve the prospects for democratic pluralization within the state and a cosmopolitanism across states."[6]

While a harried world surely has its drawbacks, then, speed reveals itself as a decidedly "ambiguous" feature of contemporary life, promoting a broad-minded sensibility even if it does make us frantic. The "ambiguities" of speed therefore advance the lives of those formerly disadvantaged by a staid, slow-moving world order whose ingrained hierarchies, belief systems, and ways of life went largely unchallenged. Thanks to the dynamism and indeed contradictions of an accelerated, interfused world, dominant paradigms now give way to "an irreducible plurality of regulative ideas."[7] Speed's vitality encouraged by a rhizomatic global interfusion is to be celebrated since it can

> improve the prospects for democratic pluralization within the state and a cosmopolitanism across states that speaks affirmatively to issues of ecology, peace, indigenous minorities, the legitimation of new identities and rights, and the protection of old rights. . . . [It can] disrupt closed models of nature, truth, and morality into which people so readily become encapsulated, doing so in ways that support new paradigms of natural science and careful reconsideration of the injuries to difference supported by dogmatic conceptions.[8]

This argument assumes a probable relationship between a slow pace of life and the inability to concede an "irreducible plurality"; slow, in other words, tends toward the provincial and clings to what it already knows. The argument assumes that a slow and curvy existence may breed prejudice and an inability to shift one's Archimedean vantage point or widen one's horizons. "Slow" becomes synonymous with a stodgy conservatism that clings to the past for the sake of the past; at the extreme, it breeds an unthinking filiopietism inhospitable to new ideas.

Yet we can make trouble for the assumed connection between a slow pace of life and the Western hegemonic sovereignty that dominated for so long, or between a slow pace of life and any provincialism unwilling to expand its intellectual and spiritual repertoire. For can we be certain that *slowness* is the culprit, that a lack of interpenetration explains the claims to superiority regarding race, religion, politics, any number of things? Perhaps other things are in play.

Connolly draws on Immanuel Kant's influential eighteenth-century writings to illustrate his point. He draws a connection between Kant's vision for an organized, cosmopolitan, peace-loving world that was undeniably Eurocentric and the slow pace of life at the time, for the slowness of things underscored the distances that separated Europe from other civilizations. These distances were geographic in nature, but they were also intellectual, theological, cultural, and linguistic. "When Kant penned his great essays on universal peace and cosmopolitanism in the 1780s and 1790s," Connolly writes, "clocks did not have a second hand; it took a week to set the print for a newspaper run, weeks to travel across Europe, more than a month to sail across the Atlantic, and close to a year to sail around the world."[9] The greatly decelerated pace of life thus helps explain the Kantian assumption that a Christian, European worldview will ultimately inform a future state of affairs led by a confederation of peaceable rulers who uphold republican principles and a respectful yet ethnocentrically tainted cosmopolitanism.

Despite its benevolent intentions, today we critique Kant's quest for universal peace using a battery of analytic tools that typify the current intellectual framework: as with other illuminati of the Western canon, we see the imprimatur of a Eurocentric worldview that took its own cultural standards as ahistorical and universal. Yet it is not clear that a critique of Eurocentrism and its attendant attributes was not *already* underway in certain quarters and among thinking individuals. The world was neither as markedly rhizomatic nor as electronically interconnected as it is today, but didn't thoughtful, careful minds look askance at claims to Western sovereignty and imperialist domination? We needn't read too far nor too wide to locate corroborating evidence that even amidst the slowness of the early modern period—that is, the period preceding Kant—thoughtful minds were not completely unaware of a Eurocentric bias positing the West as the unquestioned universal paradigm. And if that is the case, then the attribute of slowness cannot be so easily indicted for fostering a dangerous provincialism.

Shakespeare's choice of a Black Moor as the lead character in *Othello*, most likely composed in 1603 or 1604, illustrates my point. This accomplished military man promoted to general clearly commands respect and admiration among Venetians. Despite being a foreigner in the Venetian Republic, his military achievements burnish his reputation and standing, as does his recent marriage to the wealthy, well-born Desdemona. Yet Othello allows the conniving Iago to precipitate his downfall. Jealous of his military rank and command over him, Iago uses deceit to convince Othello that his wife has been unfaithful, and this proves to be the Moor's demise. For not only does Othello kill Desdemona in a fit of jealousy, but he also ultimately commits suicide when he realizes her innocence.

The elements of sexual and professional envy contained in the play surely address emotions that are universal to the human condition and help explain the play's enduring appeal. Yet the choice of including Othello's race as a factor in the plot raises questions about Shakespeare's commentary on seventeenth-century European civilization. Placing a Black Moor in the midst of the thriving Venetian Empire carries deliberate racial and geopolitical over-tones, for the protagonist's dark skin is integral to various characters' lines and could be reinterpreted using artistic license only with great difficulty. Perhaps Shakespeare's treatment of otherness can be read as a critique, a questioning rather than a confirmation of a Eurocentric worldview by liter-ally bringing a Black officer center stage and having a foreigner promoted to the rank of general while surrounded by jealous, scheming Whites eager for revenge.

True, we could read *Othello* as simply promoting pernicious early seven-teenth-century stereotypes about dark-skinned, non-Christian persons, for as Ania Loomba and Martin Orkin observe, "black-skinned people were usually typed as godless, bestial, and hideous, fit only to be saved . . . by Christians."[10] We could thus read his marriage to Desdemona as amounting to an unnatural act that allowed his "sooty bosom" and "thick lips" to enter into an unjustified and perverse union; to his enemies, Othello represents "an old black ram/tupping [a] white ewe."[11] But the Moor does not display undig-nified qualities, for Shakespeare gives ample expression to his professional accomplishments and his wife's enduring love and admiration. His "perfect soul" is clearly driven to violence thanks only to the manipulations of a preju-diced society, perhaps made insecure by its recently expanding empire and subsequent encounter with foreign cultures.

Othello's vengeful act against his wife follows only from the malevolent machinations of Iago who, overlooked for a promotion, feigns friendship with him only to destroy him. "I follow him to serve my turn upon him . . . for my peculiar end," Iago tells Roderigo, admitting his nefarious intentions to convince Othello of his wife's infidelity which will lead to her death at his hands.[12] Because of Iago's vengeful plan, can we not read the play as an indictment of ingrained prejudice, the prejudice that confers a "sooty bosom" onto a man with a "perfect soul"?[13] The Moor's racial alterity may well con-vey a worldview open to cultures beyond English borders; in fact, as Loomba suggests, the play perhaps reflects an English *tolerance* toward Moors given the politics of early empire. Recent postcolonial scholarship scrutinizes Shakespeare through this lens and interprets the bard as one cognizant of racial difference's many meanings and emotional weight in a time of colonial expansion. In Loomba's words, these early modern plays written at a time of growing empire "give us a sense of the simultaneous opening and closing of the European world," a world wherein the increasing exposure to difference and non-European cultures unsettled rather than consolidated the stable cul-tural superiority to which Connolly alludes.[14]

In fact, Loomba suggests that the playwright's English audience may have been quite tolerant of Moors, and that the play's dramatization of the resent-ful Iago may have been a means of criticizing Spain, "where Christians had warred with Moors for centuries."[15] For even Iago's name, Loomba points out, suggests the patron saint of Spain, Sant Iago (Santiago), that is, Saint James. The disdainful comments uttered throughout the play regarding Othello's racial difference may thus comment on the vagaries of early empire rather than on the playwright's inherent prejudice; perhaps Shakespeare exposes, derides, even condemns English anxieties at this moment of permeable boundaries. Even in the slow-paced world of 1604, the playwright may have chosen the Moor as his tragic central character in order to illustrate Eurocentric vulnerabilities in an expanding universe rather than consolidated power on European soil.

While such a reading has of course always been implicit in Shakespeare's text, this focus on empire and on England's newly expanding relationship with alterity brings the potential critique of Eurocentrism into special focus. Because the early modern period brought European powers increased exposure to cultures deemed exotic, European identity and its Christian beliefs may well have been destabilized rather than affirmed. "The stage was set for a drama of a nation and a global city that would prove a fertile ground for explorations of difference, diversity, and alterity," writes Jyotsna G. Singh.[16] The slow pace of life notwithstanding, perhaps early seventeenth-century minds were opened to revisiting assumptions and stereotypes; in other words, perhaps a slower world did not impede the pluralism that democratic societies value, *pace* Connolly.

Other Shakespearean dramas lend further evidence to this argument, for instance, Shylock's famous speech in *The Merchant of Venice*. Scholars have long debated whether or not the play, believed to be first performed in 1605, counts as an expression of undiluted anti-Semitism, and certainly many actors have played the role of Shylock as a tragic figure. His daughter Jessica has eloped and abandoned her Jewish identity to Christianity, and Shylock, losing his return on a loan and his threat to extract one pound of flesh in return, stands defeated. He is forced to turn over his estate upon his death and himself become a Christian.[17] Yet surely the Jew's famous and moving words about a shared humanity can be read as expressing the playwright's indictment of xenophobic claims to Western sovereignty. Without question, Shylock's references to both suffering and delight invite in all listeners as they speak of a common human condition that embraces each and all.

> Hath not a Jew eyes? Hath not a Jew hands, organs, dimensions, senses, affections, passions; fed with the same food, hurt with the same weapons, subject to the same diseases, heal'd by the same means, warm'd and cool'd by the same winter and summer, as a Christian is? If you prick us, do we not bleed? If you tickle us, do we not laugh? If you poison us, do we not die? And if you wrong us, do we not revenge? If we are like you in the rest, we will resemble you in that.[18]

Even if cultural pluralism did not claim the cachet that it does in contemporary public discourse, the bard implicitly offers a critique of European, Christian hegemony with Shylock's famous lines because, as Brandon Ambrosino argues, "the Jewish character is given the most humanizing speech in the play . . . [with] these few humanizing lines, the curtain is pulled back on Shylock's character."[19] Rather than a money-hungry individual who lacks compassion for Antonio's inability to repay a loan, he appears to be a feeling person forced to endure a hostile culture, his money-lending skills simply a way of earning a living. Because "the new gods of capitalism and colonialism" exert their power "in ways that intensify existing hierarchies," Loomba insists, those hierarchies open themselves to criticism just as easily as they receive confirmation.[20] As Shylock perhaps unwittingly reveals a common human experience that reaches across religious divides, Shakespeare may well be *opposing* the mandate that he convert, thereby challenging the claim that Christianity promises a richer human existence. As with *Othello*, it may therefore be that *The Merchant of Venice* makes trouble for speeds' progressive claims. Not a monolithic European sovereignty, but "shifts in relationship" more correctly describe the increasingly interfused worlds that open up minds as well as markets.[21] Thus a slower pace of life as was the seventeenth-century norm is itself not incompatible with the open-mindedness toward difference needed for democratic politics.

Other Shakespearean references might be enlisted to illustrate my point: the relationship between Prospero and Caliban in *The Tempest*, Cleopatra's sexual and political prowess in *Antony and Cleopatra*. Moreover, canonical authors other than Shakespeare come to mind. My eleventh-grade class pored over Montesquieu's *The Persian Letters* at length, exposing the text's many eighteenth century concerns regarding the topics of religious and cultural tolerance. The lively exchange of letters between two Persian noblemen, Usbek and Rica, traveling to France for the first time, produces biting commentary on what they observe ("The King of France is old." "[A] man who ought to be despised because he is a fool is often despised only because he wears robes"[22]). The travelers are struck by the hypocrisy of those claiming to be religious and the arrogance of those deemed educated. It is especially their Middle Eastern point of comparison that allows Montesquieu to make the thematic of tolerance central to his novel. "As we know, the theme of tolerance—its foundations, limits and what happens when it is denied—had a prominent place in Montesquieu's thought," writes Rolando Minuti. "In the *Lettres Persanes*, the need to accept religious diversity comes across as the result of the recognition of the universality of the concept of God."[23]

Minuti is not alone in recognizing the Enlightenment's sensitivity to cultural incommensurability and an anti-imperialist politics of difference. Sankar Muthu maintains that Enlightenment thinkers themselves were already attuned to cultural incommensurability and thus exerted caution in making universalizing claims. Muthu holds that thinkers such as Denis Diderot, Johann Gottfried Herder, and even Kant himself resisted positing a blueprint of human nature that would justify the imperialist aspects of Enlightenment doctrine. Kant, he argues, understood humans not as disembodied beings who drew on abstracted principles, but as culturally bound persons whose intellectual skills derived in large part from their native culture in all its grounded, historical specificity. "Kant's view is that these human skills involve the use of reason and freedom in a manner that depends, for their orientation, upon our surrounding experience—a diverse, plural, and often a socially informed experience," he writes.[24] Muthu takes issue with the claim that Kant conceives of the intellect only in universal terms, insisting instead that he values the specificities of given cultural settings in ways that acknowledge and indeed promote pluralism.

Kant thus counts among numerous "Enlightenment anti-imperialist thinkers [who] crafted nuanced and intriguingly counter-intuitive arguments about human nature, cultural diversity, cross-cultural moral judgements and political obligations."[25] As is well known, even the conservative Edmund Burke argued against the Eurocentric activities of the East India Company, insisting that it had "failed to respect the sovereignty of local Indian powers."[26] Muthu thus argues for a nuanced, variegated reading of Enlightenment thought given that human beings do not conform to one universalized model but instead are fundamentally cultural beings attuned to their social milieu. He reveals how many Enlightenment thinkers understood that we do not fit one type, European or other, but display variety and incommensurate attributes that translate from one setting to another at times with great difficulty, and sometimes not at all. Regardless of how slowly the world moved, then, the Enlightenment period was open to the attributes of a cosmopolitan tolerance attuned to difference. Like the early modern period before it, it registered the impact of incommensurate cultural realities that disallowed a homogenizing European model.

The fields of English literature and post-colonial studies thus come to my aid in countering the claim that speed typically equates with a tolerant, worldly sensibility while slow takes us back in time. Slow need not produce a provincial mindset or a dated sensibility; on the contrary, various iterations of slow that we have seen—slow fashion, Slow Food, *Cittaslow*—necessarily invoke a cosmopolitan outlook given their sensitivity to global economics and the climate crisis. They pursue a slow agenda precisely because they are aware of various far-reaching international problems. Slow fashion's invocation to wear recycled, repurposed clothing emanates from the urgent need to put fast fashion's sweat shops out of business and redistribute the wealth generated by the fashion industry. *Cittaslow* strives to keep things small and local while also creating an international web of cities "where the living is good." And Slow Food's locavore politics, shared by *Cittaslow*, emphasizes organic food that does not travel far, thereby seeking to thwart industrialized farming as it contributes to the destruction of biodiversity and global warming.

In answer to the question "What's so great about slow?" I would therefore argue that its various iterations meaningfully address urgent political problems of our times in ways that offer not just commentary, but praxis, not just a clarion call, but a how-to guide of practical advice for political democratic engagement. And of all the topics that the slow movement meaningfully confronts, none is more serious than that of climate change. Indeed, the slow movement in many ways engenders a praxis of green living that confronts the tragedy of ecocide head on. For while the topics identified by Connolly such as cosmopolitanism and a tolerant worldview surely retain their political capital, today it is climate change that takes center stage as we consider the needs of democratic societies.

Slow, Curvy, and Green

In considering the relationship between a slow and curvy philosophy and democratic politics, it is important to recognize that the demands of democratic citizenship have changed in recent years. What constitutes civic engagement, what we can expect of ourselves, and how best to channel our resources have long been questions central to democracies.[27] But while democratic debate has often focused on pluralism, tolerance, alterity, and the willingness to listen, other concerns now carry at least as much weight regarding civic duty. Otherness does not only extend to people, but includes the planet and the animal kingdom, both of which suffer critically due to our mistreatment.

Without question, the planet's vulnerability adds an important and unique dimension to civic involvement, furthering the endorsement of a closeness to nature that is of course central to a slow and curvy lifestyle. The gargantuan proportions of ecocide have produced a shared conviction that green policies must be a leading priority in need of our immediate attention given the gravity of the situation. There is an urgent need to take power out of the hands of large corporations and resistant governments that seek to thwart green policies so that forward-looking actors can gain control of the conversation. At this writing, Americans look to the Biden administration's ambitious proposals, the youthful Sunrise Movement, 350.org, other environmental organizations, and the Summit in Glasgow to offer concrete proposals regarding how the country can meaningfully lower harmful emissions and lighten our carbon footprint.

Petrini insists that "an environmentalist who is not a gastronomer is sad, but a gastronomer who is not an environmentalist is just stupid."[28] This stupidity emanates from the inability to see the connection between how a culture feeds itself and its carbon footprint, and especially the link between large-scale industrial farming and our depletion of the environment. Without question, certain hallmarks of industrial farming such as the use of pesticides, the choice of mono-farming, and the practice of transporting food great distances take the blame for upsetting a host of natural processes that keep the delicate ecosystem in balance. By advocating old-fashioned, artisanal practices still important to Indigenous Peoples, preferring small farms that eschew the use of chemicals, and insisting on biodiversity, the slow movement seeks to undo the harm done by industry and to substantially reduce our carbon footprint. Indeed, in an email conversation with me from March 2021, Petrini identified biodiversity as a crucial pillar of the Slow Food movement today, for it represents "the fertile terrain of our movement which we have defended and promoted since the beginning" [translation mine]. Similarly, in his decision to found the *Cittaslow* movement and extend Slow Food's philosophy to civic life, Saturnini emphasized the preeminence of agriculture to cities that go slow and curvy rather than conforming to a standardized model of relentless growth.

Because traditional farming methods operate more in harmony with the earth's ecological balance, things are on a smaller scale and eschew the pesticides, hybrid seeds, and chemical inputs of the Green Revolution, as well as the large-scale farm equipment that is essential to industrial farming.[29] Traditional farming typically takes the focus off the high yields that mono-farming seeks out and puts it instead on biodiversity's variety of crops and sustainable practices. According to Eric Holt-Giménez, traditional farms are "less like these standardized 'factories in the fields' and more like intensely complex, knowledge-based systems that demand lots of expertise."[30] While itself a varied and complex amalgam of different methods, older practices nearly always focus on sustaining the benefits that accompany "water conservation, high agrobiodiversity, and species richness."[31] They shun the use of synthetic nitrogen fertilizers and thereby reduce greenhouse gas emissions. Additionally, because organic farming promotes carbon storage in the soil rather than in the atmosphere, it raises productivity while avoiding any contribution to climate change.[32] While experts differ in their reading of these claims, a cohort of respectable scholars and scientists such as Vandana Shiva, Raj Patel, and Harinath Kasiganesan stalwartly defend traditional farming methods.[33]

As is well known, the advent of factory farming and its signature search for high yields began in the twentieth century, when the Green Revolution convinced many people that introducing pesticides, hybrid seeds, and various chemicals would combat world hunger by increasing output. There was great concern that population growth would create famine in many parts of the globe, and that traditional farming methods fell short in their ability to produce adequate yields. Yet, aside from their chemical damage, the long-term economic results of the Green Revolution have been extremely detrimental to nations in the Southern Hemisphere, whose indebtedness to banks and large financial institutions such as the IMF and World Bank has negatively impacted their economies. The model for "development" has often served to further impoverish countries formerly tied to colonial powers given the metrics and methods used to promote economic growth and prosperity.[34] Moreover, later Free Trade Agreements such as NAFTA further harmed farmers in the Southern Hemisphere, contributing in part to the migration of displaced persons into the United States that now so heavily impacts the American political landscape. And everywhere in the world, the power of chemical companies to overtake old-fashioned farming has been the ruin of small-scale farmers. According to Vandana Shiva, India alone has witnessed no fewer than 270,000 farmer suicides due to the loss of family farms, while Raj Patel writes compassionately about farmer suicides in Mexico as well as the United States.[35]

By now, of course, factory farming and agribusiness keynote many Americans' relationship to food since large retailers and grocery stores hold such sway over what we consume . Certain grocery chains are big business and control much about how we feed ourselves. For those who believe that citizenship in a democracy demands taking control of this topic, fighting the harm done by agribusiness therefore represents an important but difficult task. And in some ways, the battle over food is more uphill in the United States than elsewhere. For instance, nineteen member countries of the European Union have now banned genetically modified organisms, or GMOs, completely.[36] While sixty-four countries have legislation demanding that the presence of GMOs be disclosed on food labels, the United States is only now gradually introducing such laws; moreover, American laws are far less stringent than in other nations in terms of what must be reported and what is exempt.[37] Nevertheless, changes are taking place, since a preference for organically grown food and items that are non-GMO is steadily increasing.[38]

We can win the uphill battle, just as we can reprioritize the American Dream. One illustration of this occurred at the 2019 Slow Food Leaders' Summit in Denver, a large gathering of slow foodies from all over the world and all walks of life. At this gathering, Gangsta Gardener Ron Finley argued forcefully that many Americans, not only a select few, are receptive to the direction of the alternative food movement with its emphasis on organic gardening. Because the ill effects of our industrialized food system are now starkly evident, he argues, people respond to efforts to reclaim what has been colonized by corporate interests. Finley's personal commitment to communal gardening arose due to his inability to obtain fresh produce in South Central

Los Angeles; this, together with his observation that people in his neighbor-hood, a food desert, ate less well than elsewhere inspired him to take matters into his own hands. The conspicuous ill health of those around him drama-tized the class and racial issues that accompany America's unjust food sys-tem, for those who are food insecure frequently lack access to adequate health care. What he noticed, in other words, was evidence of the class warfare that typifies many food deserts, disproportionately inhabited by Black Americans and people of color.[39] This move to actively address racial issues and include persons of color in the Slow Food agenda thus constitutes an important aspect of Finley's efforts. And as will be discussed presently and in chapter six, the ways in which non-Whites have proved integral to the movement has gained increasing traction over the years.

Unhappy with the situation, Finley decided to cultivate a curbside strip of land and grow vegetables, turning a food desert into a robust "food forest" that positively impacted the neighborhood. Despite his initial arrest warrant for growing vegetables, the overall effect of his guerilla gardening has been transformational, and blossomed into The Ron Finley Project which teaches urban horticulture.[40] Cultivating a green thumb and growing one's own food represents freedom, Finley maintains, since food deserts are equivalent to food prisons.[41] He maintains that Americans need to rediscover the beauty of farming, to literally dig in and experience the joy in watching things grow and the healing that urban gardening can bring about. Gardening will bring people back to what matters, he maintains, and allow us to rethink what kind of a society we want. Finley affirmed that we need to "forget the American Dream we've been sleeping under" and get back to the land which can amply provide for our needs.

Hence Finley's transformation of his South Central food desert into an abundant food sanctuary might thus be characterized as embodying Slow Food principles *in nuce*: a neighborhood microcosm of what the movement strives to accomplish worldwide. Yet in 2020 it was estimated that 38.3 mil-lion Americans live in food-insecure households, with low-income and rural settings being especially susceptible to food deserts.[42] And if the documen-tary *A Place At the Table* is correct, the exponential growth in food pantries around the country has occurred because even middle-class Americans with steady jobs suffer from food insecurity.[43] Combatting agribusiness and mono-farming, to be replaced by an organic, "regenerative" model that sequesters the soil's carbon and reduces harmful emissions, must take into account the demands of a chemical-free approach.

While it claims no formal ties to the Slow Food movement or to *Cittaslow*, John Chester's 2018 documentary, *The Biggest Little Farm,* amply demon-strates how a commitment to biodiversity and to organic, sustainable farm-ing requires a great deal of skill and patience. The film tells of a couple's seven-year labor of love in reviving a moribund farm north of Los Angeles, transforming it from a parched, abandoned wasteland into a thriving paragon of biodiversity, not without many trials along the way. They named their 200-acre operation "Apricot Lane Farms" and set out to practice "biomimicry," seeking to mimic the dynamics of the earth's ecosystem. Drawing on the knowledge of a friend who insisted that "our goal is the highest level of biodiversity possible," John and his wife Molly worked tirelessly, painstakingly, and creatively to resuscitate a previously neglected farm whose soil was utterly desiccated. They were at times incredulous regarding the merits of biodiversity and, over the course of seven years, met with their fair share of disappointments. The hard, brittle soil which eventually flourished into Apricot Lane Farms returned only after a number of setbacks. Yet in the long run their friend's methods won out, for their efforts at repeatedly diversifying and respecting the laws of biodiversity assisted them in bringing the farm back to life.

In the course of their seven-year adventure, John and Molly learned many things about organic farming and the ways in which plants, animals, and insects balance and sustain one another in the ecosystem. For instance, they learned that planting a cover crop not only protects the soil in heavy rains, but also serves as food for sheep. When the sheep graze, their droppings and urine in turn enrich the soil. They learned that ducks eat snails, thereby helping to control a pest which, once transformed into duck droppings, then morphs into fertilizer for the trees. Chickens in turn eat maggots and contribute to reducing the population of flies. When unwelcome gophers—who nevertheless aerate the soil—appeared on the scene, they discovered that owls hunt gophers. They subsequently built bird houses for the owls in order to control the gopher population, and in one year 87 owls devoured thousands of gophers. Bringing back wildlife, diversifying crops, planting cover crops, and producing a variegated farming environment thus illustrates the merits of biodiversity, a premise that is "simple but not easy."[44] The little farm (still small by agribusiness standards) became the "biggest little farm" in keeping with the demands of biodiversity.

The couple learned that even a relatively small sustainable farm must diversify its elements in order for nature's delicate balance to be maintained. As the film recounts, the Chesters ultimately farmed no fewer than two hundred different things, since biodiversity focuses on being attuned to what is immediate and idiosyncratic. Although it demands hard work and much patience, a commitment to biodiversity avoids the uniformity of industrial farming and gives heightened attention to place, to season, and to the specifics of a given farming landscape (e.g., too many gophers, too many snails, not enough cover crop). In keeping with the philosophy of slow, it pushes back against a McDonaldized system and honors nature's preference for diversity.

Slow Food's Non-Whites: African Americans,
People of Color, Indigenous People

In his defense of speed, Connolly applauds the ability of an interfused, rhizomatic world to promote diversity and a cosmopolitan spirit. Yet we might say that Ron Finley's gangsta gardening, whose emphasis on food sovereignty aligns more readily with slow, interprets the rhizomatic literally, bringing people of color into an important conversation that was formerly less hospitable to them. Because of its focus on "good, clean, and fair," a Slow Food approach to agriculture and food politics explicitly addresses problems of food insecurity with its racial and ethnic dimensions. Jonathan Kauffman has convincingly argued that in its earliest days, the organic, back-to-the-earth movement was almost exclusively White.[45] Black Americans, Indigenous People, and people of color did not initially evince much interest in the provenance of food, and once the alignment between food politics and the hippie counterculture was solidified in the 1960s, the Black population naturally saw its most pressing political concerns lying elsewhere. The same can be said for the environmental movement and general interest in all things natural: initially, it was largely White and middle-class.

Today, however, things have changed, and we cannot discuss food politics or environmentalism without prominently featuring non-Whites in the conversation. There is much to say just on the relationship between Black America and McDonald's, as Marcia Chatelain so carefully explores in her recent *Franchise: The Golden Arches in Black America*.[46] Yet in terms of Slow Food and the slow movement generally, the analysis is simpler, for the resistance to agribusiness and processed food has always shown respect for cultures that honor traditional methods of farming and cooking. As discussed in chapter six, Slow Food has made strides in promoting racial and economic justice, always showing willingness to learn from those who have long resisted industrial farming methods.

Foremost among these are the Indigenous Peoples whose identity is inextricably linked to a preindustrial relationship to nature. A changed sensibility in the United States now insists that the injustices done to Indigenous Peoples be brought center stage in our political discourse, and that reparations toward them be taken seriously.[47] While the slow movement concurs in the legal and political battles that surround the topic of reparations, it is especially the cultural dimension and praxis of Native people that slow seeks to recuperate: it hopes to revive and revalue the understanding of nature that keynotes the Native experience. Indeed, Indigenous Peoples' agricultural and gastronomic practices have gained currency around the United States if not around the world, and efforts have begun to focus on reclaiming original food cultures as a way of reconnecting to native roots.[48] They have begun to revitalize, rehabilitate, and relearn those things central to Indigenous food culture—seeds, buffalo, salmon fishing, the many varieties of corn—in an effort to reestablish the culinary practices that define a particular tribe or nation.[49]

It is for this reason that the movement demonstrates such respect for Indigenous Peoples, those communities that revere time-honored agricultural practices yet are often disadvantaged if not destroyed by large-scale agribusiness. The slow movement insists that Indigenous Populations know more than the industrialized world does, are ahead of us, and must be respected as the repository of crucial knowledge about Mother Earth. They embody an ethos that obeys nature rather than mistakenly thinking themselves its master, and thus model behavior that must be included in twenty-first-century citizenship. "Slow Food's empathy with indigenous peoples is total," Petrini writes, since it is they who keep alive the sensibility that so much of modernity shuns.[50] "All humanity is indebted to indigenous peoples," he continues, "who kept these principles alive in their daily practices while the world was going in a completely different direction."[51]

Hence at the Denver Slow Food Leaders' Summit held in July 2019, Native Americans played a key role in the program with prayers, songs, and speeches. Members of the Lakota tribe led the summit in prayer and song, explained the centrality of nature to their worldview, and discussed the importance of food sovereignty in regaining tribal identity. Members of the Lakota also told tales about harassment and discrimination and stereotypes about Native Americans. At the accompanying festival on the streets of Denver, scheduled events included "Indigenous Languages Workshop" and "Fonio, the Ancient Miracle Grain," while the Slow Food USA website link to "Reclaiming Native Truth" offered a praxis for honoring Indigenous Peoples.

This deference shown to Native Americans aligns with the rationale behind the founding of Slow Food's Terra Madre in 2004. This arm of the movement actively seeks to give a voice and a presence to the farmers, agriculturalists, cooks, and other food connoisseurs from all over the world—from industrialized and developing countries alike—who share an interest in alternative, often artisanal ways of doing things. This branch of the movement holds that there is a great deal of wisdom to be shared, preserved, and rekindled, and that in coming together, delegates from around the world offer a counterforce to the large agribusiness corporations that in fact go against the grain of Mother Nature. Thus, in 2004, Paolo di Croce invited delegates from a number of countries to Terra Madre in Turin in what was hoped would be the first international meeting of food communities, "notably those from developing countries" who still retained traditional practices.[52] An anticipatory anxiety about the success of the gathering was widely felt; what if the event were poorly attended? Yet this worry was appeased when the five thousand chairs in Turin's *Palazzo del Lavoro* were in fact occupied, and the room showed a splendid array of various forms of international dress and adornment: Indian turbans, Native American eagle feathers, woolen ponchos, tartan kilts, knitted hats from the Andes, colorful silks and headscarves from Asia and Africa, casual attire from Canada and the United States.[53] Terra Madre has since met every two years in Turin, and in 2012 was united with the *Salone del Gusto*, a trade fair that features artisanal food, workshops, and other Slow Food products. At this writing amidst covid-19, Terra Madre is being held online over a seven-month period, featuring a vast array of virtual events that emphasize good, clean, and fair while underscoring the crucial role of food sovereignty among Indigenous Peoples.

Slow Food International has sought to bring sensitivity to Indigenous Peoples by creating the Indigenous Terra Madre Network which brings together those who "produce food in the same way as their great-great-great grandparents."[54] Meanwhile, Slow Food USA has created the BIPOC Affinity Group, which focuses on the experience of Black, Indigenous, and People of Color elements of the America population and their important histories and relationships to food that need preserving. Additionally, thanks to the pioneering work of Jim Embry and hard work of Charity Kenyon, Slow Food USA has established the Equity, Inclusion, and Justice Working Group (EIJ) with a view toward broadening Slow Food's definition of social justice to include greater racial, ethnic, and class-based awareness as well as increase the participation of minority groups. This expands the mandate of "fair" by specifying exactly what inclusiveness might look like and how the movement can more effectively address such topics as food insecurity and food deserts.

Parallel to this respect for Indigenous Peoples is the movement's esteem for other groups that are often overlooked or forgotten, either in the food chain or in society as a whole. In his writings, Petrini pays special tribute to women, children, and the elderly whose central role in sustaining cultural traditions is vital. The elderly, for instance, hold great value for they are the "stewards of memory" who represent a link between previous generations and our present-day, harried society.[55] Petrini credits them with having a worldview that is "sufficiently deep" to help reorient our conception of modernity toward something slower and curvier. Equally important is the respect for the often hidden, overlooked, underpaid workers whose frequently exploited labor ensures the delivery of food to our grocery stores. "Good, clean, *and fair*" mandates that the manner in which food is grown, delivered, bought, and sold take into consideration the labor of those who often see little of the profit; indeed, they often operate under the legal radar yet prove indispensable.

Certainly, there is now great urgency in going green, promoting agroecology, and working toward ever-increasing levels of social justice. Thus, if we ask, "what's so great about slow?" one immediate answer is that it offers a praxis for addressing leading problems of the twenty-first century. It represents an antidote to the ecocide of global warming and offers a praxis to lighten our excessively deep carbon footprint. In the following chapter, I describe how embracing the philosophy of slow in the American context makes serious demands on the time-honored American Dream of upward social mobility and expansive growth. It demands that we rethink our under-standing of "progress" and asks that we reassess our cultural heroes, perhaps discarding some of them altogether.

NOTES

1. Scheuerman, "Citizenship and Speed," in *High-Speed Society: Social Acceleration, Power, and Modernity,* edited by Harmut Rosa and William E. Scheuerman, (Philadelphia: The Pennsylvania State University Press, 2009), 288–289.

2. Scheuerman, "Citizenship and Speed," 287.

3. On this topic, see especially Ben Berger's *Attention Deficit Democracy: The Paradox of Civic Engagement,* (Princeton, NJ: Princeton University Press, 2011).

4. William E. Connolly, "Speed, Concentric Cultures, and Cosmopolitanism," in *High-Speed Society: Social Acceleration, Power, and Modernity,* edited by Harmut Rosa and William E. Scheuerman, (Philadelphia: The Pennsylvania State University Press, 2009), 261–285.

5. Virilio, *Speed and Politics,*78.

6. Connolly, "Speed, Concentric Cultures, and Cosmopolitanism," 263.

7. *Ibid.,* 284.

8. *Ibid.,* 263.

9. *Ibid.,*264.

10. Ania Loomba and Martin Orkin, "Shakespeare and the Post-Colonial Question," in *Postcolonial Shakespeares*, ed. Ania Loomba and Martin Orkin, (New York: Routledge, 1998), 91.

11. William Shakespeare, *The Tragedy of Othello, the Moor of Venice,* 1.1, quoted from *The Riverside Shakespeare*, edited by G. Blakemore Evans, (New York: Houghton Mifflin Company, 1974), 1204.

12. *Othello*, 1204.

13. *Ibid.,*, 1206.

14. Ania Loomba, *Shakespeare, Race, and Colonialism*, (Oxford: Oxford University Press, 2002), 4.

15. Loomba, *Shakespeare, Race, and Colonialism*, 104. See also Janna H. Hooke, "Racial Otherness in Shakespeare's *Othello*," https://www.academia.edu/28048057/Racial_Otherness_in_Shakespeares_Othello, accessed February 2020; Stanley Lin, "Otherness as a Dramatic Device in *The Merchant of Venice* and *Othello*, https://www.academia.edu/13506577/Otherness_as_A_Dramatic_Device_in_The_Merchant_of_Venice_and_Othello, accessed February 2020.

16. Jyotsna G. Singh, *Shakespeare and Postcolonial Theory*, (London: Bloomsbury Publishing, 2019), 71.

17. See Brandon Ambrosino, "Four Hundred Years Later, Scholars Still Debate Whether Shakespeare's'Merchant of Venice' Is Anti-Semitic," *Smithsonian Magazine*, https://www.smithsonianmag.com/arts-culture/why-scholars-still-debate-whether-or-not-shakespeares-merchant-venice-anti-semitic-180958867/, accessed June 14, 2020.

18. Shakespeare, *The Merchant of Venice*, 268.

19. Ambrosino, "Four Hundred Years Later,"

20. Loomba, 156.

21. In Jyotsna G. Singh's words, "The competing interests and cultural and racial conflicts imbricated within pervasive anti-Semitism, between the merchants and the money lender—the Christian and the Jew—can be better understood in the context of a new dependence on capital in a growing, though unpredictable mercantile economy, and attendant shifts in relationships between the two communities." See Jyotsna G. Singh, *Shakespeare and Postcolonial Theory*(London: Bloomsbury Publishing, 2019), 41.

22. Charles de Secondat Montesquieu, *Persian Letters*, translated by C. J. Betts (New York: Penguin Classics, 2004), 91, 98, 112.

23. Rolando Minuti, *Studies on Montesquieu—Mapping Political Diversity*, Springer, 2018, 160.

24. Sankar Muthu, *Enlightenment Against Empire* (Princeton, NJ: Princeton University Press, 2003), 214

25. Ibid., 14.

26. Ibid., 17.

27. For an excellent study of the confusing term "civic engagement" and the need to unpack it, see note 4.

28.https://www.azquotes.com/author/22147-Carlo_Petrini, accessed March 18, 2021.

29. By this, I do not mean that all technological advances are harmful or out of step with Mother Nature; nor do I mean to suggest that large corporations cannot, prima facia, be attuned to the larger vision of green politics. It is rather that traditional ways of farming typically respect the planet's need to sustain biodiversity and to keep a delicate ecological balance in place rather than seeking out ever larger yields, ever greater profits, and expansionist policies.

30. Eric Holt-Giménez, *A Foodie's Guide to Capitalism: Understanding the Political Economy of What We Eat*(New York: Monthly Review Press, 2017), 60.

31. Ibid.

32.This occurs thanks to "minimum tillage, the return of crop residues in the earth, the use of cover crops and rotations, and the greater integration of nitrogen fixing legumes," https://www.organicwithoutboundaries.bio/2018/09/12/climate-change-mitigation/, accessed March 18, 2020.

33. See Harinath Kasiganesan, "Doing Farming the Organic Way," TED Talk, November 12, 2019, https://www.youtube.com/watch?v=xjVHkacNkwk; Raj Patel, *Stuffed and Starved: The Hidden Battle for the World Food System*, (Brooklyn, NY: Melville House, 2012); Raj Patel and Eric Holt-Giménez, eds., *Food Rebellions:*

Crisis and the Hunger for Justice(Oakland, CA: Food First Books, 2012); Vandana Shiva, *Earth Democracy: Justice, Sustainability, and Peace (Berkeley, CA: North Atlantic Books, 2015); Reclaiming the Commons: Biodiversity, Traditional Knowledge, and the Rights of Mother Earth* (Santa Fe, NM: Synergenic Press, 2020); *Who Really Feeds the World?: The Failures of Agribusiness and the Promise of Agroecology, (Berkeley, CA: North Atlantic Books, 2016)*

34. For a discussion of how the Southern hemisphere has been adversely affected by efforts at development, see Vandana Shiva, *Stolen Harvest: The Hijacking of the Global Food Supply*, South End Press, 2000; Maria Mies and Vandana Shiva, *Ecofeminism*(London: Zed Books, 2014)..

35. See *Seeds: The Untold Story*, 2020. See also Raj Patel, *Stuffed and Starved: the Hidden Battle for the World Food System (Brooklyn, NY: Melville House, 2012)*.

36. https://ec.europa.eu/environment/europeangreencapital/countriesruleoutgmos/, accessed November 28, 2021.

37. https://www.centerforfoodsafety.org/issues/976/ge-food-labeling/international-labeling-laws. Only foods that contain more than five percent of bioengineered ingredients, and that are intended for human consumption, must comply with GMO labeling by January 1, 2022. However, certain foods are exempt from this mandate thanks to loopholes in, i.e., foods that come from animals, highly refined foods such as oil and sugar, foods consumed in a restaurant, food produced by small manufacturers, and foods not meant for human consumption.

38. See https://www.statista.com/statistics/244394/organic-sales-in-the-united-states/ accessed March 18, 2020.

39. For an excellent study of how communities can come together to face issues of food injustice, see Garrett M. Broad, *More Than Just Food: Food Justice and Community Change* (Oakland, CA: University of California Press, 2016).

40. https://www.ft.com/content/ffeaf616-d36e-11e7-a303-9060cb1e5f44, accessed October 31, 2019.

41. https://ronfinley.com/pages/about, accessed November 29, 2021.

42. See https://www.ers.usda.gov/topics/food-nutrition-assistance/food-security-in-the-us/key-statistics-graphics.aspx#foodsecure, accessed November 15, 2021, and https://www.google.com/search?q=how+many+food+deserts+are+there+in+the+US A&se_es_tkn=mtgyrpxt, accessed May 28, 2019.

43. *A Place at the Table*, Directed by Kristi Jacobson and Lori Silverbush. Brooklyn, NY: Motto Pictures/Los Angeles, CA: Participant Production Company, 2012.

44. *The Biggest Little Farm*, John Chester, 2019.

45. See chapter 1, note 48.

46. Marcia Chatelain, *Franchise: The Golden Arches in Black America*, (New York: Liveright Publishing Corporation, 2020).

47. The 574 federally recognized tribes request, among other things, restored sovereignty over the land taken from them, monetary compensation for the genocide and economic hardship they have suffered, and a rewriting of American history books such that the narrative about European settlers tells the truth about what happened. Current public debates about statues, portraits, and other monuments that revere

White settlers responsible for the harm reflect the level of seriousness with which the public now takes the topic of reparations.

48. Slow Food USA's "Recipes from Turtle Island" illustrates this by featuring recipes of Indigenous People.

49. For an exploration of this phenomenon, see *Gather: The Fight to Revitalize Our Native Foodways*, Sanjay Rawal, 2020.

50. Carlo Petrini, *Food & Freedom: How the Slow Food Movement Is Changing the World Through Gastronomy,* translated by John Irving(New York: Rizzoli Ex Libris, 2015), 120.

51. Petrini, *Food & Freedom*, 124.

52. Geoff Andrews, *The Slow Food Story: Politics and Pleasure* (Montreal: McGill-Queen's University Press, 2008), 49.

53. For a more detailed account of this first meeting of Terra Madre, see Carlo Petrini and Gigi Padovani, *Slow Food Revolution: A New Culture for Eating and Living,* translated by Francesca Santovetti (New York: Rizzoli, 2006), Chapter 8.

54. "Indigenous Terra Madre Network," https://www.slowfood.com/our-network/indigenous/, accessed December 22, 2021.

55. Petrini, *Food & Freedom,* 115.

Chapter 3

Prometheus versus Noah

A New Humanism for the Twenty-First Century

For many people, the term "progress" is sutured to the term "modernity." Both denote our ability to master nature through science and technology, and the ability to claim sovereignty over earth and space. Both indicate a successful dispelling of superstition and an Old World mentality while interpreting history in a linear, sequential fashion wherein the present prevails over what went before: modernity belittles the past, or so the thinking goes, and gives the lie to an older, inglorious worldview. Yet today our efforts to master nature have shown unambiguous signs of revenge, and in Frankenstein fashion have turned back on us with impunity in various guises. Regardless of one's political affiliation, it is clear that nature, which includes our nature, is now under duress and that much of our "progress" is to blame. According to a slow and curvy philosophy, our focus should no longer be on *controlling* nature with ingenuity (although technological ingenuity is often a good thing), but on *saving* it with patience and painstaking care.

Saving the world by acknowledging our interconnected, interpenetrated existence is integral to the new humanism implicit in the slow movement. Although this significant shift that reorients our worldview and reprioritizes our lifestyle is not always overtly acknowledged, it is key to understanding where the philosophy of slow takes us, and what a slow and curvy mindset for the twenty-first century entails. With eating as its central metaphor—the process of ingestion that relies entirely on our permeable boundaries and porous relationships, our utter dependance on things beyond our control—the new humanism demotes the time-honored mirage of human sovereignty and instead reveres an "archaic supremacy," allowing the body to pause so that the soul can catch up to it.[1]

Two iconic figures from the Western tradition clarify this shift from sovereignty to archaic supremacy, from the virus of speed to slow and curvy: Prometheus and Noah. In order to underscore the urgency with which we must shift gears and decelerate, Petrini identifies Noah, not Prometheus, as the new champion whose rise to prominence would radically rewrite modernity's narrative and seriously reorient our priorities. Noah encourages us to savor our relationship with Mother Nature in a caretaking rather than a proprietary manner, since for him the need to save the earth is paramount. And indeed, in various iterations of slow, it is often our relationship to nature—be it our own nature or our relationship to the earth—that helps us go slow and curvy: slow fashion eschews synthetic fabrics, prefering natural fibers; slow tourism encourages forms of travel that do not upset our circadian rhythms, for example by car or by boat; slow shopping reminds us we need not buy anything, thereby reducing our consumption of natural resources. In a 2009 interview with *The Independent* newspaper, Petrini thus urges a change in our choice of cultural heroes so that we will interpret "modernity" differently.

> The idea of the modern has been superceded; the challenge of today is to return to the small-scale, the handmade, to local distribution, because today what we call "modern" is out of date . . . For two centuries humanity has done everything in its power to become the master of the world. But in the third millennium, the myth of Prometheus no longer corresponds to the aspirations of contemporary man. Instead we should turn to the figure of Noah. Faced with the excesses of modernisation, we should no longer seek to change the world, but to save it.[2]

If Marx argued that we should not interpret the world but change it, Petrini argues that we should not change the world, but save it. Whether the topic be food, city life, clothing, parenting, tourism, or other, a slow and curvy lifestyle more often than not resonates with the goal of reversing ecocide and demoting the sovereign subject.

Prometheus stands pitted against Noah in their relation to Mother Nature, for they take radically different approaches to the power that she wields and the meaning she has in our lives. Importantly, both figures represent allies of humankind, persons saddled with an ennobling task that would help the human condition move forward. However, they approach this task in different ways and for different purposes, creating two distinct legacies. The former is a Greek mythological figure who dominates, tampers, and controls the earth while relying on his own native strength and intellect; he is an agent of change who makes use of nature for human ends. A descendant of the Titans, he defiantly rebels against the ruling Olympians, sets his own agenda and proceeds from there; subsequently, his love of humankind relies on an instrumentalist mindset based on formal logic. Noah, conversely, is an Old

Testament patriarch who functions as an obedient caretaker unclear as to the master plan; he works with nature in keeping with God's mandates and doesn't know how things will turn out. He operates not according to instrumental rationality but in keeping with a more intuitive, aesthetic approach trusting God's message to be implicit in nature. Unlike the instrumentalism of Prometheus, Noah's worldview reveals an aesthetic dimension whose epistemological position never claims mastery.

Visually, we imagine the former as muscular, agile, and fleet of foot. In art he is typically depicted as an athletic man whose strong limbs, rippling muscles, and thick torso exude strength and a commanding presence. There is a dynamism about him that suggests purpose, a man on a mission. The latter, on the other hand, is often represented as an elderly individual with a snowy beard and a walking stick, a benevolent soul in flowing robes and sandals. He views himself as a trusting steward of creation who interprets the natural world as rife with theological purpose, full of the (re)enchantment that for Bennett gives rise to an ethic of generosity.[3] While Prometheus intends to manipulate nature for humanistic ends, Noah's labor is marked by a docility that lets nature take the lead.

The use of mythological and Biblical figures takes us deep into the Western tradition and the many resonances that the Western experience inherits from the ancient world. Moreover, these iconic figures both reverberate with the American cultural landscape given their defining stories, for taken together they appeal to our industriousness, our admiration for lone wolf bravery, and our religiosity. Each models behavior that finds a home in Americana, bringing their ancient status forward to the present day. Indeed, as we will see, not everyone views them as polar opposites, but as differing gradations of the same thing, variations on a recurring theme.

PROMETHEUS: FIRE-STEALING TITAN OR SCIENTIST "INSENSIBLE TO THE CHARMS OF NATURE"

In many ways, Prometheus excels as an antecedent to American cultural heroes who brave the odds and defy traditions, for he is a powerful trope freighted with rugged individualist connotations. In Greek mythology, Prometheus is the industrious Titan who defies orders from above and strikes out on his own. He first appears in Hesiod's eighth-century BC poem, *Theogony,* which recounts in epic form the genealogy of the Greek gods. According to myth, Prometheus disobeys Zeus' orders and defiantly steals fire; he sets his own agenda and goes rogue in pursuit of it. This emanates from his desire to see humanity move forward by gaining agricultural, technological, and industrial know-how, allowing us to take command and no longer be subservient to the domineering Olympians. Indeed, Prometheus loves humanity more than the ruling gods; in fact, he is credited with originally shaping human beings out of mud while Athena breathed life into them. In giving humanity fire, Prometheus thus allows people to master their surroundings and control their fate, since fire enriches our lives in so many ways. Fire creates, embellishes, empowers, and refines; it is integral to metallurgy, industry, and culinary practices. As a gift to humans, fire bestows upon them the ability

> to understand their environment, to calculate, to read and to write, to build houses and sailing ships, and to tame wild animals for food, labor, and protection. Prometheus showed them treasures within Mother Earth: copper and iron, silver and gold. He taught them how, with the gift of fire, mortals could use these treasures to improve and beautify their lives. Thus, it was that man, frail as he was, became master of his environment.[4]

Prometheus, whose name means "forethought," labors valiantly on behalf of progress and humanity's effort to subdue the elements, making the latter work toward human ends. In so doing, he appeals to the traditional Protestant work ethic and belief in rags to riches, embodying the conviction that hard work is key to happiness. He believes in "progress," energy, and human ingenuity and thus refuses to bow to nay-saying powers keen on holding humanity down. His life-changing gift of fire thus defies the Olympians' authority in ways that correspond exactly to modernity's disenchantment and ability to supersede natural and supernatural forces. Promethean audacity confers agency onto human beings, allowing us to go from mere creatures of mud to creators of culture; he literally makes us stand up and walk, morphing from primitive to refined. Instead of being passive byproducts of the natural world, we become beings endowed with purpose no longer beholden to the Olympians. As Americans, we admire his bold defiance of authority and staunch self-reliance that resurfaces in the celebrated brazenness of American rugged individualism. Yet because of his daring gesture and gift to us, Prometheus was not treated kindly by Zeus: as punishment he was strapped to a mountain, his liver eaten by an eagle each day yet growing back each night for thirty thousand years.

In this tale, we see an early iteration of the mind/body split so integral to Western civilization and the subsequent devaluing of mere material reality in comparison to the workings of mind, intellect, and culture. Given his alignment with industry and technological know-how, Prometheus puts into play the power of the mind to master, control, outwit, and achieve what it wants. While he represents a cultural hero of the Western world who first formed us out of mud and then procured the wherewithal to advance, Prometheus' gift to humanity also works to reconfirm the mind/body dichotomy and subsequently, ironically, our alienation from nature. He represents drive, determination, innovation, and ingenuity; all good qualities, but do they run into trouble as they seek to surpass the immediacy of nature?

The mind/body dualism claims a long and celebrated history in the Western tradition, stretching back to antiquity and reasserting itself in those who disdain, often implicitly, the nature-body-stomach emphasis in favor of culture-mind-intellect. For those critical of this dualism, the aim is not to simply invert—and thereby reconfirm—the mind/body dualism, but to expose its falsehood. It is not that nature-body-stomach proves inferior or superior to the culture-mind-intellect side of things; rather, the juxtaposition itself is erroneous. If we understand ourselves as "creatures of Prometheus" who rely on instrumental rationality, we are predisposed toward a relationship with the earth and with ourselves that fails to perceive the continuum with nature on which we all are positioned. We fail to perceive ourselves as part of nature, and the dualistic system we have created only works against itself.[5] "What if our theoretical repertoires were to take inspiration not from thinking but from eating?" Mol asks.[6] If eating were to gain the currency traditionally awarded to thinking, surely agriculture, farming, biology, and physiology would receive pride of place, since how we grow, cook, consume, digest, and make use of food would be paramount. In other words, our status as a part of the natural would gain respect as opposed to our status as lords of creation.

To engage these ideas, however, we needn't go all the way back to Greek mythology. A nineteenth-century publication reengages the story of Prometheus and casts it along lines directly attuned to the theme of modernity addressed here. The familiar narrative of Mary Shelley's 1818 novel, *Frankenstein*, serves us well, since the novel follows naturally from a discussion of the ancient Titan trickster: its full title is *Frankenstein, or, The Modern Prometheus*. Dr. Frankenstein believes that scientific discovery will enrich human life immeasurably, and that science represents the master narrative whose creative powers trump other aspects of the humanist tradition. Theology, philosophy, art and literature all pale beside the powers of science for him, for these engage an aesthetic sensibility that, to his mind, proves less useful. To prove his point, he seeks to create a human life in his laboratory using laboratory equipment but not a woman's body. "After days and nights of incredible labour and fatigue, I succeeded in discovering the cause of generation and life: nay, more, I became myself capable of bestowing animation upon lifeless matter."[7] Yet as is well known, this project goes horribly awry and the creature-turned-monster, the would-be helper, becomes a violent, dreaded antagonist who torments its creator. In this way, Shelley plays out the central thematic of *Dialectic of Enlightenment*: namely, that our attempts to dominate nature using instrumental rationality have tragically turned back on us, not enriching, but endangering human life and the life of the planet.

Motivated by good intentions, Dr. Frankenstein is increasingly obsessed with the powers of science, with its ability to allow human ingenuity to hold sway over the natural world. He slowly loses interest in people, in conversation, in beauty, and art. He pulls away from family and friends, failing to take notice of the people around him and the changing seasons. Having become "insensible to the charms of nature," the infatuated doctor at work in his lab contrasts with his childhood friend, the foil character Henry Clerval whose passions run more toward poetry, literature, and language.[8] Dr. Frankenstein ultimately becomes oblivious to the world; as one seeking to dominate nature, its inherent beauty and rhythms mean nothing to him. Yet the horrific consequences of this hubris constitute the best-known portions of this classic story as the rebellious monster proceeds to terrorize the doctor in numerous ways.[9]

Shelley's gothic tale about a man convinced that science is capable of "almost unlimited powers" cautions against the thirst for knowledge unaccompanied by humility.[10] "You seek for knowledge and wisdom, as I once did," Dr. Frankenstein tells a companion, "and I ardently hope that the gratification of your wishes may not be a serpent to sting you, as mine has been."[11] In Prometheus, the clever yet compassionate trickster who defied the Olympians, we see the precursor of Dr. Frankenstein who unwittingly, tragically created a monster. We also see the precursor of brave American activists, inventors, and risk-takers who pioneered new territory and met with success in the interests of helping humanity progress: Benjamin Franklin flying a kite in a thunderstorm, Lewis and Clark traversing unchartered territories, Horatio Alger writing rags-to-riches stories about match boys who find prosperity. While their stories do not follow the same gothic unfolding as that of the tragic doctor, they do align America's can-do, nature-dominating spirit with the mind/body dichotomy implicit in Shelley's classic tale.

Ancient or modern—fire-bearing iconoclast or "enlightened" scientist— Prometheus emerges as an expression of human domination over nature, a well-developed theme in contemporary ecocriticism: "Human beings purchase the increase in their power with estrangement from that over which it is exerted," Horkheimer and Adorno claim. "Enlightenment stands in the same relationship to things as the dictator to human beings."[12] Perhaps, then, "enlightenment" does not reside in *mastery* over nature since the mind itself is part of the natural order, as materially grounded as are animals and plant life (yet also capable of self-reflection). Perhaps we have had things backwards for a long time, unable to see that our strength also represents our weakness; our forte is the source of our malaise. Ensconced in nature, surrounded by animals, literally at sea and thus ceding all control, benevolent Noah seemingly represents the polar opposite of fire-stealing Prometheus, ancient or gothic.

NOAH, THE WATER-LOGGED PATRIARCH

Prometheus' daring and self-determined risk-taking contrast sharply with Noah's submissive obedience to God's command. Noah is the venerable Old Testament patriarch whose dates are ambiguous, as is the question of whether the Biblical flood occurred at all. Among those who study the Old Testament and/or see evidence of the flood's existence, this diluvian event that changed the course of history took place somewhere around 2348 BC; thus, about 4,370 years ago.[13] And whether an ark filled with animals floating amidst a downpour represents an historical reality or an allegorical lesson, the person of Noah surely occupies a secure space within the Western tradition. He is the one chosen to take humanity into the redeeming waters that promise a new beginning; he lets us wash away the past and start over again with a clean slate.

Noah was a devout man living in a time of waywardness such that his benevolence contrasted markedly with the misconduct of his contemporaries. Unwaveringly devoted to God, he "found favor with the Lord" even as the rest of the world did not: "In the eyes of God the earth was corrupt and full of lawlessness."[14] Thanks to Noah's steadfast devotion, he and his family alone were spared in God's decision to wipe out humanity with a flood. He was thus assigned the task of building an ark in order to safeguard God's creation and withstand the deluge, orders which he followed dutifully despite their being unusual and uncomfortable. Whereas Prometheus' signature gesture is one of defiance in the interest of human progress moving forward, Noah's is one of obedience so that humanity can go back and start over. For in keeping with the Old Testament's account, a torrential flood drenched the earth leaving Noah and his entourage adrift for a very long time.

Scholarly interpretations of the flood's duration vary widely, but there is agreement over Noah and his entourage having spent just over one year in the ark.[15] During this time, Noah endures the tribulations of an enclosed space surrounded by animals large and small, unsure how it all will end.[16] Far from seeking to master nature, he is immersed in the animal kingdom, besieged by animal needs, overwhelmed by animal behaviors, sounds, and smells. His own willpower or decision to act never enters the equation. Noah does not control the waters but simply follows orders by working with the flood; far from seeking to enrich or embellish life, his only ambition is to keep himself and his charges alive. Indeed, he is not an individual with strong willpower: following the flood, he plants a vineyard and learns the pleasures of wine. One day he indulges this oenophilia to excess and falls asleep, "naked inside his tent," causing his sons to cover him with a robe.[17] Artists such as

Michelangelo and Pietro Liberi have portrayed this intimate familial scene of dutiful sons coming to the aid of their inebriated, incapacitated father.

While still in the ark, however, Noah exhibits sober vigilance, patiently waiting for a sign indicating that God has ended the flood and made the natural world hospitable. This long-suffering willingness to endure a trying experience surely resonates with a number of American cultural heroes whom we celebrate for their unwavering endurance and refusal to quit: George Washington surviving Valley Forge, Abraham Lincoln reading by candlelight into the wee hours, Martin Luther King, Jr. spending months in a Birmingham jail. Moreover, his waiting for a sign *in nature* is itself fraught with significance. Rather than anticipating a clear message in scientific, linguistic terms, terms that translate directly and that are unambiguous in meaning, Noah deals in birds, relying on them to convey signals and give orders. He first sends out a raven. Once that comes back without any hint of a change, he twice commissions a dove to see if the waters have abated. He looks for a sign from nature whose meanings he may or may not fully understand, for he is aware that cognition does not align perfectly with reality. There is always something different, something that the mind cannot assimilate in the natural world whose powers of enchantment stand in opposition to the powers of analysis.

This "nonidentity of being in its representations" is, as Morton Schoolman explains, central to the concept of aesthetic rationality, and it must "consistently represent in a way that *negates* representation."[18] This is just what happens when the dove returns from its second sortie with an olive branch in its mouth: Noah interprets the olive branch as designating the flood's end, yet there surely remains some element of guessing, of affective attachment, of enchanted, non-analytic response in his reading of the branch. Apprehending the world aesthetically, whose enchanted quality always leaves something unexplained or open to speculation, repeats itself famously in the form of a rainbow.[19] Is it the colors, the surprise at its appearance, the arc that it forms in the sky that designates an end to God's fury? Aesthetic rationality admits the gap between our cognitive powers and the reality we experience, thereby distinguishing itself precisely from the scientific approach in its effort to control the natural world.[20] Aesthetic rationality "can motor ethical and political change," as per Bennett, given its ability to re-enchant the world however vapid and exhausted it may appear.[21]

Indeed, an instrumentalist mindset contains some measure of hubris, since many things do not translate into terms that equate with human cognitive powers. In his study of *Dialectic of Enlightenment*, Schoolman recognizes the theological ramifications of this, for he writes that "the Judaic ban on naming God is an aesthetic recognition of the limits of thought."[22] Aesthetic rationality thus relies on an intuitive sense that contrasts with formal reason's controlling, diminishing side, for what is physically and figuratively fluid cannot be concretized. To perceive the world aesthetically is to acknowledge what is unrecognizable to human cognition: birds, olive branches, and rainbows are not singularly aligned with one idea and are not reducible to a fixed lexicon.[23]

Noah acknowledges the limits of human cognitive mastery when he permits a dove to convey messages and an olive branch to do the talking. In return for his service, God gives him a long life—"nine hundred and fifty years; then he died"[24]—and made him the patriarch of the post-diluvian world. And while the story of the ark is often used to introduce children to the Biblical elements of the Western narrative, clearly something quite serious is in play. Noah represents fluidity in more ways than one: he is cooperative, receptive, intuitive, and humble. He gives in to a slow and curvy approach to the world, recognizing that the scope and power of the flood is beyond his control. Thus, he is anything but "insensible to the charms of nature," as was the obsessed Dr. Frankenstein. And because it is impossible to tell his story without recounting his enmeshment in the forces of nature, Noah embodies the new humanism that no longer seeks to change the world, but to save it.

Health Food, Fast Food, Slow Food: The Impetus Behind Culinary Movements

The American cultural imaginary typically celebrates the daring of Prometheus more than the long-suffering of sodden Noah, for we see ourselves more as competitive innovators than as quiet caretakers. Could the Old Testament patriarch ever be our cultural hero? It seems a fair question to ask whether the country of Henry Ford, Andrew Carnegie, Thomas Edison, and Steve Jobs can reimagine itself not as a captain of industry but as a venerable steward of creation. At first blush, the aged ark builder hardly appears to jibe with the expansive energy of our leading industrialists and beacons of prosperity. The United States prides itself not merely on *surviving*, but on *thriving*. How could someone beholden to a dove ever capture our collective imagination?

Yet our list of revered icons does not emerge exclusively from industry, nor from Washington, Wall Street, Silicon Valley, or Hollywood. Numerous environmentally conscious Americans have received pride of place in our historical narrative and have significantly shaped public consciousness along slow and curvy lines. Here the biologist and author Rachel Carson deserves special applause, for through her writing she brought national attention to the endangerment of both the environment and human health given the farming industry's growing and unquestioning acceptance of harmful chemicals. Carson's 1962 best-selling publication, *Silent Spring*, roundly criticized the harmful effects of pesticides such as DDT that were being sprayed liberally on plants and insects in order to bolster yield. Stressing the interconnection of all living things, she argued forcefully that the presence of lethal chemicals in the environment and in our food will have long-lasting, devastating effects on our health and on the planet. "These sprays, dusts, and aerosols are now applied almost universally to farms, gardens, forests, and homes," she writes. "Can anyone believe it is possible to lay down such a barrage of poisons on the surface of the earth without making it unfit for all life?"[25]

Carson underscores the interconnection of all living things, warning that the reckless use of chemicals in her lifetime would have a lethal effect on future generations, especially in the form of cancers. Because she chided the scientific community for its hubris and unwillingness to more carefully research the chemicals it so liberally endorsed, she was lampooned mercilessly and even deemed a witch.[26] Yet the popularity of her book garnered her the attention of President Kennedy, who subsequently urged his Democratic Advisory Council to heed Carson's eco-manifesto and combat pollution in more environmentally protectionist ways. Thus, a shy biologist who preferred the quiet of the Maine coast now counts among our leading ecofriendly heroes, for her corpus of writings—which includes a trilogy of books about the sea—rank among the canonical heavyweights of our environmentalist movement.[27]

Other ecofriendly names join that of Carson, illustrating the breadth of the movement. Henry David Thoreau, George Perkins Marsh, John Muir, Theodore Roosevelt, Ansel Adams, and from a transcendentalist angle, Ralph Waldo Emerson deserve recognition. More recently, Al Gore and Leonardo DiCaprio are to be credited, as do other famous Americans who have transformed a general interest in environmentalism into a more concerted, time-sensitive effort to fight climate change. The rise of the Sunrise Movement, 350.org, and other organizations advocating green policies give testimony to the fact that today more Americans are convinced of the urgency of climate change and the need to mainstream ecofriendly principles. "America the beautiful" always brings to mind a repertoire of natural landscapes whose preservation is key to our national heritage: Yosemite's Half Dome, the terra cotta-hued Grand Canyon, midwestern fields of corn and wheat, the Hawaiian islands with their volcanoes, waterfalls, and coveted beaches. Moreover, in persons such as Bill Gates we have both a captain of industry and a committed environmentalist, such that a Noah-like sensibility not only partakes of an American tradition but now has the backing of industry.[28]

Yet when it comes to bringing the praxis of slow into our mainstream, do we need a hero? Without diminishing the importance of, say, Rachel Carson, it is important to remember that her ultimate goal had nothing to do with celebrity but in changing the public's unknowing acquiescence in the use of dangerous chemicals. If our larger purpose resides in rethinking and reprioritizing the American Dream, scaling back from economic largesse and embracing a new humanism based on interconnection, does it matter whose lead we follow? A Noah-like sensibility that informs a slow and curvy praxis is the goal, not a cultural icon for us to revere. In illustrating this point, it is useful to reflect on how formerly countercultural practices have ultimately become mainstream and transformed themselves from little known esoterica into our everyday language. Here, Kauffman's careful and entertaining study of "hippie food" serves as a meaningful precedent, since he also analyzes a gastronomical sea change in recent American history.

In chronicling how the organic food touted by "longhairs" became everyday American fare—how tofu and wheat germ lost their exotic veneer and became a commonplace in the American kitchen—Kauffman recounts the rise and fall of many cultural icons along the way, the gurus who instructed people about how changed dietary habits would improve their lives. Because these gurus came and went, Kauffman implicitly discounts the claim that heroes are essential to a movement's success, instead proffering the argument that social movements driven by strong principles can stand on their own. Of course, iconic figures helped galvanize the natural foods movement by bringing attention to the topic, but many of them gained a following and later were either discredited, derided, or simply faded away. Ultimately, it was not the celebrity factor that galvanized things for everyday Americans, but the strength of the argument that organic, pesticide-free, unprocessed, local food surpasses its adulterated counterpart which has often travelled a great distance before reaching us.

Kauffman chronicles a long line of health food heroes who introduced alternative culinary practices and medicinal cures in various parts of the United States. The list is long and varied: Lois Bootzin, Arnold Ehret, Paul Bragg, Gaylord Hauser, Frank and Rosalie Hurd, John Harvey Kellogg, Adelle Davis, and Frances Moore Lappé are but a sampling of those who exerted considerable influence on health-conscious Americans willing to listen. These gurus introduced organic food and farming, a vitamin-and mineral-rich diet, herbs, tonics, supplements, and a variety of exercises to enhance the health of their audiences. Through their writing and speaking engagements, they prescribed what we collectively call "hippie food" along with such regimented strictures as vegetarianism, a mucus-free diet, the steady consumption of raw foods and juices, and the recommendation that Americans make their own bread and yogurt.

The reputation of these gurus varied widely, from those deemed an eccentric fringe—the chef at Bootzin'sHealth Hut would dance in a grass skirt while her husband shook his maracas[29]—to those who were highly esteemed: Davis, for instance, was named the "high priestess of nutrition" by *Time* magazine.[30] Moreover, their dietary influence ultimately spilled over into other regimens, most notably that of exercise, spawning such cultural icons as Charles Atlas and Jack LaLanne. More recent years have witnessed a new set of diet and exercise stars, including Andrew Weil, Dr. Oz, Robert Atkins, Nathan Pritkin, Arnold Schwarzenegger, and Jane Fonda. Added to this are the many individuals who have brought yoga into our cultural mainstream.[31] Clearly, experts such as these can have widespread appeal, truly impacting the fabric of American society in long-lasting ways.

Yet one of Kauffman's most valuable insights centers around the fact that successful social movements often propagate outward on their own; they grow in rhizomatic fashion, without a leader, provided they have enough grassroots initiative and rudimentary low-level organization to sustain a compelling message. Once these social movements generate enough momentum and truly impact the collective imagination, they need not be rigidly structured in predictable administrative ways in order to proliferate; their actions need not be governed by top-heavy bureaucracy or strictly programmed mandates. Nor do they need a central figure around whom to organize; rather, they have a life of their own and inspire followers thanks to the energy that they generate and cultural cachet that propels them forward. Having interviewed many people who vividly recall the social unrest of the 1960s and early 1970s, Kauffman explains how an interest in alternative culinary practices grew out of a sense of personal betrayal and political disaffection, the feeling that American society no longer embodied one's own values and that the United States government no longer represented one's politics. These feelings of alienation subsequently generated interest in establishing a counterculture that could offer push back against mainstream America, including the latter's culinary habits. For this reason, "hippie food" garnered itself a considerable following which gradually infiltrated the society at large.

Thus emerged a grassroots movement wherein organic food took on political meaning; to eat bean sprouts was read as an act of resistance against American hypocrisy at home and imperialism abroad. Importantly, its interest in an alternative gastronomy was spurred on by the fact that those in search of the counterculture often traveled, either around the United States or abroad. They were restless and opposed the layered meanings of "settling down," of putting down roots in a society whose principles had gone astray. Carrying their life in a backpack and frequently relying on the kindness of strangers for transportation and lodgings, they transported their countercultural lifestyle and philosophy to places far and wide in ways that helped spread awareness about the virtues of organic food and back-to-the-land living. Together with the popularity of gurus such as Davis appearing on the cover of *Time* magazine, their youthful, peripatetic energy allowed the hippie food of the 1960s to gain currency throughout American culture, transporting organic, unconventional food from the fringes of society to its center.

Clearly parallels exist between the fecundity of the hippie food movement and the slow movement. Many elements within slow philosophy insist on a similar grassroots ordering, steering away from celebrity culture's hype and neoliberal profit-orientation and toward a focus on the everyday, the local, and the slow and curvy. While Petrini himself has been acknowledged as a charismatic speaker who has brought much attention to Slow Food, he himself insists that the movement remain minimally organized and reliant on input at the grassroots level. Just as slow fashion disdains the hierarchical chain of fast fashion which feeds the neoliberal ethos of for-profit production, accelerated merchandise turn-around, and escalated shopping, so do other expressions of slow seek to discourage the "vampire" of commercialism and the maw of trendy celebrity culture. For instance, slow tourism encourages us to visit fewer places and at a more leisurely pace, while slow shopping reminds us that we needn't buy anything. Slow parenting urges us to take our children outside, removing them from the mesmerizing allure of screens, while *Cittaslow* strives to provide the parks, playgrounds, bike paths, and city centers where children can play and adults can stroll.

Finally, it is worthwhile to take note of the argument that Prometheus and Noah are less antipodal than they at fist appear. Stuart Curran argues convincingly for points of overlap that unite these seemingly incongruous icons; additionally, he argues that this overlap actually links them to our American heritage.[32] True, one is Greco-Roman and the other Judeo-Christian; one defies the orders of a higher power while the other follows through. One has to wait thirty thousand years for relief while the other stays afloat for a shorter period of time; following each signature act, one suffers torment chained to a mountainside while the other enjoys the fruits of his vineyard. Yet they do mirror each other somewhat, since both seek to ameliorate the human condition and ennoble our character, whatever the source of unhappiness. And because Prometheus' son, Deucalion, serves as the surviving protagonist of the Greek diluvian story, parallels exist between the Titan and Noah despite the temporal gap. In the person of Deucalion, we have the legacy of hard-working Prometheus morphing into a Noah-like figure who safeguards humanity amidst a flood. Insisting that the confluence of attributes allows the two to bear a mutual resemblance, Curran maintains that "it is probably inevitable that the titan should be drawn into a syncretic harmony with Judeo-Christian scriptures."[33]

Moreover, in his analysis of the many cultural antecedents and political contexts in which these icons have so frequently been put into play, Curran draws out the parallels that join Prometheus not only to Noah but of all people, to George Washington, for he sees an "implicit analogy" between the father of our country and "the unflagging political commitment of Prometheus."[34] Because the "political Prometheus" is one who consistently defends the oppressed against the wages of tyranny in whatever guise, the Greek mythological figure exists as a precursor to the Founding Father who fought against colonial rule and oversaw the birth of the country. Prometheus reasserts himself in the struggle for independence, for he represents "a figure for the self-educating force of the human intellect . . . the reformulation of human ends that is America."[35] In this, the connection between Prometheus and Washington is forged, and Prometheus—claiming similarities with Noah—is Americanized.

Common sense tells us that if Noah is like Prometheus and Prometheus is like George Washington, parallels must exist between Noah and our first president. Hence, the possibility of retooling the American Dream in ways that incorporate the philosophy of slow no longer appears so out of reach. We can combine the Titan and the benevolent paterfamilias in ways that resonate with our collective conscience and think creatively about impacting our cultural imaginary, the shared narrative that defines who we are. Moreover, if we aspire to infuse the American Dream with the philosophy of slow and truly reprioritize our identity, we can learn a great deal from precisely that trend against which we take aim, indeed the trend that gave rise to slow in the first place: the fast food movement. That movement has obviously been a resounding success as it has permeated the fabric of American society and radically reshaped our relationship to food. As with hippie food of the 1960s, it also began as a relatively isolated phenomenon and then grew exponentially thanks to shrewd marketing techniques. Like tofu and granola, fast food went from being an esoteric phenomenon to being mainstream Americana, from a thrilling drive-through, single-serving experience to the everyday fare of many Americans. Clearly fast food did something right such that normalized fast food now stands side by side with normalized health food; the impetus behind both movements has successfully made them a culinary commonplace. What did fast food do right? This is the topic of the following chapter.

NOTES

1. Horkheimer and Adorno, *Dialectic of Enlightenment*, 36.

2. Peter Popham, "Carlo Petrini: the Slow Food Gourmet Who Started a Revolution." *The Independent,* December 10, 2009,www.independent.co.uk/life-style/food-and-drink/features/carlo-petrini-the-slow-food-gourmet-who-started-a-revolution-1837223.html, accessed June 5, 2018

3. Bennett argues that a re-enchantment of the natural world gives rise to a generosity that a strict instrumentalism would be incapable of grasping. See her *The Enchantment of Modern Life: Attachments, Crossings, and Ethics,* (Princeton: Princeton University Press, 2001).

4.https://www.kyrene.org/cms/lib/AZ01001083/Centricity/Domain/894/prometheus%20myth.pdf, accessed March 28, 2020.

5. For an excellent treatment of the gendered implications of this, see Timothy V. Kaufman-Osborn, *Creatures of Prometheus: Gender and the Politics of Technology,* (Lanham, MD: Rowman & Littlefield, 2000).

6. Mol, *Eating*, 3.

7. Mary Shelley, *Frankenstein, or, the Modern Prometheus*, ed. J. Paul Hunter, (New York: W. W. Norton, 1996), 30.

8. Shelley, *Frankenstein*, 32–33.

9. The hubris on display in Dr. Frankenstein's effort to master nature also plays a role in another Shelley's treatment of this story, that of Mary's husband, Percy Bysshe Shelley. His *Prometheus Unbound*, published shortly after *Frankenstein* in 1820, also engages the story of the Titan trickster and underscores the need for humility if there is to be an end to his prolonged suffering. In this version of the story, Prometheus is especially animated by his hatred of Jupiter (Zeus) who originally enslaved mankind. Following Prometheus' rebellious gesture of stealing fire in order to help mankind progress, the Titan has been tortured mercilessly, chained to a mountainside and left to the elements. Yet Percy Bysshe Shelley's Prometheus also exhibits many qualities of Jesus, for he believes that love and forgiveness are the true strength of humanity, not political power. Acting as a sequel to Aeschylus' *Prometheus Bound*, this play thus imbues Prometheus with philanthropic, humanistic attributes given his love of humankind, refusal to bow to tyranny, and willingness to take risks at our expense. The turning point arrives when the Titan develops compassion for Jupiter and views the power dynamic differently. Once Prometheus learns to pity Jupiter rather than despise him, he is ultimately freed by Heracles from the mountainside.

10. Shelley, *Frankenstein*, 28.

11. Ibid., 17

12. Horkheimer and Adorno, *Dialectic of Enlightenment*, 6.

13. https://answersingenesis.org/bible-timeline/timeline-for-the-flood/, accessed June 1, 2020.

14. *The Catholic Bible* (New York: Oxford University Press, 1995), 10, Genesis 7: 8–11.

15. https://hermeneutics.stackexchange.com/questions/50366/how-long-was-noah-and-his-family-in-the-ark, accessed December 22, 2021.

16. Scholars differ in their interpretation of how long Noah was inside the ark.

17. The *Catholic Bible,* Gen 9: 20.

18. Morton Schoolman, *Reason and Horror: Critical Theory, Democracy, and Aesthetic Individuality,* (New York: Routledge, 2001), 127.

19. Here the work of Jane Bennett proves useful, for Bennett has written cogently about the importance of enchantment to ethical behavior. See her *The Enchantment of Modern Life: Attachments, Crossings, and Ethics,* (Princeton: Princeton University Press, 2001).

20. For an excellent treatment of aesthetic rationality, see Morton Schoolman's *Reason and Horror: Critical Theory, Democracy, and Aesthetic Individuality (New York: Routledge, 2001).*

21. Bennett, *The Enchantment of Modern Life*, 91.

22. Schoolman, *Reason and Horror*, 51.

23. See note 18.

24. The *Catholic Bible*, Genesis 9:29.

25. Rachel Carson, *Silent Spring*, (New York: Mariner Books, 2002), 7–8.

26. https://daily.jstor.org/rachel-carsons-critics-called-her-a-witch/, accessed December 6, 2021.

27. In addition to her *Silent Spring*, see also Carson's trilogy of books, *Under the Sea Wind*, *The Sea Around Us*, and *The Edge of the Sea.*

28. Bill Gates, *How to Avoid a Climate Disaster*, (New York: Alfred A. Knopf, 2021).

29. Kauffman, *Hippie Food*, 21.

30. Quoted in Kauffman, *Hippie Food*, 111.

31. Ali McGraw, Tracey Rich, Ganga White, Rodney Yee, Travis Eliot and Lauren Eckstrom are but a few of those who have brought yoga into the American mainstream.

32. Stuart Curran, "The Political Prometheus," in *Studies in Romanticism*, Vol. 25, No. 3, Fall 1986, 429–455. I am indebted to Greg P. Kucich for referring me to this article.

33. Curran, "Political Prometheus," 436.

34. Ibid., 440.

35. Ibid., 400.

Chapter 4

Imagined Communities, USA

Crosses, Flags, Arches

The American Dream's expansionist, optimistic, can-do spirit is admirable for its ambition and innovation, fueled by a belief in our ability to remake ourselves at will. For many, our shared cultural imaginary invokes wide open spaces that offer room to enlarge and the possibility to start again; it offers a signature creativity supported by abundant natural resources and the contributions of a diverse melting pot. The American way of life has long defined itself in terms of its ability to grow economically, geographically, militarily, indeed in any number of ways. To be American is to think on a large scale and always assume the "more factor" to be in play: more money, more natural resources, more opportunities, more discoveries. These can all be realized thanks to the largesse of the American landscape and the power of our imagination. In Shames' words, this unfailing trust in American abundance, "the habit of more," is integral to our cultural imaginary: we assume our ability to stay ahead of the curve and to reinvent ourselves as needed.[1] Our nation is synonymous with growth and (re)invention, the knack for starting over with energy and enthusiasm, always discovering something new.

Several presidents' administrations express this penchant for grandiosity: Manifest Destiny, the New Frontier, the Great Society, and "Make America Great Again" all convey confidence in America's ongoing enlargement. Moreover, some of our cultural heroes have gained iconic status precisely because of their ability to raise a fortune and have a far-reaching impact: Andrew Carnegie, John D. Rockefeller, John Paul Getty, Joseph P. Kennedy, Sr., Steve Jobs, Bill Gates. Embarking on new frontiers—be they geographic, technological, financial, or other—is indeed integral not only to the American experience but also to our collective sense of self. Since abundance is key to our shared imagination, the reality of scarcity has often been greeted as an anomaly, even in the face of evidence to the contrary. In general, we are optimists who look forward to better days and who measure things on a scale that is larger than life. The Wild West, Texas oil fields, Hollywood, Wall Street, Silicon Valley; all of these designate immense discoveries to uncover and immense fortunes to be made thanks to ambitious individuals who think big. "Vast, varied, rough as rocks, America was the place where one never quite came to an end" for it always "offered new chances."[2] For the country to be doing well it must be growing, amplifying, going big or going home.

For some, of course, this imagined community represents no more than a pipe dream sadly out of synch with reality, and copious evidence supports their claim. Nevertheless, the American Dream has staying power, resurfacing even amidst trials and tribulations. The Hispanic-serving institution at which I teach in Southern California confirms this for me on a regular basis. The university attracts a student population drawn from first-generation immigrant homes such that my classroom displays resounding ethnic and racial diversity: Mexican, Latin and Central American, Cambodian, Vietnamese, Eastern European, African American. My students recount countless stories of their families' struggles which reconfirm the American Dream's dogged persistence even when the lived experience suggests an alternative truth. The empirical facts never diminish their belief in hard work, optimism, and staying power; they believe in upward mobility, and indeed many of them experience it. Can the muscled-up Promethean heroism so alloyed to this forward drive be renegotiated and morph into a Noah-like norm that cares for, rather than dominates, life? Assuming Curran's analysis to be correct, can the Titan trickster truly defer to the sometimes red, sometimes orange snail and start to go slow and curvy, allowing the arrogance of traditional humanism to subside?

FOOD, MEMORY, AND CULTURAL IDENTITY

The dream-like component of the imagined community in which my students so poignantly believe is also materially grounded and tangibly concrete; it relies on empirical referents and shared cultural markers, not just flights of fancy about getting rich. As Stuart Hall and Paul Du Gay write, identity is never without "its determinate conditions of existence, including the material and symbolic resources required to sustain it . . . . "[3] In mainstream American culture, baseball caps, board shorts, the Statue of Liberty and Grand Canyon fill out the optics; Jimmy Stewart, Oprah Winfrey, the Kennedys, and Barack Obama lend it personality and panache; the historical markers of the Founding, the Civil War, the 1960s, and Black Lives Matter contribute a storyline. For many, "America" invokes the visuals of the Empire State Building and Mount Rushmore; musically, we hear Frank Sinatra, Ella Fitzgerald, Miles Davis, and the Star-Spangled Banner, but also the voices and music of

Latinx, Asian Americans, and numerous other communities whose presence is integral to the American experience.

Among these concrete material referents, food plays a leading role: to a good degree, imagined communities derive from a culinary experience and the memory of taste. Without question, food represents a central player in any culture's identity as flavors, aromas, signature edibles, and favored recipes define a cultural heritage. Because food and memory are inextricably linked, food and cultural identity stand intertwined; we not only dream our Dream, but we also cook it, taste it, and inhale its aroma. Traditionally, for mainstream America—that is, for mostly White, middle-class America—this spells hot dogs and hamburgers, pot roast and apple pie; it means barbeques and picnics, pancakes, Maxwell House coffee, turkey with all the trimmings. Of course, White American fare has long been enriched by other culinary components, the contributions of rural, Southern, Southwestern, Indigenous and immigrant populations whose focus on other ingredients, other flavors, and other cooking skills brings variety to what we consider the standard American gastronomical experience. While the mainstream has historically received more press and garnered the title of "American" food, other culinary traditions have long been in play.

Today, these traditions are finally receiving recognition in all corners of American society. "This is 'American' food!" exclaims Padma Lakshmi, whose docuseries, *Taste the Nation,* visits immigrant communities with a view toward exploring their cuisines and affirming that outliers of the mainstream carry equal weight as part of the "American" culinary experience.[4] Tacos and burritos, egg rolls and fried rice, curries and samosas now partake of our gastronomical landscape and serve as reminders of how we have appropriated cultural traditions from minorities that we have not always treated kindly.[5] Yet overall and from a bird's eye view, hot dogs, hamburgers, and Coca-Cola claim a certain cachet that identifies American food around the world, much as croissants identify French cuisine and falafel spells Middle Eastern fare. They possess dense cultural currency in the lexicon of Americana. Thus, although food functions as basic fuel for the body, it also constitutes the stuff of cultural narrative. "Tell me what kind of food you eat, and I will tell you what kind of man you are," states the witty late-eighteenth, early-nineteenth century French epicurean Jean Anthelme Brillat-Savarin.[6]

Americans today are very aware of calories, nutrients, fat, and carbohydrates, all rendering us collectively overwhelmed by information about what we consume. Yet "nutritionism"—scientific knowledge and factual information about food—is only half the story, as Pollan convincingly argues.[7] Food represents a saturated signifier, a robust metaphor that fills the collective imagination as much as the individual's stomach. It appeals to the mind and heart as well as to the taste buds, and thus exceeds its constituent nutritive

value. Food is about love and togetherness, memory and loss, the deep meanings of the everyday as well as special occasions, and the importance of
pleasure. Food invokes family and friends, keeps track of time by governing
the calendar and the clock, conveys emotional temperatures and moods, and
can also recall collective hardship: for instance, the centrality of matzah to the
Jewish Seder. In her travels, Lakshmi observes that culinary traditions serve
as the "thread" that connects a community, the tie that binds and that renews
alliances. Hence the "iconic Mexican burrito" is analogous to the love of a
mother, or a blessing.[8]

The slow movement affirms this centrality of food to cultural identity and
recognizes its ability to engage memory and imagination. The term "locavore," for instance, denotes not only what is locally grown but, as *Cittaslow*
insists, what is locally meaningful, what matters to a specific environment
and history. "A cheese is as worthy of preserving as a sixteenth-century building," Petrini avers.[9] In keeping with this logic, a building that looms large in
the collective American imagination—say, the White House or Monticello—
matters as much as Wisconsin cheddar. The semiotic weight with which food
is endowed, its emotional resonances, thus plays a central role in a culture's
self-definitions, conferring great significance upon comestibles and recipes,
the latter often being handed down orally from one generation to the next.

Thus, fraught with signifying richness, food burrows deeply into the collective imagination of a society in ways that typically escape our casual
ingestion. We probably all have some American version of the Proustian
moment in our storehouse of memories wherein a specific taste or combination of tastes sets in motion a variety of powerful memories invoking our past
and former dwellings with astounding clarity. Marcel Proust's seven-volume
masterpiece, *In Search of Lost Time,* famously posits a deep connection
between taste and memory and the power of taste in stirring up feelings. The
novel accords great importance to one life-altering morsel, one solitary madeleine cookie dipped in tea that overwhelms the narrator's senses by recalling
the village of his childhood, Combray. This long-forgotten taste fuels a sublime experience that radically reorients Marcel's perceptions, allowing him to
sense "a precious essence" buried within.

> No sooner had the warm liquid, mixed with the crumbs of the cake, touched
> my palate than a shudder ran through me and I stopped, intent upon the extraor-
> dinary thing that was happening to me. An exquisite pleasure had invaded my
> senses, something isolated, detached, with no suggestion of its origin. And at
> once the vicissitudes of life had become indifferent to me, its disasters innocu-
> ous, its brevity illusory—this new sensation having had on me the effect which
> love has of filling me with a precious essence; or rather this essence was not in
> me it *was* me.[10]

During his youth, it was Aunt Léonie who dipped a madeleine cookie into her tea and then offered it to her nephew. It is the taste, not the sight of the cookie that exerts such influence on young Marcel, making him feel not that love was in him, but *was* him. "[S]uddenly the memory revealed itself," he recalls. "The taste was that of the little piece of madeleine . . . The sight of the little madeleine had recalled nothing to my mind before I tasted it."[11] Once he has tasted the morsel, Marcel remembers the houses, the streets, the pavilion, the garden, the church; in short, every detail from his time at Combray, all from a tea-soaked cookie.

This passage expresses the manner in which taste transcends an immediate sensation, fusing the taste buds with memory, emotion, and perception. For Marcel, taste takes him away from himself but also restores him; it rearranges life's meanings allowing the disasters of life to become "innocuous" and the realization of life's brevity to appear "illusory." In this way, food's ability to flood the senses and play upon the imagination cuts deeply into some of the basic premises that distinguish the Western intellectual tradition. Aunt Léonie's generosity with her madeleine highlights the false dichotomy of the mind-body split in Western philosophy, for it is taste that plays on Marcel's mind. Her sharing gesture gives the lie to the mind-body polarization, welding sensation and cognition into a unified whole. The tea-soaked cookie thus lends ballast to our theory of eating-as-trope, eating as a way of knowing, as per Mol, rather than simply ingesting. Mol concurs that "if we take inspiration from . . . stories about eating . . . the distinction between perceiving the world and sensing the self becomes blurred."[12] Both come together in a fusion that creates and recreates memory and connection.

Laura Esquivel's *Like Water for Chocolate* similarly illustrates this blurring of sensory and cognitive boundaries. Set in Mexico at the turn of the twentieth century, this novel chronicles the emotional weight of food in the life of Tita, a talented chef, and fittingly begins each chapter with a recipe: turkey mole with almonds and sesame seeds, *champandongo*, Northern-style chorizo, quails in rose petal sauce needing "12 roses, perfectly red."[13] In her community, the dishes that Tita prepares carry emotional and spiritual weight; they even facilitate telepathic communication. At one point, Tita cries despairingly into the cake she must prepare for the wedding of her beloved Pedro, now betrothed to her sister Rosaura. Distraught, Tita sheds tears into the batter which "wouldn't thicken because Tita kept crying."[14] Everyone who later eats the cake breaks down sobbing over the loss of past loves, and the wedding party devolves into a painful scene of wailing, sickness, and despair. "The moment they took their first bite of the cake, everyone was flooded with a great wave of longing . . . that seized the guests and scattered them across the patio and the grounds and in the bathrooms, all of them wailing over lost love."[15]

Of course, Esquival's genre is that of magical realism, thereby granting the author much poetic license. Yet her message about the power of taste is no less serious than that of Proust. Marcel's cookie and Tita's wedding cake make it abundantly clear that eating-as-trope draws on a profound aesthetic sensibility that renders human subjectivity not sovereign, but porous; not autonomous, but intuitive and interconnected. Here, we even have mental telepathy in play. Tasting, ingesting, swallowing, and digesting may not appear at first blush to be cognitive practices, yet if we embrace eating-as-trope, eating as a way of knowing, our attitude toward cognition changes.[16] To refute the mind-body dichotomy and subsequently recognize our relationship to food as having cognitive weight shifts the time-honored understanding of how we know: it takes us from a distanced approach to one that is enmeshed in matter and sullied, mixed up in things, messy and weighty. It takes us from the abstraction of thought to the world's immediacy, allowing the thinking process to morph from a clean, pristine enterprise to one that is embroiled in the corporeal boundary-crossing of ingestion, chewing, tasting, and digesting.[17]

Speaking before an audience, Petrini obliquely reiterates this critique of the mind-body dichotomy and thus reengages an old philosophical debate. He argues in veiled Hegelian terms that the quality of food supersedes all else, and that complaints against the expense of high-quality food are misdirected. In consuming food, he explains, what we eat literally *becomes* us as we *become* the food; we are one with what we consume as it changes form and is assimilated into our bodies. Boundaries are crossed as the subject-object poles ultimately blur the distinction between consumer and consumed, eater and eaten, and the famous phrase "you are what you eat" navigates from philosophy to digestion. In this way, our relationship to food proves more intimate than other forms of "consumption" and knowing; we can be very attached to our cell phones, yet they never become part of us in the way that food does.

Why then are we are willing to spend more on Armani underwear than on food, Petrini asks. Why the cachet surrounding undergarments, or for that matter, cell phones? "If I eat prosciutto, cheese, and some nice bread, in a few seconds that food becomes Carlo Petrini," he explains. "But Armani underwear remains outside my body."[18] Food proves crucial to our protean constitution, for even our brains respond to the nutritional quality of what we eat. Food becomes the very fiber of our being in ways that Armani underwear, cell phones, and other disposable items never will; it crosses boundaries and dismantles the atomized individual in ways that emphasize the continuum between humanity and the natural world. While the problem of food's expense presents a hurdle for many people (to be discussed in chapter 6), here the emphasis is on its quality which should not be sacrificed.

If tea-soaked cookies and wedding cake hold such cognitive and emotional potential, how does the semiotic richness of food operate specifically in the American context? If we want to entertain the possibility of advancing the slow movement's philosophy in the United States based on a new, Noah-inspired humanism, it behooves us to ponder food's deeper meanings in the American setting and find out how our specific culinary habits engage with our collective narrative, the American Dream.

Food in the American Cultural Context: Crosses, Flags, Arches

In the American context, we know the cultural imaginary to be aligned with the meanings of modernity whose forward-looking, competitive, now globalizing attributes invoke the toil of industry still connected to an agricultural heartland. Indeed, the collective American imagination traditionally draws on the ambitious workings of industry grafted onto a preindustrial nation steeped in agriculture and close to the earth. Even with today's prevalence of the service industry, the twin arenas of industry and agriculture continue to hold sway in our self-definitions. Both emphasize hard work and rugged individualism, with industry leaning toward our exemplary perseverance while agriculture errs on the side of the innate wholesomeness to be found down on the farm.

Another characteristic of the American cultural context is its rootedness not just in hard work, but in the self-denying Protestant work ethic and proscription on pleasure. Rugged individualism traditionally resists what it deems the indulgences of taste, the extravagances of epicureanism, and the privilege of taking time over food. It is only relatively recently that foodie culture has reoriented our relationship to gastronomy and encouraged Americans to think differently about how we eat. Julia Child's best-selling *Mastering the Art of French Cooking* appeared in 1961 and further galvanized the interest in fine food that James Beard and Craig Claiborne had already begun.[19] Traditionally, mainstream American cuisine (mostly White, Anglo-Saxon) downplayed the artistic end of gastronomy now celebrated in foodie culture and saw food less as a pleasurable engagement of the senses than as mere sustenance. The ethos that governed our nation for nearly two centuries—from the Founding through Child, Claiborne, Beard, and later Alice Waters—looked askance at gastronomic pleasures and the celebration of the senses that typify other cultures: epicureanism stood alongside greed, lust, and sloth as sins that corrupt the soul. Hence, the pleasure-seeking attributes that are now touted by celebrity chefs were not originally integral to the American cultural imagination.

It is within the context of these Promethean, hard-working meanings that the rise of fast food took place. Indeed, fast food resonates so deeply with the American cultural imaginary that, according to Eric Schlosser, we are *the* fast-food nation *par excellence*.[20] It is undoubtedly a combination of fast food's industrialized attributes and happy family focus that accounts for its meteoric rise, for together these create the profile of a nation of hard-working individuals who value the conveniences and the speed of ready-made fare. Leaving the wholesome cultivation of the land to those on the farm (a cultivation that is amply showcased in advertising and food packaging), fast food invokes the energy and dynamism of industry, affirming a commitment to not wasting time, to accessibility and the love of all things automated. Fast food is quintessentially American since it suggests a country on the go with no time to waste; we eat in the car with the engine idling, surfing the web, shopping online, working, or walking down the street. "Fast" describes the food's preparation, yet also suggests things about those consuming it; namely, that they are on the job, in gear and moving forward, if only vicariously through their single-serving meal. They prefer things that are family-oriented and kid-friendly, but also in tune with getting things done.

Although fast food goes back to the 1920s, its popularity exploded during the late 1940s and 1950s when the precipitous rise in automobile sales and growth of the highway system created a new way of life for Americans.[21] To be sure, fast food and the automobile are symbiotically bound, thereby resonating with the prosperous postwar economy and expansion of interstate thoroughfares. During that era, the newly designed suburbs and malls, together with the general cachet of everything automotive, meant that more Americans were traveling by car and doing things behind the wheel: dining out, watching movies at drive-ins, even going to church. Some of the earliest fast-food eateries were initially locales where one ate in the car, the food being delivered by waitresses on roller skates, called carhops. For many Americans, the automobile was not only a possession, but a symbol of success and an extension of their identity. It embodied the American spirit of forward drive and innovation, allowing chrome, steel, power steering, and Dagmar bumpers to exude patriotism. Throughout the 1950s, the design of automobiles increasingly exuded confidence in America's meanings, since the vehicles became larger, more robust, and more opulent in their presentation. For instance, the increasingly elaborate tail fins of 1950s models revealed Americans' obsession with rockets and the vast possibilities of outer space.[22]

The emerging cultural prominence of the car allowed fast food to gain exponential popularity and solidified the connection between it and modern progress. Mid-century economic largesse, the exponential rise in car sales, America's leading role in the world arena, fast/processed/frozen food: these were all of a piece, all declaring the country's unrivaled status and seemingly unlimited potential. To be processed and industrial was considered progressive; it's how modern countries operated and influenced what they ate since processed and frozen foods can be such time-savers. Indeed, much of our "food" today is still industrial, and not really food at all. As observed, a fast-food strawberry milkshake contains an array of engineered ingredients; similarly, the aromas of ready-made fare derive from chemical admixtures invoking crowd-pleasing foods such as apples, popcorn, or marshmallows.[23] Yet fast food is by now synonymous with helping move the country forward, with being a person on the go with things to do and people to see; for this reason, it qualifies as "healthy." It signals American energy and ingenuity, a confident spirit all wrapped up in a hamburger with pickles and fries. To consume a hamburger and fries thus becomes a patriotic act; to do so in a car or on the run, even better.

Until recently, we have been a country in which the value of hard work and creative industry prevail over leisurely gastronomic indulgences. The mere suggestion of a fast-food eatery sets in play a certain dynamism, for we imagine an establishment enveloped by a long line of vehicles, engines idling: cars, trucks, motorcycles, and campers driven by people with responsibilities on their shoulders and no time to waste. We see a team of employees clad in crisp uniforms working hard in a highly structured, highly disciplined fashion; inside, long lines of customers form while tables and booths fill up in no time. It's quick, it's dependable, it's always the same, and it never costs too much. Slow Food volunteers subsequently affirm that to change Americans' minds and convince them that food should take time—*take* it, not save it—represents a tall order.

Indeed, to overindulge the taste buds has traditionally been viewed as patently un-American; other nations' tendency to savor, to linger, and to refine has often been seen as a shortcoming that impedes their "progress." A Spanish proverb opines, "how lovely to do nothing and then rest afterwards," while the Chinese insist that one should not be afraid of going slowly, only of standing still. "Smile, breathe, go slowly" is a phrase that Thich Nhat Hahn, the Vietnamese Buddhist monk and peace activist, lived by, while the founder of Toaism, Lao Tzu, observes that nature never hurries yet manages to get everything done. Because Americans are self-consciously industrious, we have long looked askance at what appears to be senseless dawdling and indulgent dilly-dally, including the custom of relishing a meal that takes hours to prepare. For many, then, fast food embodies our values; it's quick, it moves, it suggests a work schedule and a commitment to output that spells "USA." Because it condenses family values, industry, and innovation into packaged food produced at top speed, it is American through and through. "Simply put, nothing else does what fast food does as well as fast food does it," Adam Chandler avers.[24]

Thus, while some food manufacturers boast of their product being "packed" with nutrition, it seems fair to argue that fast food is packed with patriotism.

"Do it for your country," Ray Kroc tells the McDonald brothers in 1954, seeking to persuade them to develop a franchise for their all-American meal.[25] By this he means that if Dick and Mac McDonald are initially unwilling to patent and expand their fast-food business out of a desire to stay small and local, they owe it to their homeland to change their mind. According to Kroc, the brothers fail to appreciate the implicit patriotism of their product and see that hamburgers in a hurry mean much more to Americans than instant energy. It's American *identity* that customers are consuming when they eat MacDonald's food, for the hamburgers embody an understanding of who we are in the world arena and what distinguishes us on the world stage. They are a saturated cultural signifier in which Kroc saw enormous patriotic appeal and commercial potential, a culinary tradition waiting to be established and a fortune waiting to be made. "Do it for America," Kroc insists in *The Founder*, recognizing that the brothers are sitting on a gold mine in the form of a modest hamburger stand in San Bernardino, California.

As a milkshake mixer salesman in the mid-1950s, Kroc knows fast food to be the wave of the future, and like the two brothers also believes that "it's all about speed" since mid-century saw a new spirit of adventure in America. He realizes that the McDonald brothers have their finger on the pulse of the country, even if they themselves are unaware of it. "Visions of McDonald's restaurants dotting crossroads all over the country paraded through my brain," he writes in *Grinding It Out: The Making of McDonald's,* chronicling his initial decision to embark on this business venture.[26] Kroc dreamed big; he envisaged a sea change in America's culinary tradition that would not remain local, but that would proliferate exponentially while carrying family-oriented, patriotic values with it wherever it went.

Kroc strives to convince Dick and Mac that the act of franchising what they serve represents an act of deep patriotism, for the USA embodies energetic innovation and productive efficiency right down to the food on Americans' plates. The individually wrapped hamburgers hold meanings that radiate out far beyond what one purchases at the counter: amber waves of grain, Superman in his billowing cape, America keeping the world safe for democracy. Yet the McDonald brothers are initially puzzled as to why hamburgers and fries might be so meaningful to the American collective imagination. Aren't they just *food*? Kroc strives to convince them that they are not thinking big enough and have not grasped the deep interconnection between food and the larger cultural narrative: what they serve helps construct the shared meanings of "America," and their timing is propitious. Instead of staying local they should reach outward from their initial hot-dog-turned-hamburger stand to something available to *all* of the United States. He encourages them to not only think along the lines of a business model, but to dream, to imagine, to situate their food within the buoyant narrative of 1950s America.

Kroc explains that as a salesman, his travels around the country have taken him to many cities, large and small, and allowed him to observe American culture from a wide angle. He has visited the urban gamut from sprawling, bustling metropolises to small, sleepy two-cow towns in his unrelenting effort to sell the Multimixer, an appliance that mixes five milkshakes at once. He has reflected on mid-century American culture and Americans' eating habits, observing the varied cultural signifiers that help define the nation. An astute observer and determined salesman, he has mulled over the lexicon of cultural signifiers that appear repeatedly around the country, and has pondered how their appearance might be of service to his shrewd business sense.

In small towns especially, Kroc has been struck by the ubiquity of two things: churches and courthouses symbolized by crosses and flags. Churches and courthouses are always present in small town America, he notices; a town doesn't seem complete without them, and they tend to be prominently displayed in the urban center. Clearly, the crosses and flags that denote these establishments are heavy with semiotic richness; they point not only to the type of building in question, but to the self-definitions of the community itself. They encapsulate many meanings about the people living there, all revolving around moral rectitude and the orderly, law-abiding foundation of the American way of life. As pillars of authority, crosses and flags denote religion and law, the rules we play by, and how we define social order. They indicate orderliness, a respect for who is in charge, how justice is carried out and why one should never go astray. They represent the physical site on which order is restored and entanglements resolved thanks to the presence of presiding authorities: God and government, paternal ministers and judges, the importance of faith and the rule of law.

The buildings' accompanying cultural signifiers, crosses and flags, are thus metaphorically dense; as Kroc explains, they represent the places where "decent, wholesome" people come together and "share values protected by that American flag."[27] Churches and courthouses embody much of the American way of life thanks to the decency and wholesomeness that they keep intact, qualities that mark the United States as comfortably ensconced within the hard-working, self-sacrificing tradition of our Protestant past. Crosses and flags loom large in the American Dream, sustaining the belief that thanks to our orderly, well-executed system there is money to be made and an affluent future to enjoy. Of course, there would be much to say about who attends which churches and in what capacity one arrives at the courthouse: the story and the locale is different for White America than for Black Americans, Indigenous Peoples, people of color, immigrants, the poor, the LGBTQIA population, etc. Yet the American Dream to which Ray Kroc refers has mostly White America in mind as it enjoys the country's booming post-war experience.

Having observed so many churches and courthouses, crosses and flags across the country, Kroc therefore sees important parallels between what McDonald's golden arches might come to mean and what churches and courthouses already mean. The latter are integral to the American Dream, invoking the traditional values that keep society together in the home, at church, and in the courthouse: crosses and flags represent the moral rectitude that undergirds America's success story. Although he realizes that his statement may sound blasphemous, Kroc convinces the McDonald brothers that their fast-food restaurant could come to symbolize something as important as crosses and flags; it could operate not merely as fuel for the body, but as a metonymic expression of modern American values. The golden arches, he insists, could possess the same cultural capital as vintage Americana; they are a treasure trove of social signification that could take their place alongside crosses and flags given the right marketing strategy. It is at McDonald's, he insists, that "decent, wholesome" people could *come together* and "share values protected by that American flag," simply by enjoying fast food. In this way, their eatery could join ranks with solid members of the community and itself become a pillar of social meaning, capitalizing on food's emotional richness and connection to memory. The golden arches, in other words, could become metaphorically dense with patriotic meaning if only Dick and Mac would franchise their humble hamburger stand.

As is well known, Kroc's powers of persuasion and dogged determination ultimately convinced the McDonald brothers that their flipped patties were a gold mine of cultural metaphor filled with patriotic meaning. McDonald's subsequently became franchised and grew into the empire that it now is, today claiming over 13,000 eateries in the United States that collectively gross in the billions.[28] The golden arches have indeed come to play as significant a role in our cultural imaginary as have crosses, flags, Elvis Presley, Walt Disney, Martin Luther King, Jr., and the Lincoln Memorial. Kroc's daring speculation that "McDonald's can be the new American church" has come true: the pair of shiny arches are as meaningful to us as a cross or a flag, and it is estimated that ninety-six percent of American children can identify Ronald McDonald.[29] The bright yellow structure carries tremendous signifying richness regarding the American Dream with all its gleaming, shiny attributes: America is optimistic, honest, efficient, clean, family-oriented, and *successful*. The arches point upward with energy, enthusiasm, and the devotion of Gothic spires; they glisten in the sunshine.

Moreover, the golden arches' rounded shape was apparently recommended by consultant and psychologist Louis Cheskin, who claimed that the curving M suggests large mammaries.[30] Hence one can persuasively argue that McDonald's symbolism subconsciously combines the American work ethic and can-do spirit with maternal connotations: abundance, warmth, unconditional love, and home. The bright, massive mammaries equate our success story with motherly love and comfort food, suggesting the welcome of home as it offers a predictable menu, entertainment, and a playground for the kids. Its iconic maternal breasts suggest *homo economicus* stopping to eat, the Protestant work ethic recharging its batteries, Americans ingesting calories so that they can remain in the lead thanks to mom's cooking.

There is even more to McDonald's success than its alignment with the values of religion, law, and motherly love. Thanks to its conveyor belt modus operandi, there is also its invocation of industry, of Fordism and Taylorism, that helps explain its popularity. Cranking out hamburgers in record time and with notable uniformity necessarily recalls the factory system and the centrality of the automobile—indeed, of industrialized machinery in general—to the American imagination. In fact, all fast food must be produced with utmost precision ensuring uniformity in what customers consume. Kroc writes of the importance of this uniformity in food preparation, for to err in this would be to lose control over the product's consistency. Hence, to Kroc, the French fry became "almost sacrosanct for me . . . its preparation a ritual to be followed religiously."[31] While mom's love and cooking constitutes a big part of the eatery's appeal, there is also the presence of American industry—Fordism, Taylorism, the factory's efficiency—rolled into the experience.

America is forward-looking in its entrepreneurial talent; our aim is to never stop growing since there is always more to be had (or so we think). Yet to ensure such growth demands discipline and tight organization. Fordism, of course, refers to the model of industrial management that places a high premium on standardized output, a high level of efficiency, and a division of labor that ensures production on a large scale. It wastes no time as it guarantees a standardized product. Taylorism emphasizes keeping the job simple—"a clear division of labor between brawn and brain"—and an established routine that also encourages a harmonious efficiency among workers.[32] It brings scientific precision to business management. Indelibly linked to the automobile and thus the expansion of American infrastructure, both Fordism and Taylorism conjure up the image of a high-functioning factory wherein workers perform narrowly specific, often low-skill tasks continuously with a view toward turning out a predictable product that will be the same everywhere. McDonald's hamburgers thus combine motherly love with the factory ethos, reenacting Fordist and Taylorist principles in an eatery as they guarantee standardization and dependability, uniformity, and fast service. Clearly the strategizing energy of instrumental rationality is at work here, the disciplined mindset that seeks system and unity above all.

The imprimatur of the factory thus looms large in any McDonald's meal, for its ideology does not allow for variations, idiosyncrasies, or the stamp of individuality. Explicitly un-locavore, its embodiment of American industriousness can be found in the rote, conforming treatment that every hamburger receives and the standardized approach to food that differs so radically from nature's biodiversity and seasonal moods. "Every hamburger has two pickles, a pinch of onions and a precise shot of ketchup and mustard," Kroc is told on an early visit to the McDonald's kitchen, learning also that "speed is the name of the game."[33] Uniformity is a valued quality that ensures healthy sales and a happy customer, a customer whose mealtime should be dependably enjoyable but never too leisurely. Without question, something that brings so many people back to McDonald's—along with its consistently low prices—is precisely the fact that they know what to expect; they know the hamburgers, fries, and milkshakes will always look and taste the same.

Added to this is the wholesomeness to which Kroc refers, eminently visible in all the ways that McDonald's and other fast-food establishments explicitly market themselves as family restaurants. This wholesomeness is conveyed not only through subliminal messages regarding mammaries, but in overt gestures and policies. The restaurant welcomes children through its use of bright primary colors, its organization of space that allows for playgrounds, toys, and other divertissements, and the prominence of cartoon characters, toys, and clowns. Happy Meals clearly appeal to children and keep them occupied while at the table. Moreover, the absence of dimmed lighting, alcohol, and secluded spaces indicates that these are family eateries, places that celebrate the familial bond and promote togetherness in ways parallel to churches and courthouses. While it would be going too far to claim that a Puritanical strain infuses fast-food establishments, a high premium is clearly placed on cleanliness, careful packaging, and a mandate that different foods do not touch. Too much touching might experiment with food and expand the restaurant's gastronomical lexicon; it might indulge creative impulses in terms of color, texture, and presentation, resonating with the things that celebrity chefs are only now bringing to the forefront of American gastronomy. If creativity in the kitchen supplants Fordism-Taylorism-motherly love, it could allow us to view food through a more artistic culinary lens (that is, foreign, imported, exotic) rather than the lens of a standardized, reliable output (that is, as fundamentally American).

Challenging Kroc's Legacy: Where to Begin?

We have to congratulate Ray Kroc, since by any standards he has succeeded brilliantly in his efforts. He has managed to insinuate a modest hamburger stand into our shared understanding of the American Dream and allowed it to burrow deeply; now, there can be no question that an Americanized worldview is a McDonaldized worldview. With the "more factor" delivering so much at such high speeds, it's hard to imagine how we might produce an equally convincing message and turn the philosophy of slow into something comparable to faith-filled crosses, law-abiding flags, and welcoming maternal arches. A worldview more aligned with a slower, greener, more locavore outlook and the theory of economic de-growth seems a hard sell indeed. Moreover, a McDonaldized worldview now applies to a great number of other fast-food eateries who have copied McDonald's methods and reproduced their modus operandi.

To be fair, however, McDonald's influence has not been wholly pernicious. In *Franchise: the Golden Arches in Black America*, Marcia Chatelain recounts in impressive detail the ways in which the McDonald's franchise has helped the entrepreneurial aspirations of Black communities, promoting "Black capitalism" in ways that allow struggling communities to experience change and growth. Thus, despite the ill effects of its food, McDonald's has played a role in advancing Blacks' civil rights. Chatelain tells "the missing piece of the story of how race, civil rights, and hamburgers converged and changed everything" given the expanding number of McDonald's owned and managed by Blacks in their home communities.[34] We cannot discount this important economic reality and what it has meant for the civil rights movement. Still, Chatelain is not insensitive to the pervasive concern over the ill-effects of fast food, a concern that gives rise to the theory that the proliferation of such eateries in predominantly Black neighborhoods reveals a malevolent indifference to the rate of diabetes, obesity, and hypertension among the customers.

If memory looms large in food's ability to connect us to a place and to a past, are we inadvertently *forgetting* when we consume not just standard American fare, but specifically industrialized food, which includes fast food, so marked by standardization and an un-locavore sameness? Pollan thinks so, for similar to Mol he argues that "eating . . . constitutes a relationship with dozens of other species—plants, animals, and fungi—with which we have coevolved to the point where our fates are deeply intertwined."For as previously remarked, "[t]o go from the chicken (*Gallus gallus*) to the Chicken McNugget is to leave this world in a journey of forgetting . . . ."[35] Yet thanks to today's various iterations of the alternative food movement, many Americans have begun to appreciate the importance of how our food is grown, picked, shipped, processed, marketed, and cooked. What began with organic hippie urgings of back-to-the-land living has mainstreamed thanks to the gastronomical turn in American society and rise of foodie culture, a culture seeking to combat the anaesthetized "forgetting" and replace it with the "right to taste" and to pleasure so central to the Slow Food movement.

But will gastronomic politics and the entire slow movement that it endorses be as successful as the fast-food revolution? The challenge in confronting the latter's resounding success clearly lies in establishing a viable counternarrative that speaks to mainstream America, competing with if not displacing fast food's maternal attributes from the drive-through and onto Mother Earth. We know the McDonaldized lifestyle to be deeply embedded in many Americans' daily routine such that unseating the reverence surrounding it will indeed pose a challenge. If the golden arches have crosses, flags, and motherly love in their corner, how can the humble snail compete with that?

One practical approach to countering all Americans' avid consumption of fast food lies in educating the public more broadly about fast food's link to a battery of physical ills, mentioned above. It has frequently been observed that its regular consumption correlates to a rise in diabetes, since it contains large amounts of sugar, salt, and saturated fats, all of which wreak havoc on the body's production of insulin.[36] Diabetes, of course, constitutes a national health crisis: in 2020, the CDC reported that no fewer than 34.2 million Americans are diabetic, with 88 million considered pre-diabetic.[37] The prevalence of this connects directly to the obesity epidemic increasingly pronounced in America; even small children are categorized as obese and suffer from diabetes. Some argue that, thanks to our diet, a biochemical imbalance exists in many of us that directly correlates with illness.[38] This imbalance results from our hefty and sustained intake of several items, most especially sugar, salt, and high fructose corn syrup which exert a ruinous impact on our metabolisms; having seen obese six-month-old infants, Dr. Robert H. Lustig does not hesitate to call high fructose corn syrup "poison." Yet the continued rise in America's obesity, along with the remarkable surge in our fast-food intake once the pandemic eased for a while, clearly indicate that we remain the fast food nation par excellence.[39] Thus when I interviewed Alice Waters via Zoom in the fall of 2021, she argued that the principles of slow food should be taught in schools as early as kindergarten. Children need to be introduced to culinary traditions grounded in locavore practices and a commitment to "good, clean, and fair" early on, she argued, since the culture at large is so steeped in fast and processed food.

Another serious topic about which Americans should be educated lies in the connection between cattle husbandry and the production of greenhouse gases. It is a well-documented fact that cattle and other forms of ruminant livestock such as sheep and goats contribute to greenhouse gases.[40] This occurs thanks to the fermentation, or "enteric fermentation," that occurs naturally with their digestion, producing methane. Needless to say, cattle husbandry has expanded exponentially with the rise of fast food, and despite intermittent dips in our consumption of beef, the overall per capita trend has been upward.[41] Cattle translates into beef: hamburgers, steaks, breakfast burritos, beef stew, standing rib roast. All of these play a leading role in the American collective imagination, for beef looms large in the American

Dream. It invokes sprawling ranches and the Wild West, John Wayne in his chaps, Yul Brenner with hired guns, Alan Ladd idolized by a young boy. It suggests Elizabeth Taylor adjusting to life with Rock Hudson in *Giant*, J. R. Ewing holding forth on the opulent Texas family estate. Because the west's wide-open spaces and consumption of beef constitutes an important part of America's defining narrative, beef occupies a revered place in our collective imagination. It is central to the transformation in Americans' gastronomical habits beginning early in the twentieth century, then expanding mid-century and finally mushrooming into an international, game-changing phenomenon that has made fast food an everyday affair.

Because it is an everyday affair, diminishing its cultural currency presents a formidable challenge. How to decouple the spirit of John Wayne and the cultural resonances of a steak? How to separate the convenient drive-through hamburger stand from the meanings of modernity, making "modern" no longer synonymous with fast food? At first blush, this seems an impossible task. Let us not forget a crucial detail from Shelley's iconic novel. When we first encounter Dr. Frankenstein, he appears nearly dead, having exhausted himself on a life-threatening trek near the North Pole. Asked why he is traversing this uninhabitable ice-covered region on a sled, he responds: "To seek one who has fled from me."[42] It is the *doctor himself*, Victor Frankenstein, who seeks the very monster who terrified him, unable to abandon his creation despite the violence and death that the monster delivered. He cannot let go of something so harmful, but embraces a neurotic *folie à deux*—madness for two—that keeps him inextricably bound to the creature that ruined his life.

Yet this *folie à deux* is not recognizable to those unconvinced that change is needed. If crosses, flags, and arches stand so deeply ensconced in the standard fare that proves harmful, the harm itself is invisible; the food is as enjoyable as it is patriotic. However, processed food's layered meanings may themselves provide a clue that is helpful to not only Slow Food, but to the slow movement in general. Clearly something is happening in American culture that has given rise to foodie culture, a culture that shares the principles of Slow Food in many ways. Perhaps the neoliberal ethos of faster, bigger, and more—the ethos implicated in hamburgers and fries— has soured on some Americans without their even knowing it, and a new sea change is underway. In the following chapter, we entertain the argument that the growth in foodie culture, which includes Slow Food, emanates from a conviction that the neoliberal doctrine is exhausting itself, or has done so already: instrumental rationality must be tempered by the beauty and deliciousness of an aesthetic sensibility that enjoys life at a slower pace. It is to this topic that we now turn.

NOTES

1. Shames, "The More Factor," 57.

2. Shames, "The More Factor," 57.

3. Hall and Du Gay, *Questions of Cultural Identity* (Thousand Oaks, CA: Sage, 1996),2–3.

4. Alison Ashton, "Padma Lakshmi Celebrates America's Flavors," *Parade, The Los Angeles Times*, June 7, 2020, 12–15.

5. See Sophie Gilbert, "Padma Lakshmi's New Food Show Is a Trojan Horse" in *The Atlantic*, https://www.theatlantic.com/culture/archive/2020/07/padma-lakshmi-hulu-taste-nation-american-cuisine/613915/, accessed October 29, 2021.

6. Jean Anthelme Brillat-Savarin, *The Physiology of Taste, or Meditations on Transcendental Gastronomy,* translated by M.F.K. Fisher (New York: Vintage Press, 2009), 15.

7. See Michael Pollan, *In Defense of Food: An Eater's Manifesto(*New York: Penguin Books, 2009).

8. *Taste the Nation*, episode one.

9. http://www.azquotes.com/author/22147-Carlo_Petrini.

10. Marcel Proust, *Swann's Way*, translated by C. K. Scott Moncrieff and Terence Kilmartin (New York: Vintage Books,1989), 48.

11. Proust, *Swann's Way*, 48–50.

12. Mol, 61.

13. Laura Esquivel, *Like Water for Chocolate: A Novel in Monthly Installment with Recipes, Romances and Home Remedies*, translated by Carol Christensen and Thomas Christensen (New York: Doubleday, 1992), 46.

14. Ibid., 30.

15. *Ibid.,* 39.

16. See, for instance, Raymond D. Boisvert and Lisa Heldke, *Philosophers At Table: On Food and Being Human* (London: Reaktion Books, 2016);; J.M. Dieterle, *Just Food: Philosophy, Justice and Food (Lanham, MD: Rowman & Littlefied International, 2015)*; David M. Kaplan, *The Philosophy of Food (Berkeley, CA: University of California Press, 2012)*; Michael Pollan, *Food Rules, An Eater's Manual* (New York: Penguin, 2009); Kevin W. Sweeney, *The Aesthetics of Food: The Philosophical Debate About What We Eat and Drink* (Lanham, MD: Rowman & Littlefield International, Ltd., 2018).

17. Raymond D. Boisvert and Lisa Heldke have convincingly argued that the distanced privilege of sight that has operated as the leading metaphor for cognition in the West endows thinking with a cleanliness that it does not deserve. In *Philosophers At Table: On Food and Being Human*, the authors emphasize the traditional juxtaposition between thinking and knowing which a worldview based on eating meaningfully subverts. Vision is 'distal' (far away), they explain, unlike taste which is 'proximal' (nearby), implying ingestion, touching, messiness, and mingling. Eating-as-knowing thus stands diametrically opposed to intellectual abstractions, and closer philosophically to the Epicurean premise that all knowledge is grounded in sense-experience as seen emanating from the madeleine and wedding cake.

18.https://cookingupastory.com/carlo-petrini-give-value-to-food-part-5. Translation mine.

19. Julia Child, Louisette Bertholle, and Simone Beck, *Mastering the Art of French Cooking* (New York: Knopf, 2009).

20. Eric Schlosser, *Fast Food Nation: The Dark Side of the All-American Meal*, Mariner Books, 2012; see also Eric Schlosser and Charles Wilson, *Chew On This: Everything You Don't Want to Know About Fast Food (New York: Houghton Mifflin, 2007)*.

21. For an authoritative history of fast food in America, see *History 101*, Episode One.

22. See Kim Kenney, "History of 1950s Cars—It Still Runs," https://itstillruns.com/history-cars-5039048.html, accessed December 10, 2021.

23. Eric Schlosser, *Fast Food Nation: the Dark Side of the All-American Meal*, Mariner Books, 2012, 125–126.

24. Adam Chandler, *Drive-Thru Dreams: A Journey Through the Heart of America's Fast Food Kingdom*," (New York: Flatiron Books, 2019), 4.

25. Quoted from *The Founder*, directed by John Lee Hancock. FilmNation Entertainment/The Combine/Faliro House Productions/S.A., 2017.

26. Ray Kroc, *Grinding It Out: The Making of McDonald's*, with Robert Anderson (Washington, D.C.: Henry Regnery Company, 1977), 9.

27. *The Founder*, see note no. 5.

28.https://www.statista.com/statistics/256040/mcdonalds-restaurants-in-north-america/, accessed December 9, 2021.

29. Ibid.

30. Eric Schlosser, *Fast Food Nation: the Dark Side of the All-American Meal*, Harper Perennial, 2004, 97–98.

31. Schlosser, 114.

32. For an excellent discussion of Taylorism in American history, see chapter 2 of Susan Clark and Woden Teachout's *Slow Democracy: Rediscovering Community, Bringing Decision Making Back Home* (White River Junction, VT: Chelsea Green Publishing, 2012).

33. *The Founder*, see note 25.

34. Marcia Chatelain, *Franchise: The Golden Arches in Black America* (New York: Liveright Publishing, 2020), 25.

35. Pollan, *Omnivore's Dilemma*, 10. See also Steve Ettlinger, *Twinkie, Deconstructed: My Journey to Discover How the Ingredients Found in Processed Foods Are Grown, Mined (Yes, Mined), and Manipulated Into What America Eats (New York: Hudson Street Press, 2007)*.

36. "High availability of fast-food restaurants across all US neighborhood types linked to higher rates of type 2 diabetes," https://www.sciencedaily.com/releases/2021/10/211029114022.htm, accessed December 10, 2021.

37. https://www.cdc.gov/diabetes/data/statistics-report/index.html, accessed November 23, 2021.

38. See, for instance, "Sugar: The Bitter Truth" https://www.youtube.com/watch?v=T8G8tLsl_A4.

39. See Aishwarya Venugopal and Hilary Russ, "McDonald's Sales Surge Amid Reopening Despite Staffing 'Challenges,'" Reuters, https://www.reuters.com/business/retail-consumer/mcdonalds-sales-surge-bts-meal-craze-easing-restrictions-2021-07-28/, accessed October 30, 2021.

40. See Veerasamy Sejian, "Global Climate Change: Role of Livestock," in *Asian Journal of Agricultural Sciences* 3(1), 2011, 19–25; Kip Andersen, *Cowspiracy*

41. For instance, see "Beef Consumption in the United States from 2002 to 2020 (in billion pounds)," https://www.statista.com/statistics/542890/beef-consumption-us/, accessed November 1, 2021.

42. Shelley, *Frankenstein*, 14.

Chapter 5

The Rescuing Ark

The Art, the Music, the Place

When it comes to food, we have seen that "nutritionism" is only part of the story: food is about much more than carbs, proteins, fibers and fats. As a metaphorically rich signifier heavy with cultural value, it plays upon memory, emotion, desire, and the collective experience of belonging. It has deep connections to family, relationships, and community. Yet while all of this is true, it is possible to overplay the collective, cultural meanings of food and overlook its personal, intimate significance. It is possible to misperceive how the relationship between eating-as-trope and the larger cultural imaginary—crosses, flags, golden arches-cum-mammaries—has an underside, a resistance striving to distance itself from "America" writ large and to contest if not subvert the received narrative. Fordism, Taylorism, hard work, increased output: instead of forever invoking and replaying the broader cultural context, food also functions as the *individual's refuge* from the increasingly demanding, increasingly accelerated outside world filled with responsibilities and headaches. Might this explain, at least in part, the rise in foodie culture?

Because food is not only rife with shared meanings, but carries intensely personal and idiosyncratic weight, it staves off the incursions of a commercialized, standardized, administered whole. While eating-as-trope dissolves the sovereign subject and underscores our interdependence with the world, this does not preclude food from having deeply private resonances. Indeed, what we ingest has the ability to celebrate what is unique and untranslatable in terms of time and place, identity, and tradition. It puts into play what does *not* conform to a received set of norms, honoring our ability to get creative and think outside the box. Instead of appealing to conformity, it highlights unique aspects of our lives, thereby defying the McDonaldized standardization implicit in Adorno's assertion that "the whole is the false."[1] Even as the new humanism's eating-as-trope underscores our dissolving boundaries that link us to nature and to one another, so does that trope call attention to the individual whose relationship to food and indeed to society at large is intensely personal. The eating subject qua eater recoups what is unique and unrepeatable, allowing the aesthetic sense to prevail. Food-as-refuge thus resists the demands of instrumental rationality and pushes back against a pre-packaged neoliberal worldview.

"WORKISM" AND THE ATROPHIED IMAGINATION

It may well be the very success of the hurried, time-compressed, workaday ethos that helps explain the rise in foodie culture, a culture that shares a commitment to aesthetics found in Slow Food and the slow movement in general. Perhaps epicurean Americans are taking an interest in gastronomy out of weariness regarding other areas of life, areas that are increasingly standardized, bureaucratized, and administered by corporate, commercial interests over which the individual has no control. Our enslavement to time and to the mandates of a neoliberal output-oriented world allows food to operate as a bastion of opposition, a refuge from the need to conform to mainstream rhythms and expectations. Treating what we eat as art—enjoying its gastronomical possibilities, the conviviality that often surrounds it, and the sheer enjoyment of taste—proclaims that we are not fully colonized by work, responsibilities, and the tyranny of time; it celebrates the immediacy of the present and our ability to find pleasure in the everyday. As against the workaday schedule there is also our internal world to consider, the world that abides with our private thoughts and imaginings, the world of desire, enjoying the here and now. "Aesthetics, ethics, epistemology, pragmatism, and even the concept of the self all inform the choices and preferences . . . of food selection and eating," writes Ferguson.[2] Food represents an alternative universe and provides a haven from a duty-driven existence, even when we eat at our desk.

Perhaps without our knowing it, then, the exponential growth in foodie culture, including Slow Food and the alternative lifestyles espoused by the slow movement, speaks of a desire to be free from rampant "workism," return to pleasure to our everyday routine (and, in some cases, combatting those aspects of the neoliberal ethos that we oppose). Positing food as oppositional pleasure therefore supports the claim that uncolonized psychic space remains, that not every aspect of the American cultural landscape has fallen prey to the Promethean mindset, for even in a workaday world we can engage the senses in ways that defy duty's call. "The focus on food and beverages, on taste in general, is a form of resistance to this increasingly administered world governed by instrumental reason," Darryl Furrow convincingly argues, insisting that it has become "an oppositional force . . . an alternative that feels more authentic."[3] If we disobey the work ethic that is so integral to the American

Dream as we have defined it—upward, outward, committed to growth—we reconnect with the imagination whose virtues engage not instrumental rationality, but the aesthetic sense, not sequential logic, but intuition.

In the twenty-first century, our workaday world obeys an ethos dominated by instrumental rationality wherein the human body morphs into Marcuse's "instrument of labor."[4] We identify deeply with work in a culture driven by utilitarian principles, by ever-increasing speed and a commitment to output. Although some argue that the global economy—and now, the pandemic—blights the individual's ability to identify meaningfully with work, we are nevertheless exhorted to work harder and "smarter" all the time in ways that increase our effectiveness on the job. My inbox often receives messages announcing new ways to make my waking hours more productive, more effective, and more output-efficient; that's what it means to "work smart." These missives are rife with the implication that time unalloyed to quantifiable, measurable outcomes is time wasted, and that we must be made increasingly aware of new and different metrics for gauging productivity. The challenge lies in transforming our waking activities into purposeful, work-related undertakings that burnish our résumés and enhance our career performances. It lies in making our individual lives mesh with a larger, homogenizing mandate that answers to productivity in an economy devoted to growth. We are urged to welcome and conform to a highly administered world that penetrates many areas of our lives: hence our work, leisure, shopping habits, and workout routines frequently align with corporate interests. Tristan Harris, a former Google employee, maintains that workism is encouraged and indeed carefully manipulated by industry which deftly seduces us into checking our cell phones roughly 150 times a day.[5]

Of course, it is preferable to "work smart" if that means not wasting valuable time. Yet some tasks do not translate into a utilitarian grid that measures progress in sequential fashion; some things have no metric with which to measure them at all. Take learning, for example. As an educator, I am encouraged to conform to an increasing number of teaching rubrics and to utilize a growing number of electronic platforms as pedagogical aids. While these aids can be useful, they risk extinguishing what is unique in my teaching and in discounting students' personal experience of the classroom. They offer advice about how to structure my lectures and how my power points should read, all of which introduces a tonality to which classtime should presumably adhere. As they further corporatize the academy, they tacitly suggest that shaping students' minds lends itself to quantifiable data and measurable outputs. Of course, certain hallmarks of an educated person *are* empirically discernable and thus quantifiable. Yet the larger task of training students' minds should never lose sight of the fact that certain aspects of education do not lend themselves to assessment; the thought process does not wholly lend itself to scrutiny. Yet I am offered training programs, templates, and a host of electronic platforms designed to help me improve as an instructor, the assumption being that the more I conform to these strictures the more effective I will be in the classroom.

One email enthusiastically announces a "revolution" in the workplace that will increase students' productivity exponentially such that *all* our time will translate into "meaningful" output. Of course, I am not alone in receiving these; other professors receive them too since it is good for students to have a uniformly consistent college experience, or so the argument goes. Those proffering these teaching aids often seek to standardize professors' pedagogical styles and instill consistency in the classroom experience in the name of higher educational standards. In the process, it also clearly implies that a corporately monitored, technologically advanced education will prove more enriching than one that is lower tech and devoid of a corporate presence, an experience of learning dominated simply by books, ideas, and conversations.

This standardized approach to pedagogy carries a potentially dangerous message to students. At the extreme, it might suggest that unique voices and maverick interpretations are not what we're after: that students' singular experiences, intellects, and sensibilities have to conform to a larger epistemic grid. It might imply that they have to sound a certain way and express certain values that correspond to a prefabricated notion of the educational experience. The site of learning is thus rife with ambiguities since those things that can surely enhance teaching—computer programs, search engines, on-line learning, pedagogical platforms—can also suggest that intelligence *equates* with technological savvy, and that critical thinking reduces to computer skills and the ability to collect information. It can deflect attention away from the mind's creativity and resilience while inflating the importance of what is merely an educational tool.

Indeed, the "common sense" of neoliberalism's instrumental rationality dictates our need to comply, to work ever harder, produce ever more, and remain indebted to the demands of the marketplace. Because neoliberalism naturalizes the free market and seeks to universalize a corporate-led Americanization of culture, it impinges on nearly every aspect of our lives by linking our work time, our free time, and everything in between to market ideology. The time-space compression that dominates our waking hours makes every day a workday, every space a workspace, every human encounter something that can be interrupted by a beep, a ring, or a pulse. In truth, the work week is now 24/7. When instrumental rationality parades as *thinking per se*, when its calculating skill gains ground on creative, original, a-systematic musings, we inhabit an intellectually pauperized universe. The slow movement advocates "losing" oneself in ways that resist instrumentalism; better to "waste" time in thought, Petrini writes, "to cultivate the ecology of the mind, the regeneration of your existence."[6] Wasting time, cultivating the imagination, going slow and curvy without any special agenda: these run counter to the Promethean work ethic so deeply ingrained in the American Dream.

Derek Thompson presents evidence that, in the United States, the ethos of *homo economicus* is not only alive and well, but has morphed into something grander than its original understanding.[7] Thompson argues persuasively that many Americans subscribe to a culture of hard work that elevates toil to the status of a religion, especially among the college-educated who indeed interpret the body as an "instrument of labor" while conferring a sanctified status on their job. While some Americans work less than their foretathers and foremothers thanks to changes in industry and in the workforce, college-educated persons have been exhorted to find their passion through work and to leave their imprint on the world, all of which causes them to view their careers as a spiritually-infused calling that gives meaning to their identities. Thompson deplores the rise of this ideology that understands life's purpose as located primarily in labor, and disdains "workism" as the sole ethos worthy of our allegiance. "What is workism?" he asks. "It is the belief that work is not only necessary to economic production, but also the centerpiece of one's identity and life's purpose; and the belief that any policy to promote human welfare must *always* encourage more work."[8]

The American Dream, when understood especially as upward mobility and economic largesse, necessarily values hard work and the ability to outperform others while setting new standards of high achievement. Yet there are copious statistics that substantiate Thompson's claim that we take things too far, demonstrating numerically how Americans today—at least, pre-covid—put in longer hours with fewer guaranteed benefits than many of our counterparts in the industrialized world. True, among those working the longest hours around the world are Mexicans, South Koreans, and the Japanese, with the latter suffering the culture of "*karoshi*, or death due to overworking oneself.[9] Nevertheless, numerous sources indicate that pre-covid, Americans typically worked a 44–47 hour week, while Germans, French, Swedes, and Italians on average work between 34–36 hours a week. The Netherlands offers roughly a 30-hour work week, and Denmark 32.[10] Added to this is the fact that the United States does not guarantee paid leave in the private sector comparable to other industrialized nations; while most Americans do receive at least ten days paid leave per year, and twelve states and Washington, DC, require paid sick leave, other countries around the world demand paid leave in the interests of work-life balance for workers.[11] At this writing, President Biden's debated legislative agenda aims to address quality-of-life issues that Americans have seen eroded since the 1970s, including devastating economic hits that families have suffered due to the recent pandemic. Indeed, Americans' hard work is tempered by the disheartening reality of how the median household income has failed to keep pace with the economy over the last fifty years, and how Americans have endured increasing levels of income inequality.

Yet many of us *are* enamored of our careers, willingly ensconced in a life-style that raises our jobs to the status of a religion. And to be fair, work can be pleasurable and deeply rewarding, not simply a means of earning an income. Yet work does not always allow for the relaxed and deliberate approach to life that is so central to the slow philosophy; more often than not, it stands rooted in sequential, chronological time rather than in the amplitude of cairos, and thus remains bound to a sense of duty that always pushes forward. Thompson most notably observes that "our elitist institutions are minting coed workists" who worship what they do, even though "our desks were never meant to be our altars."[12] I find ample evidence to suggest that today, being "educated" is synonymous with being job-ready, hirable, eager to earn money. For many, an education translates into job training, the acquisition of knowledge about how to succeed in the workplace where one will be successful and well-liked. Indeed, when other cultures refer to the "Americanization" of their tradi-tional, often slower lifestyle, they have in mind such things as the working lunch, two weeks of paid vacation per year, comparatively fewer holidays, and a general orientation of their five-day work week around time spent in labor, with offices open ample hours, if not 24/7, for customer satisfaction. The American cultural ethos so influential in the globalizing world economy prides itself on its intense organization and high-yielding output: as the McDonald brothers explain, "it's all about speed."[13]

As previously noted, one distinguishing attribute of "Americanization" is the focus on standardization, a love of uniformity and predictability that becomes synonymous with a thriving, expanding economy. It is key to a McDonaldized worldview which, in George Ritzer's words, promotes "an increasingly omnipresent process not only in the world of fast food . . . but in many other aspects of the social world . . . . "[14] It promotes uniformity, predictability, standardization, and the globalization of "nothing," mean-ing that those who cooperate in a franchise simply imitate what someone else has already established; there is no original thinking.[15] In many ways, Ritzer's McDonaldization was foreshadowed by Horkheimer and Adorno's jeremiad concerning the culture industry, an industry whose commercial-ized and commercializing influence was already felt in the 1940s when *Dialectic of Enlightenment* appeared. Modern "culture" was characterized by a numbing, disheartening standardization, they argued, that tied its poten-tially creative, oppositional force to the interests of industry and the reigning political regime. Dominated in this way, the liberating power of aesthetics had been captured and colonized such that its most crucial social function had been coopted. No longer did it give rise to the critical faculty capable of gaining distance on society; instead, it partook in appeasement and skillfully indoctrinated those now simply deemed consumers. What had been a bastion of resistance was thus deprived of its contrapuntal power, and instead served the interests of commercial and political players who expertly domesticated culture's ability to challenge rather than affirm the status quo. The authors thus write of an "insatiable uniformity," a deadening quality that cripples the contrapuntal element and coerces everything into supporting the system.[16]

> Culture today is infecting everything with sameness. Film, radio, and magazine form a system. Each branch of culture is unanimous within itself, and all are unanimous together. Even the aesthetic manifestations of political opposites proclaim the same inflexible rhythm . . . All mass culture under monopoly is identical . . . . [17]

Thus, infected with sameness, culture fails to perform its designated function of offering a fresh vantage point on the mainstream; its maverick role capitulates to the status quo and dissolves the distinction between culture and commercialism. As consumers of this industry, we thus erase any vestige of critique as we unknowingly acquiesce in our own intellectual deflation. Adorno goes further in his denunciation of what the culture industry delivers: not only standardization, but de-humanization; not only poor aesthetic quality, but violence. "If culture is defined as the de-barbarization of man [*sic*] . . . then culture is a total failure . . . It is no coincidence that he is still capable of barbarous outbursts . . . he welcomes the trash of the culture industry with outstretched arms."[18]

Such outstretched arms lamentably convey the tragedy of a completely eclipsed critical faculty that no longer has distance on its own indoctrination, and indeed desires what numbs its perception. They clarify the power of the administered state as it succeeds in colonizing every aspect of cognition, transforming what might defy the system into acquiescence. In "Free Time," Adorno expresses incredulity regarding the very existence of uncolonized mental space. Even in the mid-twentieth century, he already perceived that every corner of our interior landscape had been conquered by Promethean demands such that a truly oppositional viewpoint is now impossible. Distinguishing free time from leisure, he argues that the freedom previously afforded by leisure has now been appropriated by the encompassing culture industry that successfully, surreptitiously binds us to the needs of an administered system. "Free time is shackled to its opposite," he insists, such that what appears recreational in fact obeys the demands of labor."[19] The ethos of hard work and greater output is smuggled into the realm of free time,[20] such that even our efforts to think outside the box are confined to its parameters. Believing ourselves to be renegades, we are in fact obedient lackies.

Such obedience to the prevailing order can only take place if the meaning of leisure has been radically altered. If we understand leisure as the possibility of imagining, even encountering something truly oppositional and unalloyed to the administered state, then it represents an element largely missing from modern society. The culture industry proves adept at diminishing the mind's oppositional force, Adorno maintains, and skillfully curtails the heterogeneous, subversive potential of free thought. It replaces truly liberated thought with "boredom," the inability to conceive of anything untouched by the demands of (today's) neoliberal order and unalloyed to corporate, administered ends.

Boredom and the Importance of "Losing" Oneself

The perils of boredom that in fact reveal a depleted imagination partakes of a long tradition in the West that emanates from various, often incongruous locales. Even pre-modern and early modern philosophy recognized the importance of respite and the mind's liberation from the demands of conforming labor. Josef Pieper's influential *Leisure: The Basis of Culture,* published in 1952, helped revive a twentieth-century interest in Aquinian philosophy rooted in ancient philosophical and medieval theological worldviews.[21] As implied in his title, Pieper valorizes our ability to detach from the programmatic intentionality of industrial civilization; for him, philosophizing operates against the grain of instrumental rationality and thus "transcends the world of work."[22] In the nineteenth century, Charles Baudelaire posited boredom, *ennui,* as a malaise that the modern world knew intimately yet often failed to perceive thanks to its infatuation with "the new." *Ennui* plagues the modern sensibility, Baudelaire implies, since the modern world has undergone a severance from the deep roots of the ancient and medieval sensibilities, replacing these with an infatuation with the peripatetic crowd (*la foule*), the changing cityscape, and the fleeting sensations that accompany urban dynamism.

More recently, feminist scholarship has asked why an uncritical endorsement of hard work and professionalism has captivated so many otherwise maverick thinkers. Kathi Weeks probes the deeper question regarding why a work ethic has been so highly valorized in the Western tradition, and why we so often fail to see the emotional and economic senselessness of our excessive toil. Weeks comments on the workism of contemporary post-Fordist culture:

> One consequence of these developments is that more and more of workers' subjectivities become folded into and fused with their identities as workers. To configure work as the center of our identity requires a reconfiguration of the self in its relationship to work. This is facilitated by the fact that . . . [w]aged work and its values have . . . come to dominate ever more our time and energy.[23]

In an effort to valorize a "post-work" economy, Weeks argues that the many schools of feminist thought have not sufficiently probed this basic question of why our identity should be so tied to our job. Equal opportunity, equal pay, and the work/home balance have understandably been crucial to feminist scholarship, yet weeks regrets that these have not been tempered by a skepticism regarding neoliberal values and the naturalization of market relations. Social movements meant to subvert the status quo have often unwittingly reproduced its central tenets, failing to reevaluate what is wrongly accepted as the unassailable truth.

Of course, we work because we need a paycheck. Today, however, our paychecks don't go as far as they did several decades ago. The well-publicized squeezing of the middle class underway since the 1970s readily explains why many of us cherish our jobs; moreover, the globalized economy with its attendant job insecurity makes it more likely that Americans will lose their source of income and need to retrain or start over on another career path. Such tenuous employment security, greatly exacerbated by covid-19, surely explains why many of us make job performance a high priority.

Yet this bleak, seemingly totalized picture of the contemporary cultural landscape offers redemption in the form of art which, we have seen, may take the form of food. *Pace* Adorno, art's *continued* ability to retain its renegade, nonconformist quality and perform its true calling affirms its subversive quality and revives hope in an otherwise colonized world. Aesthetics, including the aesthetics of food, represents a bastion of opposition, a repository for the imagination to perceive something beyond the administered world. Because aesthetics necessarily draws upon the inventiveness of imagination rather than the regimented logic of instrumental rationality, it retains the ability to grasp something unconventional and refreshingly novel, an alternative truth as of yet uncontrolled by prevailing forces. "Art desires what has not yet been," Adorno explains in *Aesthetic Theory*, going so far as to say that "each artwork is a utopia . . . No artwork cedes to another."[24] The uniqueness, the inability to be repeated in a way that resists homogeneity thus represents a vital element of the aesthetic realm, for its highly idiosyncratic quality disallows appropriation by the ruling system, thereby endowing it with liberationist power. Unscathed by infecting sameness, it proclaims an alternative society.

Many scholars and cultural critics analyze the aesthetic dimension in terms easily recognizable as art: painting, sculpture, film, music. Yet Furrow's brilliant insight lies in his ability to see that this same argument about the liberatory powers of art also extends to foodie culture in the twenty-first century (and, I would argue, to Slow Food and other exponents of the slow movement). For just as art announces the possibility that we can resist the standardizing forces of commercialized capitalism, so does the creativity of gastronomical art imply our desire to remain free from the pressures of an increasingly controlling, invasive, bureaucratic social whole that demands our conformity. Culinary creativity operates in much the same way that bohemian defiance does, or the privileged intellect of the cultural critic who sees in the artwork the imprimatur of an alternative truth unalloyed to the status quo. "I am a great artist!" exclaims Babette, a French chef in Isak Dinesen's short story, "Babette's Feast." Having spent ten thousand francs on a meal prepared for her Norwegian friends who had heretofore "renounced the pleasures of this world," the Parisian epicurean and caretaker gives them an unforgettably elegant meal designed to change their lives and unite the community.[25] Thus food, like other expressions of slow philosophy, "represents our happy alienation from the utilitarian world outside."[26]

The current explosion in the culinary arts may therefore relate directly to the growth in an administered reality aided by technology and social media whose pervasive presence insinuates itself into our lives 24/7. I find persuasive Furrow's claim that it results from the fact that we can now work anywhere, anytime, turning every space into an office, that we have immediate access to a vast amount of information, and that we can be in touch with work associates, family and friends with the tap of a speed dial. What others diagnosed as an infecting sameness in the twentieth century Furrow today sees repeated in our society's "increasingly administered, standardized public world in which efficiency, profit, and measurable success at a task are all that matters."[27] But food rescues what is unique and unadministered, safeguarding an aesthetic element grounded in pleasure against the often aggressive intrusions of our twenty-first-century bureaucratized, fast-paced world. The glamor that now surrounds cooking and eating in American foodie culture—and in the Slow Food movement itself with its focus on "the delicious"—clearly reveals a revered aesthetic dimension long missing from our relationship to food, an experience of pleasure that staves off the incursions of an encroaching system and instead engages the deeper resonances of food: imagination, intuition, memory, emotion.

Even a cursory perusal of the many cookbooks, magazines, and television shows that celebrate gastronomical creativity clarify the aesthetic importance of food today and our collective conviction that cooking is an *art*, an expression of love, imagination, even resistance, not merely a way to refuel. Perhaps cooking shows demonstrate this fact most clearly, for with so many of them competing for audience attention, their mandate to be creative, original, and entertaining has increased tremendously. While we all remain indebted to the trailblazing work of Julia Child whose culinary instructions were delivered with charm, the focus today carries forward her tradition with a high premium on audience accessibility, spontaneity in the kitchen, and an element of surprise. Cooking show titles alone illustrate my point: *Kitchen Criminals, The F Word, How to Boil Water, Dinner: Impossible.*

We should take seriously the possibility that America's rise in gastronomical interests expresses a deep-seated desire to *escape* the hurried, homogenized world that we live in and to seek refuge in a culinary haven unalloyed to *homo economicus*. Seeking to controvert the ubiquitous sameness and task orientation that we daily confront, that haven preserves what is unique, unrepeatable, and protects against the banality of the predictable. And what foodie culture promotes in the realm of comestibles the slow movement expresses elsewhere: that is, it is not only through food that we might seek respite from our harried pace and standardized experience, but in many other aspects of contemporary life. *Cittaslow*'s unique urban spaces, slow fashion's one-of-a-kind garments, slow parenting's decision to listen to one's children and trust oneself rather than compete with other families: these controvert a standardized neoliberal experience and reinforce the long-standing distinction between industry and culture, between instrumental and aesthetic rationalities. Petrini himself promotes "losing" oneself in ways that resist instrumentalism; better to "waste" time in thought, he writes, "to cultivate the ecology of the mind, the regeneration of your existence."[28]

Rescuing the Special: O'Keeffe's Doors and Churro Sheep

In the highly acclaimed, award-winning television series, *Breaking Bad*, Jesse Pinkman remains mystified over Georgia O'Keeffe's paintings of doors, and tries to understand why variations on a door—the same door viewed differently—should hold his interest. Having visited an art gallery with his girlfriend, Jane, he is unclear as to why O'Keeffe painted the same thing over and over, but always from different angles, with different colors and lighting, and altered details. He finds the repeated subject matter monotonous and uninspiring and asks, "Why would anyone paint a picture of a door over and over again, like, dozens of times;that's not psycho to you?" Jesse doesn't understand how the repetition of an everyday object is not equal to a monotonous expression of boredom. He fails to grasp the deliberate focusing on the same subject with a view toward highlighting how each encounter with the door is unique, unrepeatable. It is precisely the repetition that allows the unique aesthetic quality of each separate encounter to stand out in relief, a new experience looked at with fresh eyes. It is this uniqueness that O'Keeffe captures on canvas, rendering each painting distinguishable from the others, unpredictable.

Jane explains that the repetition of the image does not constitute monotony, but underscores the originality of every experience of the door which is different every time. Far from expressing homogenization, O'Keefe's paintings exalt the specialness of each experience, capturing what is singular to each new encounter with the door that can never be repeated. The paintings are

Figure 5.1 Georgia O'Keeffe, *Black Door With Red*, 1954. © 2022 Georgia O'Keeffe Museum / Artists Rights Society (ARS), New York.

not "infected with sameness," but call forth the idiosyncracies freighted with meaning that distinguish each new experience of that part of the home. This is why each painting displays different colors, different lighting, a different angle, and various unrepeated details. "The light was different, her mood was different," Jane explains in the artist's defense. "She saw something new every time . . . why should we do anything more than once? Should I just smoke this one cigarette? Maybe we should only have sex once, if it's the

Figure 5.2 Georgia O'Keeffe, *Wall With Green Door*, 1953. © 2022 Georgia O'Keeffe Museum / Artists Rights Society (ARS), New York

Figure 5.3 Georgia O'Keeffe, *My Last Door*, 1954. © 2022 Georgia O'Keeffe Museum / Artists Rights Society (ARS), New York.

same thing." Jesse remains unpersuaded by the power of aesthetic reasoning and sees only the dogged repetition of subject matter: "I will say it again. A door." But Jane clearly understands the importance of what cannot be colonized and remains elusively unrepeatable, for "[t]hat door was her home and she loved it."[29]

The uniqueness of place, situation, season, lighting and color, the combination of ingredients: all contribute to Slow Food's rescuing ark (and other iterations of slow), the effort to resist the Promethean "more" factor so reliant on the Fordist/Taylorist/McDonaldized uniformity that drives American workism and sustains the American Dream. Ferguson argues that a cook can only be successful by exercising "close attention to both the diversity of the individuals and the needs and desires of the collective" for which she is cooking; losing a sense of specificity will ruin the reception of food.[30] As against the predictability of administered culture, then, we can state that slow aims for a new dynamism, allowing the local, the unique, and the *unrepeatable* to countervail and even subvert the more generalized categories endorsed by the global. With its emphasis on one-of-a-kind artisanal products, seasonal produce, biodiversity and locavore living, the philosophy of slow, like art, "has sought to rescue the special," since for Adorno "[s]uccessful works have always been those in which specification has flourished most extensively."[31] With its focus on the unrepeatable that resists generalization, slow living offers resistance to mass culture which deadens our ability to engage in oppositional thinking and imagine something other than globalization's patterns of uniformity. Freeze his Burgundian snails so that they can be transported year-round to chefs far and wide? For Jean-François Vadot, a snail rancher who adheres to traditional French practices, freezing is the "f word." "There is simply no comparison between the rubbery, flat taste of a frozen snail and the tenderness of a real one," Vadot insists. "These are endearing little fellows."[32]

Rescuing the special is clearly integral to foodie culture whose celebrity chefs work hard to further awaken America's interest in gastronomy as art. Yet it is also at work in Slow Food's and *Cittaslow's* efforts to combat the ills of industrial farming's monoculture and disregard for biodiversity. This mission is especially encapsulated in two arms of the Slow Food movement: the Ark of Taste and the Presidia. Together, these organizations literally rescue the special by keeping alive the biodiversity of nature that industrial farming necessarily destroys. The Ark of Taste, whose very name captures the image of Noah afloat with a variety of animals, catalogs endangered heritage foods that have been forgotten or overshadowed by corporate big sellers such as corn, soy, and beef, and thus keeps a record of plants and animals that have nearly disappeared from the collective imagination. By tracking these endangered things on the verge of extinction, the Ark of Taste preserves their existence and ensures their inclusion in a culture's culinary experience. At this writing, there are more than 200 items registered in the Ark for the United States alone. The Hog Island fig, the Jersey Buff turkey, the Marrowfat pea, and the purple straw wheat are but four items that Americans typically don't find on their grocery shelf but that share in a regional culinary tradition worth saving and nurturing. Other countries contribute their own endangered items such as the Bilimbi fruit from Tanzania, the Toheroa clam from New Zealand, the cloudberry from Finland, the Pehuenche Araucaria pine nut of Brazil. At this writing, these items total 5698 Ark of Taste entries.

The devotion to biodiversity embodied in the Ark of Taste works in conjunction with Slow Food's Presidia. This arm of the movement actively keeps endangered foods alive by working with farmers, fishermen, chefs, grocers, and others who deliberately use traditional production techniques and artisanal methods. The Presidia acts upon the information catalogued in the Ark and, following established guidelines for preserving nearly-extinct foods, promotes the Slow Food mantra of "good, clean, and fair" as it strengthens a community's connection to place. At this writing, there are 624 Presidia worldwide, all of which work with local infrastructure to obtain less processed, more artisanal and high-quality food that factors so prominently in a community's collective imagination. The team of volunteers in Phoenix, for instance, has been instrumental in preserving the existence of the Navajo-churro sheep and Sonoran white wheat, both of which are important to the Navajo, Hopi, and Tohono O'odham Native American communities of the Southwest. Brought to North America by the Spanish explorers in the sixteenth century, the hardy, wooly Navajo-churro sheep has nearly gone extinct

Figure 5.4 The Pehuenche Araucaria pine nut of Brazil is sacred to the Pehuenche people. Source: Photo courtesy of Slow Food Italy

twice; in the 1970s there were as few as 450 of them left. Yet together with other grassroots organizations concerned about the sheep, the Presidia has ensured the sustainability of these creatures with long, curling horns whose copious supply of wool has been used by the Navajo Indians in weaving. In twice rescuing this breed from extinction, the movements involved helped protect Navajo identity and spiritual beliefs. In "Diné" philosophy, as it is called, churro sheep play an integral role and are crucial to "Diné be´iiná," or the Navajo Way of Life. They represent the ability to live in harmony with nature and practice sustainability, and thus function as a spiritually meaningful creature that cements and defends Navajo identity. The Navajo Lifeway, or Diné be´iiná organization, thus celebrate the "Sheep Is Life! A Celebration of Shepherds and Weavers" event annually with the exception of a hiatus caused by covid.

Mesquite pancake breakfasts are another tool used by Slow Food volunteers of the Southwest as a way of showcasing locavore gastronomy while respecting the earth's variations. Mesquite flour replaces the standardized packaged pancake mix and educates people about native traditions via their taste buds. "[M]onoculture is the hallmark of the industrial food chain," Pollan observes, "something nature never does, always and for good reasons practicing diversity instead."[33] Indeed, in my conversations with volunteers at Slow Food USA, their efforts to get creative with locavore eating and biodiversity frequently comes up. Because "[t]he whole is the false,"[34] that which expresses uniqueness and a refusal to be mass produced steers us away from homogeneity. Thus, volunteers devise ways to present previously endangered products to the public; for instance, in 2017 the Bodega Red Potato became the "go-to" potato on Northern California farms, and its popularity spread. The tuber had been rescued from near-extinction by an anonymous donation of just a few potatoes, and after geneticists studied the plant, Slow Food was able to deliver 2,000 pounds of seed potatoes to growers.[35]

As discussed earlier, *Cittaslow* embraces a similar thinking, seeking to emphasize the uniqueness of communities and enhance their individuality. During my meeting with Oliveti, he spoke frequently of the "soul" of a town that needs to be rehabilitated and revived, the unique personality of an urban space often vanquished by modernity yet capable of being restored. In its emphasis on urban personality and the singularity of locale, he argued, *Cittaslow* seeks to unearth and draw attention to the qualities that modern life tends to diminish with its big box chain stores, its predictable corporate presence, familiar commercial logos, and universally recognizable advertising slogans. The movement strives to replace a generalized, depersonalized set of conventions with a unique urban spirit whose chemistry brings people together. "The art, the music, the place" as per one food critic; the architecture, the town center, the incorporation of natural beauty; all serve the larger purpose of either retaining what is unique to an urban setting or of reviving what the faceless imprimatur of modernization unwittingly destroyed.[36] Hence in Wando, South Korea, the principles of *Cittaslow* are brought to life in the annual Slow Walking Festival which celebrates a leisurely gait among its participants who literally stop and smell the flowering plants.[37] And when Kesennuma, Japan hosted a *Cittaslow* Festival in November 2021, it featured traditional Japanese theater, food, music, and crafts, and was attended by 25,000 people.

The desired outcome of *Cittaslow's* presence is always to create community and encourage a sense of belonging among the residents. Thus, before visiting the mayor's office in Alphen-Chaam, The Netherlands, in fall of 2019, I went into a café to pass the time. I had come to Alphen-Chaam in order to discuss that city's adherence to *Cittaslow* principles and to witness the philosophy in action. Having just arrived in town not more than an hour earlier, I had taken a walk and noticed the *Cittaslow* orange snail in various arrangements of tiles on the sidewalk. I then picked that café haphazardly based on its proximity to the mayor's office. Inside was a lively gathering of mostly middle-aged and elderly people who drank coffee, played cards and a board game, and chatted noisily. A small town, friendly-grapevine feeling permeated the room, and it seemed apparent that everyone knew everyone else, as well as the local news and neighborhood gossip. This urban coziness came into sharp focus when, upon serving me coffee, the friendly waiter asked, "You're the lady from *Cittaslow,* aren't you?" Apparently, word had gotten around that I was coming. The waiter then explained that he was a friend of the mayor and had known him for many years. He then pointed out that this very gathering was an expression of *Cittaslow* philosophy, since it is a weekly event sponsored by the mayor's office designed to encourage retired persons to get out of the house and socialize. The idea is to bring the community together, to get the focus off routine matters while encouraging fun and conviviality. In its adherence to *Cittaslow* philosophy, the waiter explained, Alphen-Chaam deliberately keeps things at the level of kaffeeklatsch and board games, cherishing its small-town culture. Later that day, I ran into the waiter again as he peddled back home on his bicycle.

In conversation with the mayor, Joerie Minses, and his assistant Bart van Strien, they relayed their hopes of enlarging on this kaffeeklatsch practice, and of sponsoring visits to communal gardens followed by dinners at people's homes. The visits to the gardens are meant to encourage an interest in locavore food so that people grow more of what they consume. The mayor's office also graciously served me lunch and explained how all of its constituent parts were made from local produce and local ingredients cultivated in an environment that practices biodiversity. As will discussed further in chapter six, The Netherlands is a pioneer in green, cutting edge agricultural practices and is the second largest food exporter in the world.

The championing of the unique as exemplified in the Ark of Taste, the Presidia, and Alphen-Chaam's lively café thus deepens the analysis of Slow Food, *Cittaslow*, and other expressions of the slow movement by clarifying the impact that resistance to the globalizing world economy carries with it. It would be easy to view "rescuing the special" as simply an invitation to cherish local produce, artisanal clothing and crafts, and recycled garments that were manufactured during our parents' generation. Yet returning to the mandate that we not only change the world, but *save* it, the aesthetics of slow remains tied to a politics that directly addresses the urgent needs of the twenty-first century. "Rescuing the special" does not simply represent an aesthetic preference but is tied to a political praxis that helps in this regard. Going locavore and biodiverse, recycling and repurposing garments, traveling less far and taking in fewer sights, not buying our children yet another expensive electronic device: all of these lighten our carbon footprint in keeping with a Noah-like respect for the earth. All of them resonate with eating-as-trope and the reconceived humanism that understands humanity as part of nature, not above it.

Given the rise in foodie culture and its natural connection to slow, it would seem that America is ready to develop an aesthetic sensibility unaligned with modernity's hurry. It would seem that a Fordist/Taylorist/McDonalidized worldview might be receding for some in favor of a rescuing ark that safeguards "the art, the music, the place." Yet if we think it through, a problem arises for advocates of slow: what if twenty-first century citizens who grew up on hamburgers and fries do not want to be part of the rescuing ark? What if fast and processed food are themselves their repository of memory, emotion, and a sense of belonging? After all, these culinary creations originated in mid-twentieth-century America; thus, many people have been eating them all their lives and undoubtedly experience them as "the art, the music, the place." It is in hamburgers and fries that many Americans encounter their Proustian moment wherein taste and memory interconnect, just as other forms of highly processed items spell "mother" to them. Having been raised on this food, what if they enjoy not only the predictability of drive-through meals, but the rush of a harried schedule, the friendly standardization of replicated urban space, and the thrill of competing with other people, other families, and other people's children in the race of life? What if they are content with the neoliberal world whose earthly survival they are somewhat concerned about, yet not enough to go slow and curvy? To some, the "vampire" of commercialism, as Petrini calls it, proves kinder than his diagnosis, and a McDonaldized worldview may bring stability. Who are we to judge?

In addition to this, it is not obvious that in seeking to convince such people of the virtues of slow, an apprehensive end-of-the-world narrative will prove effective. We can invoke Noah's ark as a metaphorically rich concept signaling an ominous future, but the argument about the earth's vulnerability has already been made numerous times and with utmost clarity. There is nothing we can add to Greta Thunberg's impassioned plea for radically changed policies that will reduce greenhouse gases to desirable levels; she has already done so with aplomb. Scores of scientists have corroborated Thunberg's position and warned us about the urgency of the matter. If slow only appears as a utopian pipe dream rooted in nostalgia for a pre-industrial society, a wish-fulfilment that cannot cope with the realities of globalization, it seems improbable that it should ever become mainstream, especially in the United States.

To be sure, advocates of slow could easily become discouraged, as I was myself in speaking to my fellow traveler in Paris. But the picture changes, along with my mood, when I speak directly to those involved in the slow movement who see real, rubber-hits-the-road change occurring and real potential for the future. From inside the movement, these encouraging voices paint a different picture, and see a burgeoning interest in the slow movement even among young people. Their hopefulness concurs in Petrini's exhortation, "If you want to change the world, don't do it with sadness, do it with joy!"[38] It is to this topic that we now turn.

NOTES

1. Adorno, *Minima Moralia: Reflections on a Damaged Life* (London: Verso, 2005), 50.

2. Kennan Ferguson, *Cookbook Politics*, University of Pennsylvania Press, 2020, 15.

3. Darryl Furrow, *American Foodie: Taste, Art, and the Cultural Revolution* (Lanham, MD: Rowman & Littlefield, 2016), 37.

4. I take the phrase "an instrument of labor" from Herbert Marcuse's *One-Dimensional Man (Boston: Beacon Press, 1964/1991).*

5. https://www.pbs.org/newshour/show/phone-trying-control-life, accessed November 14, 2021.

6. Quoted in Maggie Berg and Barbara K. Seeber, *The Slow Professor: Challenging the Culture of Speed (Toronto: University of Toronto Press, 2016), 60.*

7. https://www.theatlantic.com/ideas/archive/2019/02/religion-workism-making-americans-miserable/583441/

8. See note 7.

9. See Danielle Demetriou, "How The Japanese Are Putting An End to the Extreme Work Week, https://www.bbc.com/worklife/article/20200114-how-the-japanese-are-putting-an-end-to-death-from-overwork, accessed July 7, 2020.

10. See Michael Guta, "Business Owners Can Now Compare Their Working Hours With Global Averages (INFOGRAPHIC), https://smallbiztrends.com/2018/11/working-hours.html, accessed July 7, 2020.

11. See G.E. Miller, "The U.S. Is the Most Overworked Developed Nation In the World," 20somethingfinance, https://20somethingfinance.com/american-hours-worked-productivity-vacation/, accessed July 7, 2020.

12. https://www.theatlantic.com/ideas/archive/2019/02/religion-workism-making-americans-miserable/583441/.

13. *The Founder*, The Weinstein Company and Filmnation Entertainment, 2016.

14. George Ritzer, *The McDonaldization of Society: Into the Digital Age*, 10th Edition (Los Angeles: SAGE Publications, 2021), 162.

15. See Ritzer, Chapter 7.

16. H & A, Dof E, p. 96

17. Ibid.,94–95.

18. Adorno, "Culture and Administration," in *The Culture Industry: Selected Essays on Mass Culture* (London: Routledge, 1991), 126.

19. Adorno, "Free Time," in *The Culture Industry: Selected Essays on Mass Culture*, edited by J.M. Bernstein (London: Routledge, 1991), 187.

20. Adorno, "Free Time," 190.

21. Joseph Pieper, *Leisure, the Basis of Culture* (San Francisco, CA: Ignatius Press, 2009).

22. Pieper, 75–76.

23. Quoted in Kathi Weeks "Down With Love: Feminist Critique and the New Ideologies of Work," in *Women's Studies Quarterly*, Vol. 45, Iss. 3/4., 2017, pp.37–5, https://www-proquest-com.csulb.idm.oclc.org/docview/1950417958/63F71475373B45F0PQ/25?accountid=10351, accessed March 27, 2021.

24. Adorno, *Aesthetic Theory*, translated by Robert Hullot-Kentor (Minneapolis: University of Minneapolis Press, 1997), 134–135.

25. Isak Dinesen, "Babette's Feast," in *Anecdotes of Destiny* (New York: Random House, 1958), 23-68.

26. Furrow, 27.

27. Furrow, 28.

28. Quoted in Maggie Berg and Barbara K. Seeber, *The Slow Professor: Challenging the Culture of Speed (Toronto: University of Toronto Press, 2016), 60.*

29. https://www.quotes.net/mquote/692746, accessed December 3, 2019.

30. Ferguson, 15

31.Theodor Adorno, *Aesthetic Theory*, translated by Robert Hullot-Kentor (Minneapolis: University of Minnesota Press, 1997), 201.

32.Mort Rosenblum, *A Goose in Toulouse and Other Culinary Adventures in France* (New York: Hyperion, 2000), 104.

33. Michael Pollan, *The Omnivore's Dilemma: the Natural History of Four Meals* (New York: The Penguin Press, 2006), 8-9.

34. Theodor Adorno, *Minima Moralia: Reflections on a Damaged Life,* translated by E.F.N. Jephcott (London: Verso, 1951/2005), 50.

35.https://www.fondazioneslowfood.com/en/slow-food-presidia/bodega-red-potato/, accessed December 14, 2021.

36. *Chef's Table*, created by David Gelb, Netflix, Episode 1.

37. I am grateful to Sun-Young Kwak for this information.

38.https://www.slowfood.com/press-release/slow-food-usa-launches-slow-food-nations/ accessed December 13, 2021.

Chapter 6

Conversations with Snailblazers and the Charge of Elitism

Stories from the front prove useful in examining America's relationship with slow and curvy. The real-life, rubber-hits-the-road testimonials tell of persons in the trenches who strive to bring this philosophy to life and into the collective American imagination. For this reason, conversations with people who are actively involved in the movement greatly enrich our inquiry and allow us to move from theory to praxis, from a conceptualized new humanism to its realization in practice. Their hands-on experience proves invaluable in helping us gain insight into the larger question that drives this study: viz., could the philosophy of slow, the philosophy that drives Slow Food, *Cittaslow,* and other offshoots,ever become mainstream in the United States? Could the slow and curvy lifestyle that disdains the frenzy potentially, imaginably be the wave of America's future?

Since beginning this project in 2015, I have had conversations with over fifty people committed to this philosophy and involved in various aspects of Slow Food, *Cittaslow,* and other iterations. Our interviews have lasted roughly fifty-five hours, and I have been impressed with the information and anecdotes that those involved with the philosophy of slow have been willing to share. These committed activists affectionately dubbed "snailblazers" do commendable, often unpaid work. In speaking with them, I have learned so much about the movements' internal dynamics, successes and failures, growing pains, and hopes for the future. Like any social movement that is widely dispersed, slow has played out differently in different places, has gone through various stages, and has itself felt the impact of larger social and economic phenomena. Both Slow Food and *Cittaslow* have felt the financial debacle of 2008 and the global downturn caused by covid-19; they have seen membership rise and fall and, to date, have seen experiments in *Cittaslow* fail to take deep root in American culture. And while it is impossible to issue definitive, broad pronouncements about the movement as a whole or to make easy predictions about its future, my conversations with snailblazers allow me to make observations that are useful and, I think, hopeful regarding the future.

The Slow Food movement in the United States is by now well organized and well-articulated, even if it still not a household word. Slow Food USA was founded in 1999 and, according to Mulè, now claims over 115 chapters around the country. Its governing document, a national statute, is renewed every four years. While the administrative center of Slow Food USA is now online with staff in various cities around the country, the movement as a whole emphasizes the grassroots nature of its politics, for this resonates with the red snail's focus on biodiversity, respect for local cultures, and the need to connect to a unique place—values consistent with the orange snail of *Cittaslow*. While the central offices do important work handling administrative duties and supporting the network as a whole, volunteers are key to sustaining the movement and helping it grow. As stated on the Slow Food USA website, engaging in a Slow Food chapter allows participants to "taste, celebrate, and champion the foods and food traditions that are important to their regions."[1]

In speaking with Mulè via Zoom in November 2020, she stressed the manner in which the movement has changed over time, placing increased focus on Indigenous Persons and other underrepresented groups, ramping up its efforts to be inclusive. It is important to preserve the delicious, Mulè affirms, and never lose the element of fun. Nevertheless, Slow Food has changed since its early days and has grown increasingly committed to embedding equity, inclusion, and justice into each pillar of "good, clean, and fair." From online, Mulè organizes and engages with a vast array of campaigns, networks, and partnering relationships that promote the movement's message in myriad and creative ways, some via governmental support, some via local venues such as restaurant kitchens. In this way, Slow Food principles are promoted at all levels in connection with numerous partners whose interests vary but whose concern with food, its relationship to human health, and its relationship to the planet, overlaps with the movement's mission. For instance, Mulè's involvement ranges from federal farm policies to rural coalitions, from championing Meatless Monday Ambassadors to encouraging kids to plant a seed and watch their tomato plant grow. Among other things, it comprises Slow Meat, Slow Fish, Slow Seed, and Slow Books, and cooperates with the international gatherings organized by Slow Food International. Indeed, Slow Food USA's reach is by now extensive; as an organization, it is admirably and efficiently run. In all my dealings with its various divisions, I have been impressed with its singularity of purpose and team morale. The optimism among its employees embodies Petrini's conviction that it is important to be organized without going overboard into a micromanaged labyrinth.

SLOW FOOD CHAPTERS: REACHING
AND TEACHING THE PUBLIC

Every Slow Food USA chapter is unique, claiming a good deal of autonomy from the administrative offices. The common emphasis on a locavore lifestyle and the needs of biodiversity necessitate decentralization, allowing different chapters to pursue an agenda that makes sense in terms of their area. True, many chapters participate in the Ark of Taste, the Presidia, and the Slow Food Nations food festival typically hosted in Denver. Many also participate in the biennial Terra Madre Salone del Gusto, a forum of exchange for farmers, chefs, wine growers, and other foodies who are committed to artisanal and small-scale practices based on good, clean, and fair. (In 2020, both the Slow Food Nations Leaders' Summit and Terra Madre were held online.) Yet even amidst international involvement, the central task of volunteers is to engage the surrounding community and educate people locally about the philosophy and practice of slow. Their job is to clarify Slow Food's pertinence to the specific locale, disabusing people of the notion that the movement exists as a high-priced foreign affair established for affluent foodies; rather, it's a loca-vore lifestyle open to everyone.

There are numerous ways in which Slow Food USA volunteers strive to teach and reach Americans about the movement. Bethany, a restauranteur in Atlanta, makes use of her menu and natural wines to help educate her clien-tele about the virtues of slow. Customers are intrigued by the term "natural wine," she explains, which allows her to discuss the movement's principles. Similarly, Hannah, a volunteer in Denver, recounts that her chapter also coop-erates with local wineries, breweries, and restaurants in order to advertise the Slow Food name and explain its philosophy to customers. At wineries and breweries, representatives from the movement are invited to come speak about its philosophy and explain what makes an alcoholic beverage "slow." A discussion about wine or beer can then expand to include a conversation about climate change, our collective need to go green, and the beauty in slowing down.

At restaurants, participating chefs at times invent a new menu item drawing from the Ark of Taste, thereby allowing nearly-extinct food items to go from obscurity to the advertised special of the day. It also allows the staff to explain what the Ark of Taste is when curious customers inquire. I had evidence of this practice in Florence at the restaurant section of Eataly. Various menu items had the words *Presidi di Slow Food,* "Presidia of Slow Food," written next to them along with a colorful little drawing.

Slow Food Denver takes an active role in the school gardens program there. This project, widely practiced by other Slow Food chapters as well as schools unaffiliated with the organization, follows Alice Waters' Edible Schoolyard Project begun in 1995. More recently, Slow Food has produced an official School Garden Program organized around the principles of good, clean, and fair, offering a blueprint of the Program's aims and what it recommends for schools at the primary, middle, and high school levels. I spoke with Kim and Neha about the Program, two of its three "tri chairs." The driving principle behind it consists in educating children and young adults about the pleasures of gardening and the gastronomical benefits of growing one's own food. The learning blueprints and classroom activities that accompany the "good" and "clean" principles are carefully laid out in curricula publications, pairing the learning objectives of the movement with activities that go on in the classroom and school garden. (Slow Food USA is now fundraising in order to get "fair" up and running.) They supply specific assignments and learning objectives at the elementary, middle, and high school levels, clarifying how the School Gardens Program will enrich and diversify the school curriculum by educating students about sustainability and biodiversity while generating enthusiasm around healthful food more generally.

For instance, students are encouraged to plant seeds and explore different varieties of fruits and vegetables, resulting in homework on their "Tomato" or "Cucumber" Worksheets. They are asked to taste a variety of apples and then to make a chart plotting the gamut of "appley" tastes: sweeter, more tart, more chewy. This develops their "sensory education," which is supplemented with "kitchen skills." Students are also encouraged to research the history behind the seeds they plant, and to learn about the Indigenous People who originally cultivated them. Thus, the assignments combine planting and tasting with standard academic subjects such as history, writing, organizing one's thoughts, and drawing.[2]

Volunteers in Arizona also put energy into involvement with the young. Beverly, an activist in Prescott, finds great value in Slow Food's efforts to teach children how to harvest worm beds, allowing them to grow microgreens in the classroom. This brings in instructors from the Rocky Mountain Seed Alliance, an organization that teaches people how to save seeds and thus combat industrial farming. In all her work, Beverly draws attention to the rich agricultural and culinary heritage of the Southwest that contributes many items to the Ark of Taste: Aunt Ruby's German Green tomatoes, the Black Sphinx Date, Green Striped Cushaw, and the Spanish Goat count among these.

In January 2017, I visited a Southern California community project and was given a tour of the many separate gardens that coordinate with schools. Joanne explained to me that children and teenagers are encouraged to get creative in how they present their gardens, which subsequently display painted stones and tiles, scarecrows, birdhouses, decorated wheel barrels, repurposed trash cans, and retired lawn mowers as props that help make their gardens interesting. Some gardens have a theme or a featured topic, and they exhibit a sign that explains certain aspects of gardening such as the pollinating role of butterflies or bees. Some schools participate with farmers' markets or purchase the gardens' produce themselves, thereby allowing the students to turn a profit on the food items they grow.

I later met with an Orange County master gardener who explained that while the school system is crucial to the gardening project, other organizations such as the Girl and Boy Scouts, and Boys' and Girls' Clubs, also participate. According to him, the endorsement of such youth-centered organizations is vital to the future of the alternative food movement. For children, the emphasis has to be on fun; Slow Food will only be able to keep its momentum and continue to draw in new people, young and old, if it keeps the focus on *pleasure*. He insists that enjoyment can be found just as easily in simple "mom and pop" food as it can in haute cuisine; the red snail can qualify as Americana and utterly shed its foreign resonances if need be. It is his conviction that equating Slow Food with expensive meals at high end restaurants will only hurt the cause; the movement should aim at keeping things local, familiar, and simple, playing on our memories and the emotional weight of food. He argues, in other words, that Slow Food should tap into the genius of Ray Kroc's claims to wholesomeness and convince people that "good, clean, and fair" is *American* food to the core, right up there with crosses, flags, and arches. Slow Food is American food.

Volunteers in Louisville, Kentucky agree that they have seen evidence of how far fun can take you. The Slow Cocktail Challenge, Fried Chicken Throwdown, Best Dessert Award, and bread making demonstrations really succeed in bringing people in, creating a captive audience in front of which Slow Foodies can hold forth about their philosophy. Charity, a volunteer in Sacramento, agrees that the battle can be won through increased visibility in the community via familiar American venues and cultural referents. This means collaborating with organizations and events that are already underway, such as fairs and festivals, in order to showcase the Slow Food presence. In Sacramento, roughly thirty-one restaurants, twenty-five food and beverage producers, and twelve "supporters"—e.g., groceries, farmers markets, literacy centers—have won the "Snail of Approval" label, meaning that their activities, such as the Farm-to-Fork Festival and participation in the Annual National Heirloom Exposition, align with the movement's philosophy. The chapter has also tabled at Earth Day and World Food Day events on campuses and taken part in a Native American food event. Charity's emphasis is on creating a profile of the movement that underplays its foreign attributes, thereby integrating it into the fabric of American society.

Many Slow Food chapters around the country make use of social media and newsletter blasts to be in touch with interested persons. In Chicago, volunteers explain that a monthly, sometimes bi-monthly newsletter blast advertises the many activities that the movement hosts in the area: e.g., a food book club, Disco Soup evenings, seed saving lessons, veggie bingo. It also sponsors fundraisers that provide travel scholarships for members to participate in Terra Madre and Slow Food Nations. They explained that this philanthropic aspect of involvement resonates with the movement's grassroots emphasis since it is important that not only the economically comfortable be allowed to experience these important events.

Chicago volunteers are not alone in their conviction that "fair" deserves ample attention. For as stated, critics of the movement often dismiss it as a fad tailored to wealthy foodies. They complain that the movement does not speak to the scores of Americans whose earning power has shrunk considerably since the 1970s and whose effort to make ends meet renders fast food an attractive if not indispensable staple. These class-related issues also carry a racial element since people of color are adversely affected in far greater numbers than Whites. Hence, in speaking with many volunteers, a consensus emerges that the movement must straightforwardly address the classist and racist dimensions of America's food insecurities, making "good, clean, and fair" a reality for everyone.

The volunteers with whom I spoke all register a hopeful tone about the future of the movement. While Slow Food USA responds to pressure as does any other social movement, volunteers appear convinced that the general trajectory is forward and up, and that a Noah-like sensibility will ultimately at least temper if not replace the Promethean, McDonaldized ethos that has dominated the United States for over sixty years. However, as we will see presently, this optimism differs radically from the outlook for *Cittaslow* in the United States, where former volunteers express doubts about the outgrowth's ever really taking root on American soil.

The Understandable but Undeserved Charge of Elitism

The interwoven politics of class, race, ethnicity, and legal status concern all iterations of the slow movement and go directly to the question of who will reap the benefits of a Noah-inspired world. For whom should the right to pleasure be safeguarded? How can a person go slow and curvy when working two or three jobs? The charge of elitism is brought most forcefully against Slow Food, although slow fashion, slow travel, slow parenting, and other iterations of slow also bring class-related issues to the fore. Given its efforts to oppose the culture of inexpensive processed comestibles and revive an older sensibility regarding taste, eating, and locavore living, Slow Food especially cannot help but appear elitist for a number of reasons. And to be fair, we can see why: it exists as a foreign import, its delectable products sold at Eataly are expensive, Prince Charles is an advocate, and Petrini argues that food *should* cost more than Armani underwear. Moreover, at this historical juncture, food insecurity is a reality for many Americans who visit food pantries and shelters regularly, and as is well known, this food insecurity is far more prevalent among Indigenous People, Black Americans, and people of color. Hence "the right to pleasure" cannot help but sound like the gilded entitlement of high society that many cannot enjoy. In this setting, will the Slow Food philosophy make an impact in America?

Slow Foodie restauranteurs sometimes express doubt. While in Amsterdam in the fall of 2019, I visited a famous Slow Food restaurant, De Kas, located in Frankendael Park, and met with a chef and co-owner, Jos Timmer, who works alongside Wim de Beer. Sipping an espresso in the restaurant's greenhouse while taking a break, Jos explained to me that while De Kas has been in business for twenty years, he and Wim only recently took charge and have successfully focused on organic dining that makes ample use of Slow Food products. The restaurant represents an exemplary farm-to-table establishment, using produce from its three gardens and other local foods. The repurposed greenhouse setting and scrupulous attention given to food's presentation make for an elegant dining experience. "Food here is poetry," one blogger asserts.[3] Importantly, though, Jos recognizes that his garden-to-table luxury caters to the well-to-do, and he would like to see this change. People of every socio-economic profile deserve the attractive, inventive meals that the restaurant offers, he argues, suggesting that the government should step in to address food insecurity.

So the criticism is fair. At least under current conditions, what the movement proffers can be enjoyed by those with sufficient funds, which excludes many Americans. But is it *accurate* to say that the movement's agenda centers around spending more on food than we can afford, that it is elitist at heart? Is arguing that food is more important than fancy underwear and cell phones tantamount to arguing that only the wealthy should be able to afford it? Surely advocating "good, clean, and fair" need not be synonymous with a generous food allowance, for lavish spending has nothing to do with the movement's original, Noah-inspired principles. Many volunteers implicitly reference the Noah-like principles that guide the movement and that underscore its democratic ambitions, for their work's connection to locavore food, artisanal products, small-scale biodiverse farming, and preserving endangered species in fact forges connections with the more vulnerable elements of society.

Volunteers maintain that because all the long-term goals of the movement center around agroecology, the movement by definition supports an inclusive agenda without class-based, racial, ethnic, or other barriers. With agriculture at its core, all sectors of society and all walks of life partake in the project; as chef Dan Barber asserts, it *all* comes together in a plate of food. Cooking today represents "an ethical act," Barber maintains, one whose importance is now more politically charged than ever before. The ethical component of cooking affords a chef much creativity as so many aspects of life converge around the topic of food. Politics, economics, nutrition, agriculture, biology, ecology: "all come together in that plate of food" and thus have the ability to spearhead cultural reform.[4] "It's about seasonality, locality, and direct relationship with your farmer," he writes of locavore politics. "It's also about better-tasting food, which is why chefs have been so influential in broadening the movement . . . A growing number of chefs have joined the ranks of activists . . . ."[5] Just as Gangsta Gardener Ron Finley began curbside growing as a response to inner city food deserts, so does Barber posit the centrality of agroecology as the main rebuttal to the charge of elitism. Hence while a Slow Food utopia would surely feature some expensive restaurants, another reality would exist alongside it: namely, that gently treated, gently raised foods would be widely available and thus more affordable.

Slow Food's commitment to democratic principles and an anti-elitist praxis reveals itself clearly in the movement's "Thousand Gardens in Africa" project. Launched in 2010, this undertaking sought to create one thousand sustainable gardens throughout Africa with a view toward helping local economies achieve food sovereignty and preserve endangered varieties of foods through cooperation with the Ark of Taste and Presidia. The aim is to support small-scale farmers with modest funding and some managerial help from Slow Food, Italy while guiding those in Africa to follow the movement's principles. The gardens instruct those involved in how to preserve local culture, grow their economy, empower the community, and protect indigenous foods against the incursions of large-scale mono-farming. This undertaking has been called "Slow Food's most important project" given its aim to increase African farmers' knowledge, skills, productivity, and most importantly "their faith in themselves."[6] It allows them to be in control of their seeds and not become indebted to large corporations. The gardens themselves need not be large and are often in very unlikely places such as on a rooftop or beside a walkway.

Terra Madre initially oversaw this project in twenty-six African countries, and its enormously successful outcome surpassed initial expectations. Therefore, the decision was made in 2014 to expand this model, and instead of building one thousand gardens, it strove for ten thousand. The focus on empowering African farmers and affirming the great value in their gardens, however small, challenges the charge of foodie snobbery, for indeed the movement insists that *we* learn *from them* and their artisanal practices. Hence the Slow Food Foundation now sponsors "Ten Thousand Gardens in Africa," and has at this writing succeeded in constructing 3,411 gardens. Petrini subsequently savors the memory of "the people who had looked at me as if I were punch-drunk, carried away by my umpteenth utopia, when I told them of my scheme for a thousand gardens in Africa."[7]

While the term "foodie" may carry elitist implications, then, there can be little doubt that Slow Food, and indeed the slow movement more generally, responds to the intersectional politics of race, class, ethnicity, religion, and other divisions that separate privileged from underprivileged sectors of the population. In a Noah-inspired world, it is caring for the earth and stopping the ill effects of neoliberalism's global reach that matters. Still, many volunteers argue that the movement should reach out more energetically to lower income communities, people of color, and Indigenous persons in order to make the movement more inclusive.

Jim in Louisville, Kentucky, argues that Slow Food USA has every chance of becoming a truly transformative social movement thanks to its connection to the earth; because food has such far reach, it can bring fundamental change to our society. Yet he insists that the movement needs to make a concerted effort to reach out to those less likely to be persuaded by its gastronomic appeal and focus on pleasure. Highly enthusiastic about the movement overall, Jim admits that thus far Slow Food USA has fallen short in terms of race relations and general inclusivity; it needs to shed whatever upper-crust image some continue to see and be proactively engaged with the economically vulnerable. The demographics of his local Slow Food chapter, for instance, scarcely resembles that of the surrounding community in eastern Kentucky, for those closer to him suffer the effects of food insecurity and food deserts.[8]

Despite this shortcoming, Jim sounds a hopeful note about the future of Slow Food USA and Slow Food International. He therefore helped draft the crucial "Slow Food Equity, Inclusion, and Justice" document that stresses the integral relationship between the mission of Slow Food and the need to end racism, discrimination against Indigenous Peoples, abuse of migrant workers and of the earth, and our responsibility to act on the movement's principles for everyone. Because inclusion proves crucial to the red snail's philosophy, he argues that Slow Food USA should more closely resemble the Terra Madre gatherings in Turin, Italy: that is, it should "bring the whole world in." Such inclusivity should operate as the movement's ultimate goal, he insists, as opposed to the "silos" principle that now typifies how things are run.

The University of Gastronomic Sciences (UNISG)

A group of honorary snailblazers reside in Petrini's native region of Piedmont, in Northwestern Italy, and approach the movement from both an academic and practical angle. The University of Gastronomic Sciences (UNISG) in

Pollenzo, Italy represents an academic arm of Slow Food open to students from all around the world. While there is no formal, official relationship between UNISG and the Slow Food movement, it is well known that Petrini first conceived of this educational establishment and that the ideas that drive its agenda mostly align with those of the movement. The university opened its doors in 2004. It is committed to training students both academically and practically in gastronomic sciences in ways attuned to the slow philosophy. A private university that receives a small amount of state funding, UNISG offers bachelor's and master's degrees, and just recently began a PhD program. Its library contains over 24,000 books that address various aspects of gastronomy, and its "educational gardens," or *l'orto didattico*, allows students to have a hands-on, farm-to-table experience. Also for pedagogical purposes, the University brings in internationally renowned guest chefs to give lectures and presentations.

Since 2015, I have visited the University twice, and each time have been favorably impressed with its thoughtful academic agenda, its resolve to combine academic and practical knowledge, and its insistence on a global outlook. Pollenzo is a small city and its landscape features the beautifully restored summer home of King Charles Albert of Savoy, a UNESCO world heritage site dating from 1832, which now houses the University. The fact that Petrini succeeded in procuring financial aid from roughly 350 companies in order to undertake this refurbishment indicates the confidence that he inspired in his donors. "It was a large, indeed enormous, royal farm, neo-Gothic outside and neo-classic inside with a square ground plan," he writes. "The first time I saw it inside, it was in a sorry state . . . The building, very beautiful and very grand, was falling to bits and it was going to cost a fortune to repair it."[9] Photographs now on display in one area of UNISG illustrate the estate's pronounced dilapidation before Petrini's project got underway, contrasting sharply with its current state-of-the-art condition.

There are now between 450–500 students at UNISG from 90 different countries: roughly 44% are Italian, 10% American, with the remaining coming from the rest of the world. The university, which also sponsors an artfully photographed magazine, *The New Gastronome*, proudly displays the high percentage of students who readily find employment in their selected field of study. It describes itself as an institution that "forms gastronomes, new professional figures with multi-disciplinary skills and knowledge in the fields of science, culture, politics, economics and ecology of food, working to apply them to production, distribution and sustainable consumption."[10]

Two students from my home campus, Tien and Victoria, are graduates of UNISG. Tien pursued the Master of Gastronomy: World Food Cultures and Mobility program, while Victoria was a student in the Master of Food Culture, Communication, and Marketing Program. Both appreciated the seriousness of the university's approach to food studies and found that, in addition to being academically challenging and comprehensive in perspective, the school fostered a comradery among the students thanks to its extra-curricular projects. These included The Gastronomic Society, an off-campus countryside venue that features two communal dining spaces, a professional kitchen and pantry, a "teaching garden," and a large courtyard, all of which serve the purpose of encouraging "everyday gastronomy." In addition to the Society, the university features the student association, ASSG (*Associazione Studenti di Scienze Gastronomiche*), the UNISG Slow Food Convivium which connects students to Slow Food events such as Terra Madre and Salone del Gusto, and GAS-La Credenza, an organization that seeks to connect consumers directly with producers of local, sustainable products.

A mandatory feature of both Tien and Victoria's master's degree were three study trips aimed at broadening students' knowledge of different cuisines and gastronomical cultures. Tien's trips took her to Campania, in Southern Italy, to the Basque region of Spain, and to Thailand where she visited a water buffalo farm, a rice field, and a fishing community. She also had the opportunity to engage in hands-on weaving and had an internship harvesting seaweed. Victoria also had a study trip to the regions of Campania and Basilicata in Southern Italy, the Netherlands, and Japan. Her final study trip to Japan is memorable for its focus on medicinal herbs, as well as for meeting women pearl divers known as "*ama.*"

UNISG strives to incorporate both a liberal arts and scientific approach to food that provides students with a broad perspective on the field of gastronomy. Any degree pursued at the university therefore combines the elements of cross-disciplinary learning, practical experience, and international study trips so that students come to appreciate food culturally as well as scientifically. Julia is an employee of UNISG who graciously met with me both times that I visited the university, once in 2016 and once in 2019. She explained how the connection to memory and emotion is foregrounded by the Sensory Analysis Lab which seeks to educate students in the aspects of taste; it asks them to detect a flavor without being told what it is. Thus, either the room is blackened as the food is brought in, or the students wear dark glasses which prevent them from seeing clearly. Students gain experience in this lab as well as in the classroom, in the gardens and kitchens, and visiting other countries. Moreover, available areas of study are organized not only around food but also around communications and marketing, food innovation and management, world food cultures and mobility, agroecology and food sovereignty.

On my second visit to UNISG in November 2019, Julia explained that she now works in the International Relations and Executive Training Division. In this position, she designs and organizes courses that teach corporate executives about sustainability, educating them in how to make their commercial food production, packaging, and advertising more closely align with the principles of Slow Food. The corporate world now comes to her seeking guidance on how to go green in its methods and bring a more sustainable corporate model to fruition, even though they need not use that title explicitly. The fact that this position exists at all, and that UNISG cooperates so closely with corporate giants eager to learn about sustainability, illustrates the strides that Slow Food and other allies in the alternative food movement have made into mainstream society. It signals an important shift in corporate sensibility and lends further evidence to the belief of one former Slow Food USA employee that "we are winning." And progress is of course aided by the many American universities which today feature Food Studies programs that train students in ways similar to UNISG.

CITTASLOW, HERE AND ABROAD

The optimistic, expansive feeling that keynotes UNISG and the growth of foodie culture does not sustain itself when we consider *Cittaslow,* USA. In my exchanges with snailblazers intent on bringing the slow philosophy to urban life, the mood is decidedly different and stands diametrically opposed to the optimism that characterizes my conversations about *Cittaslow* abroad. For as I have chronicled, this outgrowth of the Slow Food movement begun by Paolo Saturnini in Tuscany has met with much success on foreign soil and has expanded to comprise participating cities in thirty-two countries around the globe. At this writing, there are 282 cities in the world that carry the movement's mascot, yet none of them are on American soil.

My 2020 conversations with persons formerly involved in *Cittaslow* USA register a note of exhaustion, even though individuals committed to this cause have worked hard on its behalf and still believe in its principles. Their stories about courageous attempts to introduce the movement to the United States reveal how enthusiastic they were, and still are, about the philosophy that purports "there is no smart without slow." They did have a run in Northern California, where at its peak three cities earned the *Cittaslow* mascot of an orange snail with a rounded urban cityscape on its back: Sebastopol, Fairfax, and Sonoma. But by now those who volunteered their time and energy to *Cittaslow,* USA have either moved away or simply relinquished their responsibilities, convinced that, while the movement had its moment, it never took root in city life enough to make it flourish. While it was well-received during its heyday, *Cittaslow* never gained the grassroots support necessary to allow a movement to embed itself into the fabric of city life. It never became *American.*

I spoke with several volunteers from Northern California and met with one in Long Beach. All spoke enthusiastically about the ideas that guide this movement and their conviction that, when it is done properly, it makes a real difference in the quality of urban life. They had all been actively involved at the grassroots level in Northern California and had witnessed what they hoped would be the introduction of *Cittaslow* into mainstream American life. They described their efforts to encourage a small-town, close-knit feel to the cities by focusing on such things as bike paths, paths allowing people to walk to school and work, support for local entrepreneurs, and discouragement of chain stores or big box retailers. They fought to protect local supermarkets rather than recognized names that carry major food brands, and managed to keep out the familiar, big name coffee shops that now populate every major urban setting in the country. They wanted to preserve what was unique to each place, to rescue the special and escape the homogenizing influence of commercialism. And while these volunteers feel that they indeed achieved some measure of success in bringing the ideas of Saturnini to fruition on American soil, the lifespan of *Cittaslow* in these cities simply did not endure. The volunteersadmitted to burnout, and never found that there was sufficient enthusiasm in the urban centers to sustain what they had begun.

David spoke with me twice about *Cittaslow*, once in the summer of 2020 and once in the fall of 2021. He explained that he had given much time and energy to the experiment in Fairfax, which was successful for a while. But when the mayor responsible for obtaining the *Cittaslow* label moved on, the enthusiasm dwindled among those remaining. David had been to the Netherlands to attend a *Cittaslow* event and was impressed by how deeply embedded the movement was in the everyday life of cities carrying the label; according to David, it seemed to come more naturally to them. "It's not a reach for them," he said, as it is for the USA given our Promethean, McDonaldized culture. Even though David does see evidence of the slow movement gaining support around him, he feels that few *Cittaslow* principles have really taken hold in his community in a lasting way.

Pam concurs in David's assessment, stressing that at least for now the United States lacks both the political structure and the historical memory to sustain *Cittaslow* for long. Thus, while the mayor of Alphen-Chaam, Joeri Minses, demands that proposals seeking approval from his office abide by various *Cittaslow* criteria, Pam explains that American mayors eager to implement *Cittaslow* practices had difficulty obtaining cooperation from the surrounding business community. Because so much of the American Dream focuses on progress and economic expansiveness, leaning forward into industry rather than backward into artisanal craftsmanship, it meshes with the principles of slow only with difficulty. Of course, we have historical societies and other collectives eager to safeguard the past, but according to the veterans of *Cittaslow* USA, the interests of the business community are often pitted against them.

Those promoting the urban arm of the slow movement thus experienced fatigue among its ranks that has stymied the undertaking. Along with Oliveti, they too hope that the effort will revive in the future with new blood and new enthusiasm. "I am waiting for the United States!" [*aspetto gli Stati Uniti*!] Oliveti exclaimed during our interview, throwing his arms open. For now, however, the undertaking has entered a dormant period.

My encounters with *Cittaslow* mayors in Italy, France, and the Netherlands, as well as my virtual correspondence with those in the United Kingdom and research on numerous other countries, affirm that maintaining the movement's presence in a city takes a good deal of organized teamwork. It involves myriad areas of life and levels of bureaucracy: e.g., city planning, architecture and restoration, efforts to protect small farms while discouraging large supermarkets, helping the elderly, the retired, and the unemployed, educating children about *Cittaslow*, planning festivals and fairs, and making use of the Ark of Taste and Presidia in an effort to protect endangered species of plants and animals. For instance, the mayor of Mirande, France, Pierre Beaudran, is proud of his slow activities in the realms of residential living, agriculture, culture, and education. I visited Mirande in the fall of 2019 along with my traveling companion who helped me navigate the medieval streets of Occitanie, some of which were so narrow that we had to back up our economy car and reroute several times. In Mirande, Mayor Beaudran has spearheaded numerous activities that revolve around slow living and efforts to create community bonds. He showcases the small residential community made up of closely situated, contiguous homes conceived in an effort to bring together the aging and young families since the presence of small children proves beneficial to the health of the elderly. The mayor and his assistant, Gisèle Beuste, took us to see one residential community where young and old live side by side in homes that face one another surrounding a courtyard. We came upon a group of aged persons playing cards. The mayor explained that the physical layout of the community affords a feeling of protection to those who are vulnerable.

Mayor Beaudran also stressed agriculture and the emphasis that the slow philosophy places upon preserving biodiversity. He is especially proud of the large, portly "Mirandaise" cows, the Gascon Black Pigs whose floppy ears cover their eyes (referred to as an "ancient" and "exceptional" pig), and the Gascon chickens that the city has protected and helped nurture. Indeed, in the 1950s the hens of the region began to dwindle in number due to industrialized farming, but a small group of committed farmers and nature enthusiasts managed to reverse this trend, even founding an organization, *la Poule Gasconne*, devoted to saving this bird. We visited a nearby farm with Mayor Beaudran and Madame Beuste, slipping plastic bags over our shoes in order to wade through the mud and visit the animals.

In nearby Saint-Antonin-Noble-Val, also in the Occitanie, sustainable agriculture similarly factors prominently in its adherence to *Cittaslow* principles. This charming medieval town prides itself on its Sunday farmers' market, an important and lively event that brings out the whole town and then some. When we visited the office of Denis Ferté, then the mayor's assistant and now the mayor, he explained that efforts to introduce a supermarket in Saint-Antonin met with clear disdain. The area cherishes its locally grown products, including lavender and its damson plum which came to France during the Crusades and has not been cross-bred since. I was sent away with a jar for my journey.

Interviews conducted in Holland, France, the United Kingdom, Positano, San Miniato, Florence, and Piedmont, Italy, all returned to the centrality of agriculture. No one had nice things to say about mono-farming on a large scale, and at the extreme some persons targeted it as a leading culprit behind the erosion of local identities and a sense of community. Indeed, Saturnini maintained that his eagerness to extend the philosophy of Slow Food to city life as expressed in *Cittaslow* originated with his personal concern that the disappearance of small farms would cause the extinction of various products. He agreed with Petrini that small farms and the preservation of traditional farming methods are crucial in resisting the incursions of agrifarming and globalization, a resistance evidenced in the recent uptake in shepherding as a chosen lifestyle among young Italians.[11]

Several volunteers concede that a phenomenon like *Cittaslow* is better tailored to civilizations that are older than the United States, and that have a past rooted in an older, ancient or medieval framework. Take the example of artisanal products, which in the United States often carry kitschy, hipster connotations. While some efforts to revive low-tech practices earnestly seek to sustain or reclaim the past—for instance, making candles identical to those in the early days of the republic, or promoting Native American jewelry—artisanal products on American soil often suggest a countercultural strain defiant of the mainstream. Yet when I met with two Florentine women in order to learn about their "Historiam Firenze," an organization committed to reproducing sauces consumed in antiquity, clearly something else was at play. This revival of a gastronomical past was less a defiant act of counterculture and more a culinary excavation; it was a less an expression of dissent and more a celebration of ancient gourmandizing. The founders of this organization met with me in Florence in December 2019. They explained that Historiam Firenze is an innovative undertaking that devotes itself to *"salse antiche,"* or ancient sauces, such as those consumed by the ancient Etruscans and ancient Romans. Their ambition is in part to revive Old World recipes worth retaining, while also seeking to further the growing cultural trend of cherishing artisanal creations.[12]

The women insist that Italians are eager to learn about older cooking techniques and artisanal products, both out of interest in the past and a desire to escape the standardization that accompanies modernization. While Historiam Firenze claims no formal ties to Slow Food, the women maintain that their organization is "one way of going slow," of connecting to the past and enriching the present. The recent uptake in shepherding as a chosen lifestyle among young Italians also suggests as much. The pay is poor, but the work is steady and provides "fresh air and as much pecorino cheese as you can eat."[13] Yet such artisanal enrichments are read differently on American soil where they present themselves more as an expression of disaffection with homogenized culture than an eagerness to connect to a past.

My conversations with *Cittaslow* USA advocates clearly register a degree of defeatism, since the movement here simply hasn't gotten off the ground as it has elsewhere. Yet we have seen that other expressions of slow register more optimism, confident that a "slow and curvy" philosophy might take root in the twenty-first century. Taking the long view I see reasons for optimism, which I will summarize in the Conclusion.

NOTES

1. https://slowfoodusa.org/network/chapters/, accessed June 8, 2020.

2. Across the country, these efforts are funded by various sources, many of them private. Yet all receive the guidance of "Agriculture in the Classroom," a project that comes under the aegis of the USDA as well as the National Agriculture in the Classroom Organization. In California, state-wide funding for school gardens also existed during the Schwarzenegger administration thanks to the impetus of First Lady Maria Shriver whose book, *Gardens for Learning: Creating and Sustaining Your School Gardens*, inspired many to get involved. (Maria Shriver, *Gardens for Learning: Creating and Sustaining Your School Gardens,* California School Garden Network, 2006). And as is well known, First Lady Michelle Obama carried this tradition forward at the national level by inviting children to help her plant a garden at the White House, an experience she describes as a balm for her spirit thanks to the enthusiastic inquisitiveness and disarming manner of the children. Although there was nothing explicitly "Slow Food" about Mrs. Obama's garden, her eagerness to stem the growing tide of childhood obesity and diabetes and encourage children to take an interest in healthful habits surely dovetails with the movement's ambitions.

3. "Amsterdam Wonderland" blog.

4. *Chef's Table*, Episode Two.

5. Dan Barber, *The Third Plate: Field Notes on the Future of Food* (New York: The Penguin Press, 2014), 10. .

6. http://www.slowfoodphilly.org/wp-content/uploads/A-Thousand-Gardens-in-Africa.pdf, accessed June 17, 2020.

7.Petrini, *Food and Freedom*, 225.

8. In this, Jim resembles the argument made in Garret M. Broad's *More Than Just Food: Food Justice and Community Change,* University of California Press, 2016.

9. Petrini, *Food and Freedom,* 55.

10. https://www.unisg.it/en/administration/history-mission/, accessed July 18, 2020.

11. https://www.telegraph.co.uk/finance/jobs/9244441/Young-Italians-flock-to-become-shepherds.html, accessed December 30, 2019.

12. The webpage for Historiam Firenze explains that their sauces are made from local ingredients, contain nothing artificial, and follow the recipes supplied by the ancient Roman gourmet, Marcus Gavius Apicius. Marcus Gavius was a member of the educated Roman elite who lived in the first century A.D., under the reign of the Emperor Tiberius. He was famous for his luxuriant dinners such that Tertullian dubbed him the patron saint of cooks; subsequently, the ancient cookbook, *Apicio*, is named after him. True, it may be that the name "Apicius" attributes itself to an earlier gastronome who lived in the first century B.C., and whose love of fine food caused his name to morph into a generalized nickname for anyone enamored of the culinary arts and entertaining. Whatever its genealogy, the cookbook *Apicio* represents the source of Historiam Firenze's ancient sauces.

A staple of the ancient Etruscan and Roman cuisines was the sauce known as "garum," a strong-tasting concoction derived from fish, fish innards, and herbs that has been allowed to ferment in the Mediterranean sun. Garum served as a flavoring in many dishes and was even put in the water. It was used as an antidote to an array of maladies, from earaches to tonsillitis to aching joints. For Katia and Francesca's business, however, they use a variation on garum known as "allec" derived from the more solid portion of garum. In addition to allec they offer three flavorful sauces. "Salsa di vaso Apicio" errs on the side of aromatic herbs and delicate spices rather than the stronger flavors preferred in antiquity. "Epytirum" is a dip made from olives and spices not unlike tapenade. Recognizing that many philosophers and scholars have ruminated about the inspiring olive, Katia and Francesca have chosen to stay close to Cato's recipe for epytirum: olives, fennel, rue, mint, coriander, cumin, and oil. There is also *"piccatiglio rosso"* for "lovers of decisive taste" which, thanks to its use of tomatoes, demonstrates the entrepreneurs' willingness to adapt ancient recipes to modern taste buds, since tomatoes only reached Europe around 1550. The recipe combines tomatoes with chili peppers, capers, vinegar, and herbs.

Katia and Francesca sell their products online, work with gastronomical tours, and take part in tabling events such as Christmas bazaars and wine tastings. They also participate in the purchasing cooperative mentioned earlier, GAS, with which UNISG also joins forces in an effort to fight corporate profit-seeking and bring consumers closer to producers.

13. https://www.telegraph.co.uk/finance/jobs/9244441/Young-Italians-flock-to-become-shepherds.html, accessed December 30, 2019.

Conclusion

A New Humanism: Forging a Revolution at a Snail's Pace

Americans can learn so much from the philosophy of slow. Whether it becomes our official way of life or simply remains an influential social movement, there is so much in its teachings that can benefit our culture, especially when we finally emerge from the ravages of covid-19 and regain momentum after the latter's physical, economic, and emotional devastation. Moreover, as the critical vulnerability of our planet reveals itself in ever more worrisome fashion, the new humanism proposed in these pages offers a needed corrective to the carbon-heavy footprint of the American Dream. It offers a blueprint for going forward in ways that not only reduce our harmful impact on the earth but redefines the time-honored narrative of human sovereignty that places human agency and control at the center of things. By displacing this human-centered approach and placing human life on a continuum with the natural world, this reoriented vantage point necessarily diminishes our footprint in ways that are not only propitious, but essential for our shared survival.

Given the degree to which a McDonaldized worldview has burrowed into our shared narrative and collective imagination, there is reason to doubt that the Noah-like sensibility that Petrini advocates will replace the Promethean ethos that typifies America's persona. Despite the imprint that environmental activists such as Rachel Carson, John Muir, Wendell Berry, and others have made on our society, our current perilous state indicates that the harm of our collective footprint outweighs any helpful change forged by progressive green forces. Moreover, the sheer success of fast and processed foods, the staggering volume of fast fashion, the pervasiveness of determined helicopter parenting and other offshoots of the virus of speed all point to the fact that slow is hardly mainstream Americana. Added to this is *Cittaslow's* lack of long term success on American soil despite the efforts of committed enthusiasts who believe in its philosophy. In light of this reality, one might conclude that an aesthetic sensibility that proceeds in slow and curvy fashion will never supplant the aggressive forward drive of the current American

Dream and allow a new humanism to take root. For advocates of slow, then, the optimistic pronouncement that "we are winning" might sound quixotic. At the moment, slow is an outlier, a dissident position yet to occupy center stage.

Yet three things allow me to retain a hopeful outlook. Even if the specific organizational labels addressed in these pages are never explicitly embraced—for instance, even if Slow Food or *Cittaslow* per se never become mainstream Americana—various changes in our culture since the twentieth century lead me to believe that another sea change is possible. Because our country has come under the sway of various social movements in the past and has experienced seismic shifts under their influence, I see hope for the future of slow on American soil. Specifically, these movements include precisely the three examined in these pages: the sensational spread of fast and processed food since the 1950s, the successful infiltration of "hippie food" since roughly the 1960s, and the more recent growth in foodie culture that now captures so many Americans' attention. So deeply embedded are these culinary trends in mainstream America today that we easily forget how, not so long ago, they represented the renegade tastes of an iconoclastic culture outside the mainstream. They used to be the outliers. Yet their influence ultimately took hold of the culture at large and gradually infiltrated the sensibilities of great swathes of the population; they went from being outsiders to being gastronomic staples that today define many Americans' lifestyle. Given this history, there is hope for other gastronomic sea changes to come.

Moreover, between the devastating impact of covid-19 and the pronounced vulnerability of our planet, this may be a propitious time for Americans to heed the philosophy of slow. The difficult and at times tragic realities in which we find ourselves ensconced may help propel a change, for especially when it comes to our imperiled planet, we know that a dramatic reorientation of our lifestyle is needed. Whether we call it a "new humanism" or not, we know that a reprioritizing in our relationship to Mother Nature is in order, for as Petrini affirms, "a gastronome who is not an environmentalist is surely stupid."[1]

As we have seen, the social movements discussed in these pages all had momentum behind them that helped catapult the advocated change. For instance, the success of fast food was greatly facilitated by the growth in automobile sales, the expansion of the American highway system, and the cultural cachet that surrounded the car in the post-war years. It was our nation's infatuation with the automobile that played a large role in cementing the affinities among crosses, flags, and fast food, as per Ray Kroc. In mid-century America, being behind the wheel became an extension of one's identity and declared one's patriotism; it expressed one's status and belief in the American way of life. Thus, when fast food began to feature the drive-through, its meanings extended far beyond the hamburgers and fries purchased at the window: now it spoke of the nation's prosperity and growth in the post-war years. Kroc was quick to perceive the cultural capital to be found in fast food and cashed in on its signifying richness. The same is true of the general explosion in consumer goods that accompanied the growing popularity of fast and frozen foods; these time-savers went hand in hand with a country on the go, making progress and moving forward both literally and figuratively.

If the rise of fast and processed food was propelled by discernable prosperity and optimism, the success of healthful hippie food benefited from an opposing sentiment: the fact that many early advocates committed to countercultural trends felt betrayed by their country and disaffected by its politics. As Jonathan Kauffman convincingly argues, the food originally consumed by longhairs, war resisters, and those interested in communal living represented the repast of persons who opposed the meanings behind the USA in the 1960s and 1970s. Despite the fact that health-oriented precursors to hippie fare were supportive of the mainstream and eager to identify as American, the hippie movement saw itself as roundly oppositional to the reigning American Dream. Everything from the hippies' peripatetic mobility to their unconventional dress to their preferences in food became an expression of opposition to the mainstream, a youthful blowback against the staid authority. Indeed, the hippie movement's healthful alternative to processed and fast foods became synonymous with protest against the Vietnam War, the spread of American imperialism, our domestic racial tensions, and the economic reality of Michael Harrington's "other America."[2] Hippie identity helped catapult an interest in organic food whose meanings initially condemned capitalist ideology and America's hegemonic standing in the world arena; organic, chemical-free comestibles low on the food chain came to represent countercultural push back against the industries that dominated Americans' relationship to food. Going back to the land paralleled the hippie claim that, as a nation, we needed to go back to the basics of our ideology and redefine who we are; having strayed too far from our better selves, it was time to rethink the prevalent iteration of the American Dream.

Yet this disillusionment with the mainstream that gave rise to a gastronomic ideology eventually found its way into our everyday culinary repertoire, and what was exotic then has by now become a commonplace in our grocery store shopping carts. Reading Kauffman's informative book clarifies how, in the early days of the hippie movement, items such a yogurt, bean sprouts, and wheat germ were rarified, to be found only in health food stores stocking esoteric, unusual foods that most Americans never consumed. They were heavily infused with countercultural connotations: love beads, marijuana, peace signs, and VW vans. Yet over time, little by little, these items ingratiated themselves into our collective palate as our interest in better health expanded. They shed their hippie veneer and gained admission to the mainstream. The fact that they are now easily available in grocery stores everywhere offers insight into how radically America's culinary habits have changed, along with the general interest in nutrition—"nutritionism"—that by now represents big business. And importantly, it was mainstream America that gradually took an interest in hippie comestibles, not the counterculture that pandered to the mainstream. That such change is possible offers hope to the slow movement, clarifying how what appears esoteric one day can become commonplace the next. Although still unknown to many Americans, the roughly 115 chapters of Slow Food USA may thus experience an incorporation into the mainstream parallel to that of countercultural hippie food now gone mainstream.

Added to these changes that occurred in the mid-twentieth century—the rise of fast and processed food as well as healthful organic cuisine—is the sea change that we are currently witnessing: the exploding popularity of foodie culture and widespread interest in celebrity chefs. Without question, the art of gastronomy is establishing a firm foothold in mainstream America as the population at large evinces an unprecedented fascination with the art of cooking and eating well. Gastronomy is without question a current American fascination, a cultural trend that has burrowed deeply into our collective conscience and captured our imagination. The meteoric rise in foodie culture hardly confines itself to an economic or epicurean elite, illustrating the difference between today's widespread epicureanism and the smaller, former côterie of connoisseurs who watched Julia Child's television show, read *Gourmet* magazine, and learned about wine. Today's epicureans hail from all segments of society and different age groups; even younger Americans are on board with this new sensibility, many approaching gastronomy as an issue of democratic principles and social justice.[3] They view a serious interest in food as an expression of social activism and a commitment to change: vegetarianism, veganism, going organic, and other practices stand on par with avoiding plastic, discrediting all cruelty to animals, and lightening our carbon footprint through a reduction in our consumption of beef. Foodie culture indeed has widespread appeal, for it resonates with gastronomic passions as well as social and political convictions. Kamp is right, this *is* a great time to be an eater in America, since the food just keeps getting better.

Darryl Furrow's *American Foodie* takes us deeper into this explosion in gastronomy all across the country: why has epicureanism so captured the American imagination at this moment in our history? Why have celebrity chefs garnered such attention as they seek to both educate and entertain in their kitchens and on their road trips, exploring culinary experiences that Americans are eager to learn about and to reproduce at home? As we have seen, Furrow's insightful reading of the situation connects our newfound passion to the excessive incursions of the administered state, now present in our lives 24/7 thanks to the power and reach of both media culture and social media that are ever-present in our lives. Furrow perceives a pervasive need to escape the intrusive reach of bureaucracy's arm and to eschew the dictates of instrumental rationality, to be replaced instead by beauty, pleasure, and the intensely personal meanings of cooking, recipes, and favorite foods. A gastronomic preference is on the rise in America, he maintains, precisely because we are fatigued by the regulative forces that constantly invade our lives and connect us to impersonal administration devoid of aesthetic appeal. We crave pleasure, in other words, and seek out the satisfaction to be found in gastronomy's treatment of food as art. Furrow persuasively links a cultural phenomenon to a pervasive spiritual exhaustion, a desire to parry the ubiquity of instrumental rationality and replace it with the comforting nuance of aesthetics that views food as poetry. In different guises and from different angles, this same aesthetic craving expresses itself in other iterations of the slow movement, each advocating slow and curvy in its own way.

If the legacy of these three sea changes in American culinary habits is any indicator, it appears eminently possible that the slow movement might burrow deeply into our collective conscious and make a significant impact on how we live. It might contribute to a retooling and reprioritizing of the American Dream in ways that favor a Noah-like sensibility, urging us away from the ideology of constant growth and toward a dethroned human sovereignty that humbly prefers a continuum with the natural world. In ways consistent with Mol's analysis, it might augment our sensitivity to the ways in which we are all interconnected and intimately connected to the earth, such that porous boundaries and permeable identities replace humanism's sovereign subject, allowing a new humanism of interrelationship to prevail. This implicit shift from humanist sovereignty to a new humanism that takes eating as its governing trope may be the biggest contribution of slow. Slow Food, *Cittaslow,* slow fashion, travel, parenting, and other iterations all emphasize our interconnected, interfused identities in ways that underscore our dependence on the other; in this way, they contribute to Horkheimer and Adorno's desired agenda "to prepare a positive concept of enlightenment which liberates its entanglement in blind domination."[4] In the best scenario, the new humanism frees us from this entanglement. Hopefully, we will move in that direction bearing in mind Petrini's prescription not to do so with sadness, but with joy and humor, taking delight in what we do.

NOTES

1. Petrini, *Food & Freedom*, 27.
2. Michael Harrington, The Other America: Poverty in the United States (New York: Scribner, 1997).

3. See especially Stephen Schneider, "Good, Clean, Fair: The Rhetoric of the Slow Food Movement," in *College English*, Vol. 70, No. 4, March 1, 2008, 384–402.

4. Horkheimer and Adorno, *Dialectic of Enlightenment*, Preface, xviii.

Bibliography

Adorno, Theodor. *Aesthetic Theory*. Translated by Robert Hullot-Kentor. Minneapolis: University of Minnesota Press, 1997.

———. "Free Time." In *The Culture Industry: Selected Essays on Mass Culture*. Ed. J. M. Bernstein. London: Verso, 1991. 187–197.

———. *Minima Moralia: Reflections on a Damaged Life*. Translated by E. F. N. Jephcott. London: Verso, 2005.

Ambrosino, Brandon. "Four Hundred Years Later, Scholars Still Debate Whether Shakespeare's 'Merchant of Venice' Is Anti-Semitic." *Smithsonian Magazine*, https://www.smithsonianmag.com/arts-culture/why-scholars-still-debate-whether-or-not-shakespeares-merchant-venice-anti-semitic-180958867/, accessed June 14, 2020.

Amsterdam Wonderland blog. https://amsterdamwonderland.com.

Andersen, Kip. *Cowspiracy, the Sustainability Secret*. Kip Andersen and Keegan Kuhn. Santa Rosa, CA: A.U.M. Films and Media/First Spark, 2014.

Anderson, Benedict. *Imagined Communities: Reflections on the Origin and Spread of Nationalism*. London: Verso, 2006.

Andrews, Geoff. *The Slow Food Story: Politics and Pleasure*. Montreal: Montreal-Queens University Press, 2008.

Archer, John. "The Resilience of Myth: The Politics of the American Dream." *Traditional Dwelling and Settlements Review*, Vol. 25, No. 2, Spring 2014, 7–21.

Ashton, Alison. "Padma Lakshmi Celebrates America's Flavors." *Parade, Los Angeles Times*, June 7, 2020, 12–15.

Barber, Dan. *The Third Plate: Field Notes on the Future of Food*. New York: Penguin Press, 2014.

"Beef Consumption in the United States from 2002 to 2020 (in billion pounds)." https://www.statista.com/statistics/542890/beef-consumption-us/, accessed November 1, 2021.

Benjamin, Walter. "The Work of Art in the Age of Mechanical Reproduction," In *Illuminations: Essays and Reflections. Translated by Harry Zohn. New York*: Schocken Books, 1968/2007.

———. "Theses on the Philosophy of History." In *Illuminations*. Translated by Harry Zohn. New York: Harcourt Brace Jovanovich, 1968. 253–264.

Bennett, Jane. *The Enchantment of Modern Life: Attachments, Crossings, and Ethics.* Princeton: Princeton University Press, 2001.

Berg, Maggie, and Barbara K. Seeber. *The Slow Professor: Challenging the Culture of Speed.* Toronto: University of Toronto Press, 2016.

Berger, Ben. *Attention Deficit Democracy: The Paradox of Civic Engagement.* Princeton, NJ: Princeton University Press, 2011.

Berman, Marshall. *All That Is Solid Melts into Air: the Experience of Modernity.* New York: Penguin, 1988.

Bhabha, Homi. *The Location of Culture.* London: Routledge, 1994.

Bobrow-Strain, Aaron. *White Bread: A Social History of the Store-Bought Loaf.* Boston: Beacon Press, 2012.

Boisvert, Raymond D., and Lisa Heldke. *Philosophers At Table: On Food and Being Human.* London: Reaktion Books, 2016.

Brillat-Savarin, Jean Anthelme. The Physiology of Taste, or Meditations on Transcendental Gastronomy. Translated by M. F. K. Fisher. New York: Vintage Classics, 2009.

Broad, Garret M. *More Than Just Food: Food Justice and Community Change.* Berkeley, CA: University of California Press, 2016.

Brown, Wendy. *Undoing the Demos: Neoliberalism's Stealth Revolution. Brooklyn:* Zone Books, 2016.

Caputi, Mary. "'An Idiot With a Spoon': Adorno, Petrini, and the Oppositional Politics of Slow Food." *Reading Adorno: The Endless Road Edited by Amirhosein Khandizani.* New York: Palgrave Macmillan, 2019.

Carr, Nicholas. *The Shallows: What the Internet Is Doing to Our Brains.*" New York: W.W. Norton & Co., 2020.

Carson, Rachel. *Silent Spring.* New York: Mariner Books, 2002.

———. *The Edge of the Sea.* Boston: Mariner Books, 1998.

———. *The Sea Around Us.* New York: Oxford University Press, 2018.

———. *Under the Sea Wind.* New York: Penguin Classics, 2007.

Castelhanos, Liliana. "Fast Fashion vs. Slow Fashion," https://www.youtube.com/watch?v=nkjsdNlVnAI&t=2s, accessed September 4, 2021.

Castiglione, Baldassare. *The Book of the Courtier.* Translated by George Bull. New York: Penguin, 1976.

Chandler, Adam. *Drive-Thru Dreams: A Journey Through the Heart of America's Fast Food Kingdom.*" New York: Flatiron Books, 2019.

Chatelain, Marcia. *Franchise: The Golden Arches in Black America.* New York: Liveright Publishing Corporation, 2020.

Chef's Table. Season One, Episode One. "Massimo Bottura." David Gelb. Netflix, April 26, 2015.

Chef's Table. Season One, Episode Two. "Dan Barber." David Gelb. Netflix, April 26, 2015.

Chertkovskaya, Ekaterina, Alexander Paulsson, and Stefania Barca, eds. *Toward a Political Economy of Degrowth (Transforming Capitalism).* Lanham, MD: Rowman & Littlefield, 2019.

Chignell, Andrew, Terence Cuneo, and Matthew C. Halteman, eds. *Philosophy Comes to Dinner*. New York: Routledge, 2016.

Child, Julia, Louisette Bertholle, and Simone Beck. *Mastering the Art of French Cooking*. New York: Alfred A. Knopf, 2009.

———. *My Life in France*, with Alex Prud'homme. New York: Alfred A. Knopf, 2006.

"Cittaslow International Charter." Accessed March 27, 2020, https://www.cittaslow. org/sites/default/files/content/page/files/257/charter_cittaslow_en_05_18.pdf.

Clancy, Michael. "Practicing Slow: Political and Ethical Implications." In *Slow Tourism, Food, and Cities: Pace and the Search for 'the Good Life.'* Edited by Michael Clancy. New York: Routledge, 2019, 63–73.

Clark, Susan, and Woden Teachout. *Slow Democracy. Rediscovering Community, Bringing Decision-Making Back Home*. White River Junction, VT: Chelsea Green Publishing, 2012.

Connolly, William E. "Speed, Concentric Cultures, and Cosmopolitanism." In *High-Speed Society: Social Acceleration, Power, and Modernity.* Edited by Harmut Rosa and William E. Scheuerman. Philadelphia: Pennsylvania State University Press, 2009, 261–285.

Cowspiracy: The Sustainability Secret. Directed by Kip Andersen and Keegan Kuhn. Santa Rosa, CA: A.U.M. Films and Media/First Spark, 2014.

Cullen, Jim. *The American Dream: A Short History of an Idea That Shaped a Nation*. Oxford: Oxford University Press, 2004.

Curran, Stuart. "The Political Prometheus." *Studies in Romanticism*, Vol. 25, No. 3, Fall 1986, 429–455.

Demetriou, Danielle."How the Japanese Are Putting an End to the Extreme Work Week." https://www.bbc.com/worklife/article/20200114-how-the-japanese-are-putting-an-end-to-death-from-overwork, accessed July 7, 2020.

Dieterle, J. M. *Just Food: Philosophy, Justice and Food.* Lanham, MD: Rowman & Littlefield Publishers, 2015.

Dinesen, Isak."Babette's Feast." In Anecdotes of Destiny. New York: Random House, 1958.

Danielle Demetriou, "How The Japanese Are Putting An End to the Extreme Work Week, https://www.bbc.com/worklife/article/20200114-how-the-japanese-are-putting-an-end-to-death-from-overwork, accessed July 7, 2020.

Dreher, Rod. *Crunchy Cons: How Birkenstocked Burkeans, gun-loving organic gardeners, evangelical free-range farmers, hip homeschooling mamas, right-wing lovers, and their diverse tribe of counter-cultural conservatives plan to save American (or at least the Republican Party).* New York: Crown Forum, 2006.

Epicurus "Letter to Menoeceus." In *Classics of Moral and Political Theory. Edited by Michael L. Morgan. Indianapolis, IN: Hackett, 2005.*

Esquivel, Laura. *Like Water for Chocolate: A Novel in Monthly Installments with Recipes, Romances, and Home Remedies*. Translated by Carol Christensen and Thomas Christensen. New York: Doubleday, 1989.

Ettlinger, Steve. *Twinkie, Deconstructed: My Journey to Discover How the Ingredients Found in Processed Foods Are Grown, Mined (Yes, Mined), and Manipulated into What America Eats.* New York: Hudson Street Press, 2007.

Ferguson, Kennan. *Cookbook Politics.* Philadelphia: University of Pennsylvania Press, 2020.

"Fueling Food Sovereignty in Puerto Rico." https://slowfoodusa.org/fueling-food-sovereignty-in-puerto-rico/, December 16, 2021. Accessed December 18, 2021.

Furrow, Dwight. *American Foodie: Taste, Art, and the Cultural Revolution.* Lanham, MD: Rowman & Littlefield, 2016.

Galvin, Gaby. "The Obesity Rate Now Tops 40%." U.S. News and World Report, February 27, 2020. https://www.usnews.com/news/healthiest-communities/articles/2020-02-27/us-obesity-rate-passes-40-percent, accessed June 4, 2020.

Gates, Bill. *How to Avoid a Climate Disaster.* New York: Alfred A. Knopf, 2021.

Gilbert, Sophie. "Padma Lakshmi's New Food Show Is a Trojan Horse." *Atlantic,* https://www.theatlantic.com/culture/archive/2020/07/padma-lakshmi-hulu-taste-nation-american-cuisine/613915/, accessed October 29, 2021.

Gilson, Dave. "Overworked America: 12 Charts That Will Make Your Blood Boil." *Mother Jones,* July/August 2011, https://www.motherjones.com/politics/2011/05/speedup-americans-working-harder-charts/

"Good, Clean, and Fair: the Slow Food Manifesto for Quality." https://www.slowfood.com/wp-content/uploads/2015/07/Manifesto_Quality_ENG.pdf, accessed August 2, 2021.

Guta, Michael. "Business Owners Can Now Compare Their Working Hours with Global Averages (INFOGRAPHIC)." https://smallbiztrends.com/2018/11/working-hours.html,accessed July 7, 2020.

Hall, Stuart. *Representation: Cultural Representations and Signifying Practices (Culture Media and Identities Series).* London: Sage Publications, 1997.

———. and Paul Du Gay. *Questions of Cultural Identity.* Thousand Oaks, CA: Sage Publications, 1996.

Hanson, Sandra L., and John Kenneth White, eds. *The American Dream in the 21st Century.* Philadelphia: Temple University Press, 2011.

Harrington, Michael. The Other America: Poverty in the United States. New York: Scribner,

Harvey, David. *The Condition of Postmodernity: An Enquiry into the Origins of Cultural Change.* Cambridge, MA: Blackwell, 1990.

Hawken, Paul, ed. *Drawdown: The Most Comprehensive Plan Ever Proposed to Reverse Global Warming.* New York: Penguin Books, 2017.

Hickman, Leo. "Slow Food: Have We Lost Our Appetite?" *Guardian,* February 4, 2009. https://www.theguardian.com/environment/2009/feb/04/slow-food-carlo-petrini, accessed September 20, 2021.

History 101, Episode One, "Fast Food." Laura Stevens. Netflix, May 20, 2020.

Holt-Giménez, Eric. *A Foodie's Guide to Capitalism: Understanding the Political Economy of What We Eat. New York: Monthly Review Press, 2017.*

Honoré, Carl. *In Praise of Slowness: How a Worldwide Movement Is Challenging the Cult of Speed.* New York: HarperCollins Publishers, 2004.

————. *Under Pressure: Rescuing Our Childhood from the Culture of Hyper-Parenting.* New York: HarperCollins Publishers, 2008.

Hooke, Janna H. "Racial Otherness Is Shakespeare's *Othello.*" https://www.academia.edu/28048057/Racial_Otherness_in_Shakespeares_Othello, accessed February 2020.

Horkheimer, Max, and Theodor Adorno. *Dialectic of Enlightenment.* Translated by Edmund Jephcott. Stanford: Stanford University Press, 2002.

Hoskins, Tansy E. *Stitched Up: The Anti-Capitalist Book of Fashion.* London: Pluto Press, 2014.

https://answersingenesis.org/bible-timeline/timeline-for-the-flood/.

https://cookingupastory.com/carlo-petrini-give-value-to-food-part-5.

https://hermeneutics.stackexchange.com/questions/50366/how-long-was-noah-and-his-family-in-the-ark, accessed December 22, 2021.

http://slowfood.com/filemanager/Convivium%20Leader%20Area/Manifesto_ENG.pdf.

https://slowfoodusa.org/network/chapters/, accessed June 8, 2020.

http://www.azquotes.com/author/22147-Carlo_Petrini. Accessed June 15, 2018.

https://www.cdc.gov/diabetes/data/statistics-report/index.html, accessed November 23, 2021.

https://www.cdc.gov/diabetes/data/statistics-report/index.html, accessed November 23, 2021.

https://www.cdc.gov/obesity/data/adult.html.

https://www.cittaslow.org/, accessed March 27, 2020.

https://www.cittaslow.org/sites/default/files/content/page/files/257/charter_cittaslow_en_05_18.pdf.

https://www.commondreams.org/news/2018/12/04/we-have-not-come-here-beg-world-leaders-care-15-year-old-greta-thunberg-tells-cop24?gclid=CjwKCAjwqpP2BRBTEiwAfpiD-92qbAAP6jo-wLHBKLTf5CzVcqm68M_nm8_ngHJh4YaEQTbcoAgXXhoCjTkQAvD_BwE, accessed May 28, 2020.

https://www.cowspiracy.com/blog/2015/11/30/earthtoparis-meat-consumption-and-animal-agriculture-need-to-be-addressed, accessed June 29, 2020.

https://www.google.com/search?q=how+many+food+deserts+are+there+in+the+USA&se_es_tkn=mtgyrpxt.

https://www.historiamfirenze.com/.

https://www.kyrene.org/cms/lib/AZ01001083/Centricity/Domain/894/prometheus%20myth.pdf, accessed March 28, 2020.

http://www.nytimes.com/1986/05/05/style/romans-protest-mcdonald-s.html.

https://www.nytimes.com/2016/08/09/us/politics/donald-trump-diet.html.

https://www.organicwithoutboundaries.bio/2018/09/12/climate-change-mitigation/, accessed March 18, 2020.

https://www.pbs.org/newshour/show/phone-trying-control-life, accessed November 14, 2021.

https://www.quotes.net/mquote/692746, accessed December 3, 2019.

https://www.sciencedaily.com/releases/2021/10/211029114022.htm, accessed December 10, 2021.

https://www.slowfood.com/press-release/slow-food-usa-launches-slow-food-nations/ accessed December 13, 2021.

https://www.slowfood.com/about_us/img_sito/pdf/Companion08_ENG.pdf,accessed.

https://www.slowfood.com/embrace-joy-justice-at-slow-food-nations-2019/.

http://slowfood.com/filemanager/Convivium%20Leader%20Area/Manifesto_ENG.pdf.

https://www.slowfood.com/wp-content/uploads/2015/07/Manifesto_Quality_ENG.pdf, accessed August 2, 2021.

http://www.slowfoodphilly.org/wp-content/uploads/A-Thousand-Gardens-in-Africa.pdf, accessed June 17, 2020.

https://www.slowfoodusa.org/manifesto.

https://slowfoodusa.org/network/chapters/.

http://www.slowfoodphilly.org/wp-content/uploads/A-Thousand-Gardens-in-Africa.pdf, accessed September 15, 2021.

https://www.statista.com/statistics/256040/mcdonalds-restaurants-in-north-america/, accessed December 9, 2021.

https://www.statista.com/statistics/244394/organic-sales-in-the-united-states/, accessed March 18, 2020.

https://www.ted.com/talks/carl_honore_praises_slowness, accessed October 2, 2019.

https://www.telegraph.co.uk/finance/jobs/9244441/Young-Italians-flock-to-become-shepherds.html, accessed November 26, 2019.

https://www.theatlantic.com/ideas/archive/2019/02/religion-workism-making-americans-miserable/583441/.

https://www.theverge.com/interface/2019/4/24/18513450/tristan-harris-downgrading-center-humane-tech.

https://www.unisg.it/en/administration/history-mission/, accessed July 18, 2020.

https://www.youtube.com/watch?v=kyNdzzHUqC4, accessed September 6, 2021.

"Indigenous Terra Madre Network." https://www.slowfood.com/our-network/indigenous/, accessed December 22, 2021.

"Innovation by Tradition," *Cittaslow* in-house publication.

A Place At the Table. Directed by Kristi Jacobson and Lori Silverbush. Brooklyn, NY: Motto Pictures/Los Angeles, CA: Participant Production Company, 2012.

Junker, Yohana Agra. "On Covid-19, U.S. Uprisings, and Black Lives: A Mandate to Regenerate All Our Relations." *Journal of Feminist Studies in Religion*, Vol. 36, No. 2, Fall 2020.

Kamp, David. *The United States of Arugula: How We Became a Gourmet Nation.* New York: Broadway Books, 2006.

Kaplan, David M. *The Philosophy of Food. Berkeley: University* of California Press, 2012.

Kasiganesan, Harinath. "Doing Farming the Organic Way." TED Talk, November 12, 2019, https://www.youtube.com/watch?v=xjVHkacNkwk.

Kauffman, Jonathan. *Hippie Food: How Back-To-The-Landers, Longhairs, and Revolutionaries Changed The Way We Eat.* New York: William Morrow, 2018.

Kaufman-Osborn, Timothy V. *Creatures of Prometheus: Gender and the Politics of Technology. Lanham, MD:*Rowman & Littlefield, 2000.

Kaur, Harmeet. "The coronavirus pandemic is hitting black and brown Americans especially hard on all fronts." CNN, May 8, 2020.

Kenney, Kim. "History of 1950s Cars—It Still Runs." https://itstillruns.com/history-cars-5039048.html, accessed December 10, 2021.

Kow, Simon. "Enlightenment Universalism? Bayle and Montesquieu on China." *The European Legacy: Toward New Paradigms, Vol. 19, No. 3,* 347–358.

Kroc, Ray, with Robert Anderson. *Grinding It Out: The Making of McDonald's. Washington, DC:* Henry Regnery Company, 1977.

Latouche, Serge. *Farewell to Growth.* Translated by David Macey. Cambridge, UK: Polity Press, 2009.

"Leader of Nobel Peace Prize-winning World Food Programme on Global Starvation Crisis." *PBS Newshour,* Amna Nawaz, October 9, 2020.

Lin, Stanley. "Otherness as a Dramatic Device in *The Merchant of Venice* and *Othello.*" https://www.academia.edu/13506577/Otherness_as_A_Dramatic_Device_in_The_Merchant_of_Venice_and_Othello_, accessed February 2020.

Lindholm, Charles, and Siv B. Lie. "You Eat What You Are: Cultivated Taste and the Pursuit of Authenticity in the Slow Food Movement." In *Culture of the Slow: Social Deceleration in an Accelerated World.* Edited by Nick Obaldiston. London: Palgrave Macmillan, 2013. 52–70.

Little, Tyler. *The Future of Fashion: Understanding Sustainability in the Fashion Industry.* Potomac, MD: New Degree Press, 2018.

Loomba, Ania. *Shakespeare, Race, and Colonialism. Oxford:* University Press, 2002.

———, and Martin Orkin. "Shakespeare and the Postcolonial Question." In *Postcolonial Shakespeares.* Edited by Ania Loomba and Martin Orkin. New York: Routledge, 2004, 1–19.

Manella, Gabriele. "*Cittaslow*, the Emilia-Romagna Case." In *Slow Tourism, Food and Cities: Pace and the Search for the Good Life.* Edited by Michael Clancy. London: Routledge, 2018, 145–165.

———. Eros and Civilization: A Philosophical Inquiry Into Freud. Boston: Beacon Press, 1974.

Marcuse, Herbert. *An Essay on Liberation.* Boston: Beacon Press, 1969.

———. *One-Dimensional Man.* Boston: Beacon Press, 1991.

Miller, G.E. "The U.S. Is the Most Over worked Developed Nation in the World."20somethingfinance,https://20somethingfinance.com/american-hours-worked-productivity-vacation

Minney, Safia. *Slave to Fashion.*Oxford, UK: New Internationalist Publications Ltd, 2017.

———. *Slow: Aesthetic Meets Ethics.* Oxford, UK: New Internationalist Publications Ltd. 2016.

Minuti, Rolando. *Studies on Montesquieu: Mapping Political Diversity. New York:* Springer, 2018.

Mol, Annemarie. *Eating in Theory.* Durham: Duke University Press, 2021.

Montanari, Massimo. *Italian Identity in the Kitchen, or Food and the Nation.* Translated by Beth Archer Brombert. New York: Columbia University Press, 2013.

Montesquieu, Charles de Secondat. *Persian Letters.* Translated by C. J. Betts. New York: Penguin Classics, 2004.

Muoio, Anna. "We All Go to The Same Place. Let Us Go There Slowly." Fast Company, https://www.fastcompany.com/40068/we-all-go-same-place-let-us-go-there-slowly

Muthu, Sankar. *Enlightenment Against Empire. Princeton, NJ:* University Press, 2003.

Otero, Gerardo. *The Neoliberal Diet: Healthy Profits, Unhealthy People. Austin: University* of Texas Press, 2018.

Parker, Ashley. "Donald Trump's Diet: He'll Have Fries with That." www.nytimes.com/2016/08/09/us/politics/donald-trump-diet.html, accessed June 3, 2018.

Parkins, Wendy, and Geoffrey Craig. *Slow Living.* Oxford: Berg, 2006.

Patel, Raj, and Eric Holt-Giménez, eds. *Food Rebellions: Crisis and the Hunger for Justice. Oakland, CA:* Food First Books, 2012.

———. *Stuffed and Starved: The Hidden Battle for the World Food System.* Brooklyn, NY: Melville House, 2012.

Petrini, Carlo. *Food and Freedom: How the Slow Food Movement Is Changing the World through Gastronomy.* Translated by John Irving. New York: Rizzoli Ex Libris, 2015.

———, and Gigi Padovani. *Slow Food Revolution: A New Culture for Eating and Living.* Translated by Francesca Santovetti. New York: Rizzoli, 2006.

———. *Slow Food: The Case for Taste.* Translated by William McCuaig. New York: Columbia University Press, 2001.

———. *Slow Food Nation: Why Our Food Should Be Good, Clean, and Fair.* Translated by Carla Furlan and Jonathan Hunt. New York: Rizzoli Ex Libris, 2013.

———. *Terrafutura, Dialoghi con Papa Francesco Sull'Ecologia Integrale.* (Florence/Milan/Bra: Giunti/www.slowfoodeditore.it: Slow Food Editore, 2020).

Pieper, Josef. *Leisure: The Basis of Culture.* Translated by Alexander Dru. New York: Pantheon Books, 1964.

Pollan, Michael. *Food Rules: An Eater's Manual.* New York: Penguin, 2009.

———. *In Defense of Food: An Eater's Manifesto.* New York: Penguin Books, 2009.

———. *Omnivore's Dilemma: A Natural History of Four Meals.* New York: Penguin, 2007.

Popham, Peter. "Carlo Petrini: The Slow Food Gourmet Who Started a Revolution." *Independent,* December 10, 2009, www.independent.co.uk/lifestyle/food-and-drink/features/carlo-petrini-the-slow-food-gourmet-who-started-a-revolution-1837223.html, accessed June 5, 2018.

Press, Clare. *Wardrobe Crisis: How We Went from Sunday Best to Fast Fashion.* New York: Skyhorse Publishing, 2018.

Proust, Marcel. *Swann's Way.* Translated by C. K. Scott Moncrieff and Terence Kilmartin. New York: Vintage Books, 1989.

Putnam, Robert D. *Our Kids: The American Dream in Crisis.* New York: Simon & Schuster, 2015.

Rawal, Sanjay. *Gather: The Fight to Revitalize Our Native Foodways.* 2020.

Ritzer, George. *The McDonaldization of Society.* Thousand Oaks, CA: Sage Publications, 2013.

Rockhill, Gabriel. *Interventions in Contemporary Thought: History, Politics, Aesthetics*. Edinburgh: Edinburgh University Press, 2016.

Rosa, Hartmut. *Social Acceleration: A New Theory of Modernity*. Translated by Jonathan Trejo-Mathys. New York: Columbia University Press, 2015.

Rosenblum, Mort. *A Goose in Toulouse and Other Culinary Adventures in France*. New York: Hyperion, 2000.

Ross, Robert. *Slaves to Fashion: Poverty and Abuse in the New Sweatshops*. Ann Arbor, MI: University of Michigan Press, 2004.

Samuel, Lawrence R. *The America Dream: A Cultural History*. Syracuse: Syracuse University Press, 2014.

Scheuerman, William E. "Citizenship and Speed." In *High-Speed Society: Social Acceleration, Power, and Modernity*. Edited by Harmut Rosa and William E. Scheuerman. Philadelphia: Pennsylvania State University Press, 2009, 287–306.

Schlosser, Eric. *Fast Food Nation: The Dark Side of the All-American Meal*. New York: Harper Perennial, 2004.

———. and Charles Wilson. *Chew on This: Everything You Don't Want to Know About Fast Food*. Boston: Houghton Mifflin, 2007.

Schneider, Stephen. "Good, Clean, Fair: the Rhetoric of the Slow Food Movement." *College English*, vol. 70 (4), March 1, 2008, 384–402.

Schoolman, Morton. *Reason and Horror: Critical Theory, Democracy, and Aesthetic Individuality*, Routledge, 2001.

Schor, Juliet R. *True Wealth: How and Why Millions of Americans Are Creating a Time-Rich, Ecologically Light, Small Scale, High-Satisfaction Economy*, Penguin Books, 2010.

Searching for Italy. Episodes 1–6. Stanley Tucci, Raw Television, February 14– March 21, 2021.

Seeds: The Untold Story. 2020.

Sejian, Veerasamy. "Global Climate Change: Role of Livestock." *Asian Journal of Agricultural Sciences* 3(1), 2011, 19–25.

Shakespeare, William. *The Merchant of Venice*. In *The Riverside Shakespeare*, edited by G. Blakemore Evans. New York: Houghton Mifflin Company, 1974, 250–285.

———. *The Tragedy of Othello, the Moor of Venice*. In *The Riverside Shakespeare*, edited by G. Blakemore Evans, Houghton Mifflin Company, 1974, 1203–1248.

Shames, Laurence. "The More Factor," in *Signs of Life in the USA*.Edited by Sonia Maasik and Jack Solomon. Boston: Bedford/St. Martin's, 2003. 56–63.

Shelley, Mary. *Frankenstein, or The Modern Prometheus*. Edited by J. Paul Hunter. New York: W. W. Norton & Company, 1996.

Shelley, Percy Bysshe. *Prometheus Unbound: A Lyrical Drama in Four Acts*, (Los Angeles: Black Box Press, 2007).

Shiva, Vandana. *Biopiracy: The Plunder of Nature and Knowledge*. Brooklyn, NY: South End Press, 1999.

———. *Earth Democracy: Justice, Sustainability, and Peace*. Berkeley, CA: North Atlantic Books, 2015.

———. *Reclaiming the Commons: Biodiversity, Traditional Knowledge, and the Rights of Mother Earth*. Santa Fe, NM: Synergenic Press, 2020.

————. *Stolen Harvest: The Hijacking of the Global Food Supply.* Lexington, KY: University Press of Kentucky, 2016.

————. *Who Really Feeds the World?: The Failures of Agribusiness and the Promise of Agroecology.* Berkeley, CA: North Atlantic Books, 2016.

Shriver, Maria. *Gardens for Learning: Creating and Sustaining Your School Garden.* Irvine, CA: California School Garden Network, 2006.

Singh, Jyotsna G. *Shakespeare and Postcolonial Theory. London:* Bloomsbury, 2019.

slowfood.com/filemanager/Convivium%20Leader%20Area/Manifesto_ENG.pdf, accessed October 28, 2016.

Sohn, Dehyun, Hee-Jung Jang, and Timothy Jung. *Go Slow and Curvy: Understanding the Philosophy of the Cittaslow^slowcity Phenomenon.* Cham, Switzerland: Springer, 2015.

Sparks, Jennifer M. *Slow Travel: Escape the Grind and Explore the World. Garden City, NY:* Morgan James Publishing, 2019.

Steakin, William. https://www.aol.com/article/news/2017/07/27/scaramucci-says-trump-s-love-for-burgers-and-pizza-proves-hes-n/23052702.

Stille, Alexander. *The Sack of Rome*: *How a Beautiful European Country with a Fabled History and a Storied Culture Was Taken Over by a Man Named Silvio Berlusconi. New York:* Penguin, 2006.

"Sugar: The Bitter Truth." https://www.youtube.com/watch?v=T8G8tLsl_A4.

Suro, Mary Davis. "Romans Protest McDonald's." *New York Times.* May 5, 1986, accessed July 28, 2017, http://www.nytimes.com/1986/05/05/style/romans-protest-mcdonald-s.html.

Sweeney, Kevin W. *The Aesthetics of Food: The Philosophical Debate about What We Eat and Drink. Lanham, MD:* Rowman & Littlefield International, 2018.

Tasch, Woody. *Inquiries into the Nature of Slow Money: Investing As If Food, Farms and Fertility Mattered. White River Junction, VT:* Chelsea Green Publishing, 2010.

Taste the Nation. Episode One.

The Biggest Little Farm. Sandra Keats and John Chester, Moorpark, CA: FarmLore Films, Los Angeles, C: LD Entertainment, New York: Impact Partners. Artemis Rising Foundation, 2019.

The Catholic Bible. New York: Oxford University Press, 1995.

"The *Cittaslow* Manifesto." *Cittaslow*: International Network of Cities Where the Living Is Good, https://www.cittaslow.org/content/cittaslow-manifesto, accessed December 16, 2021.

"The Deeply Unequal Consequences of the Pandemic." *The PBS Newshour*, Amna Navaz, October 2, 2020.

The Founder. John Lee Hancock. FilmNation Entertainment/The Combine/Faliro House Productions/S.A., 2016.

The PBS Newshour. January 30, 2017.

The PBS Newshour. June 13, 2018.

The PBS Newshour, Amna Nawaz,. "Leader of Nobel Peace Prize-winning World Food Programme on Global Starvation Crisis," October 9, 2020.

The PBS Newhour, Amna Nawaz. "The Deeply Unequal Consequences of the Pandemic," October 2, 2020.

The PBS Newshour, Amna Nawaz. "Leader of Nobel Peace Prize-winning World Food Programme on Global Starvation Crisis," October 9, 2020.

"The Slow Food Manifesto." http://slowfood.com/filemanager/Convivium%20 Leader%20Area/Manifesto_ENG.pdf, accessed August 18, 2018.

Thomas, Dana. *Fashionopolis: The Price of Fast Fashion—and the Future of Clothes*. New York: Penguin Press, 2019.

Thompson, Derek. "Workism Is Making Americans Miserable." *Atlantic*, February 24, 2019.

Tickell, Josh. *Kiss the Ground: How the Food You Eat Can Reverse Climate Change, Heal Your Body & Ultimately Save Our World*. New York: Atria/Enliven Books, 2018.

Tocci, Giovanni. "Slow and Intelligent Cities: When Slow Is Also Smart." In *Slow Tourism, Food and Cities. Edited by Michael Clancy. London: Routledge*, 2019, 110–128.

Venugopal, Aishwarya, and Hilary Russ. "McDonald's Sales Surge Amid Reopening Despite Staffing 'Challenges.'" Reuters, https://www.reuters.com/business/retail-consumer/mcdonalds-sales-surge-bts-meal-craze-easing-restrictions-2021-07-28/, accessed October 30, 2021.

Virilio, Paul. *Speed and Politics*. Translated by Mark Polizzotti. Los Angeles, CA: Semiotext(e), 2007.

Walker, Michelle Boulous. *Slow Philosophy: Reading Against the Institution*. London, UK: Bloomsbury, 2017.

Waters, Alice. *We Are What We Eat: A Slow Food Manifesto*. New York: Penguin, 2021.

Watson, Penny. *Slow Travel: A Movement. Richmond, Australia:* Hardie Grant, 2019.

Weeks, Kathi. "Down with Love: Feminist Critique and the New Ideologies of Work." *Women's Studies Quarterly,* Vol. 45, No. 3/4, (Fall/Winter 2017), 37–58.

———. *The Problem With Work: Feminism, Marxism, Antiwork Politics, and Postwork Imaginaries.* Durham, NC: Duke University Press, 2011.

Weiss, Allen S. *Feast and Folly: Cuisine, Intoxication, and the Poetics of the Sublime.* Albany, NY: State University of New York Press, 2002.

Weston, Phoebe. "'This Is No Damn Hobby': The 'Gansta Gardener' Transforming Los Angeles." Guardian, April 28, 2020, https://www.theguardian.com/environment/2020/apr/28/ron-finley-gangsta-gardener-transforming-los-angeles, accessed July 9, 2020.

Whiting, Tabitha. "'Sustainable Style': The Truth Behind the Marketing of H&M's Conscious Collection." Accessed September 2, 2021, https://tabitha-whiting.medium.com/sustainable-style-the-truth-behind-the-marketing-of-h-ms-conscious-collection-805eb7432002.

Witkin, Robert W. *Adorno on Popular Culture. London:*Routledge, 2002.

Wollenberg, Eva, Alison Nihart, Marja-Liisa Tapio-Bistrom, and Maryanne Grieg-Gran, eds. *Climate Change Mitigation and Agriculture. London:* Routledge, 2012.

www.aol.com/article/news/2017/07/27/scaramucci-says-trump-s-love-for-burgers-and-pizza-proves-hes-n/23052702/, accessed July 30, 2017.

Index

Adams, Ansel, 8, 86
Adorno, Theodor, 35–36, 81–82, 84–85,
  118–19, 121, 127, 157
Aeschylus, 91n9
aesthetic rationality, 84–85
aesthetics: of *Cittaslow,* 43–44; of food,
  17, 22, 121–23; of foodie culture,
  121, 131; instrumental rationality
  and, 43, 48, 79, 109; Noah and, 79;
  of slow fashion, 45–46
Aesthetic Theory (Adorno), 121
Africa, 142–43
African Americans/Blacks: food
  insecurity of, 141; McDonald's
  and, 70, 107
Agent Orange, 26
agriculture: *Cittaslow* and, 66; Slow
  Food and, 3, 10, 141–42. *See also*
  industrial farming; organic farming;
  traditional farming
Agriculture in the Classroom, 150n2
Alger, Horatio, 6, 82
alpha children, 49
American Dream, 93–109; carbon
  footprint of, 153; covid-19 pandemic
  and, 14–15; crosses and flags in,
  103–4; de-growth in, 6–7; different
  ones, 4–5; fast food and, 34; food in,
  94–110; hippie food and, 155; home

ownership in, 5; Noah and, 90, 157;
  poverty and, 6; slow culture and,
  55–56; Slow Food and, 2, 4, 51n31;
  social media and, 4; upward mobility
  in, 5; workism and, 114–20
American Foodie (Furrow), 17, 156–57
Americanization: implications of,
  31–32; standardization in, 118–19;
  on television, 30; workism and, 118
Annual National Heirloom
  Exposition, 139
anti-Semitism, 74n21
Antony and Cleopatra (Shakespeare), 63
Apricot Lane Farms, 69
Archer, John, 5
Arcigola, 28–30
Ark of Taste, 27, 127–29, 142
artisanal farming: by Indigenous
  Peoples, 66
*Associazione Studenti di Scienze
  Gastronomiche* (ASSG), 145
Atkins, Robert, 88
Atlas, Charles, 87
automation, 15, 16
automobiles, fast food and, 100–
  101, 154–55

"Babette's Feast" (Dinesen), 122
Barber, Dan, 2, 142

About the Author

Mary Caputi is professor of political theory at California State University, Long Beach, where she teaches courses in modern political thought, feminism, critical theory, and postcolonialism. Her research interests focus on the intersections of gender, first-generation Frankfurt School scholars, modern French philosophy, postcolonial studies, and contemporary American politics and culture. Her books include *Voluptuous Yearnings: A Feminist Theory of the Obscene* (Rowman & Littlefield, 1994), *A Kinder, Gentler America: Melancholia and the Mythical 1950s* (University of Minnesota Press, 2005), *Feminism and Power: The Need for Critical Theory* (Lexington Books, 2013), as well as *David Riesman and Critical Theory*, co-authored with Amirhosein Khandizaji (Palgrave, 2021). With Vincent Del Casino, Jr., she also co-edited and contributed to *Derrida and the Future of the Liberal Arts: Professions of Faith* (Bloomsbury, 2013).